The Last Civilized Place

The Last Civilized Place

Sijilmasa and Its Saharan Destiny

BY RONALD A. MESSIER AND JAMES A. MILLER

University of Texas Press ◆ *Austin*

First edition, 2015
First paperback printing, 2016

♾ The paper used in this book meets the minimum requirements of ANSI/NISO Z39.48-1992 (R1997) (Permanence of Paper).

Library of Congress Cataloging-in-Publication Data
Messier, Ronald A.
The last civilized place : Sijilmasa and its Saharan destiny /
by Ronald A. Messier and James A. Miller. — First edition.
    pages   cm
    Includes bibliographical references and index.
    ISBN 978-0-292-76665-5 (cloth : alk. paper)
1. Sijilmasa (Extinct city)   2. Excavations (Archaeology)—
Morocco.   I. Miller, James Andrew, author.   II. Title.
    DT329.S57M47   2015
    964.502—dc23

                                        2014026620

ISBN 978-1-4773-1135-6, paperback
doi:10.7560/766655

For Emily, Ron's wife, whose encouragement, patience, and limitless love and willingness to share Sijilmasa with her husband have made Ron's work possible

and

for Mary and Martha, James's sisters, for their strength and wisdom through the years.

Contents

Notes on Dates and Transliteration

All dates for events in the narrative, unless otherwise specified, are in AD style and use numbers only, without the AD designation—for example, 1055. If there is any chance for ambiguity, then "BC" or "AH" (referring to the Muslim calendar, *hijra* dates) is used. If two dates are given for the same event, they are in the form AH/AD, but without the designations AH and AD—for example, 140/757–758. Dates for sources are given only as AD dates.

Transliterations of Arabic words into Latin script are simplified. For example, the *ta marbuta*, the terminal Arabic silent *t* rendered as an *h* in English, is generally not used here. Initial hamzas (') and 'ayns (') are omitted, as are dots below and above consonants, and macrons above long vowels. Words that are commonly seen in English, such as "Quran" and "vizier," appear in that form and are not italicized. Words that often appear in French, such as *oued* rather than "wadi," are kept in French. Names of recent authors are written as the authors render their own names in Latin script. Names of places and persons that are still used today are written as they are in the country where they are located, for example, Meknes rather than Maknaas, Marrakech rather than Marrakush. Foreign words that are part of proper names are not italicized. In endnotes and in the bibliography, the rules for uppercase and lowercase in English are applied to all titles.

Acknowledgments

In May 2011, the Royal Library of the Kingdom of Morocco (Bibliothèque Nationale du Royaume du Maroc; BNRM) organized a daylong seminar in honor of Ron Messier's lifelong dedication to the history and archaeology of Morocco. The "Homage à Ronald Messier" day was planned by four friends and colleagues who have worked with Ron for over twenty years—Abdallah Fili, Lahcen Taouchikht, Saïd Ennahid, and me, James Miller. In the splendid setting of the BNRM, a day of presentations and personal memories recreated for an intimate public the road that led Ron from graduate school at the University of Michigan and the classroom at Middle Tennessee State University (MTSU) to the Tafilalt oasis in Morocco and the site of Sijilmasa. It is a long story, and here we wish to thank those who have worked with us, debated with us, assisted us financially and morally, and discovered, like us, the world in which Sijilmasa existed over its long career as a place and as a people connecting worlds nearly forgotten across the strata of time.

Thanks, first, like that fine May day, to our closest colleagues and friends, those who have worked with us in the field and who have accompanied us on our intellectual journey. Our long relationship with INSAP (the Institut National des Sciences d'Archéologie et du Patrimoine; National Institute of Archaeology and Heritage), in Rabat, began with the signing of an agreement with the Ministry of Culture for the archaeological exploration of the Sijilmasa site in 1988. Mohammed Ben Aissa, then minister of culture, was among the first to recognize the significance of Morocco's medieval heritage and the need for archaeological exploration. We thank him deeply for his encouragement and support. At INSAP, our deepest thanks go to Mme. Joudia Hassar-Benslimane, the institute's director and a signatory of the agreement with Ron Messier and MTSU that established the Moroccan-American Project at Sijilmasa (MAPS). Mme. Benslimane's lifelong dedication to archaeology in Morocco is unparalleled. At the Ministry of Culture, we thank Abdulaziz Touri for his wisdom and advice through the years, from Ron's first exploratory visit in 1986 through the completion of our field work in 1998. His support has been indispensable.

From the faculty at INSAP, Elarbi Erbati served as our Moroccan counterpart. We thank a special group of INSAP students who worked under our direction and whose development as professionals has given us great joy. There were dozens; we name in particular Mohammed Choukri, Saïd Ennahid, Khadija Bourchouk, Naima Keddane, Choukri Heddouchi, and especially Abdallah Fili, who has continued to share his deep knowledge of archaeology, Moroccan history, and Moroccan ceramics and who has contributed to several of our Sijilmasa articles. The newest recruit to the MAPS team is Chloé Capel, a PhD student at the Sorbonne, Paris I, whose dissertation is largely focused on Sijilmasa. In addition to her many thoughtful comments, Chloé provided invaluable service in fine-tuning many of our illustrations.

In Rissani, our gratitude goes to the directors at the Centre d'Etudes et de Recherches Alaouites, which provided us with laboratory and office facilities. We first met Lahcen Taouchikht in 1988 as a PhD student (in Aix-en-Provence) working on his native Tafilalt before he became director of the center in Rissani, where he worked with us side by side in our first two seasons, 1988 and 1992. Rissani itself, our second home during the six seasons of excavations, is forever sealed in our hearts and minds. We are grateful to many people in Rissani and the Tafilalt in different ways, but over the years, some individuals were especially helpful. Abdelsellam Taouchikht was our purchaser, the person we could rely on to find a way through what was for us sometimes the unknown. He provided solutions that kept our operation running each season. And that operation was big, with over thirty people in the field. At the heart of our excavations were our local workers, whose hands and eyes took on the expertise that dedicated archaeologists develop. We thank especially the eldest among them, Bel-'Aid Ben Barek, and remember them all for their dedication and their sense of what to do next at the surface of the site or the bottom of a trench.

The dig, the lab, the students, the Earthwatchers, and others: a cast of several hundred people joined us at Sijilmasa over the years. In the core team, Neal Mackenzie, our field director, was with us for ten years and in every season. His direction of the excavations was key to our project in every way. Jim Knudstadt was with us during the 1992 season, bringing his extraordinary skills as an archaeologist and his worldwide reputation earned during a long career all over the Middle East.

Complementing the staff of MAPS, Stephen W. Brown and John Runkle translated their skills in historic preservation and architecture into maps and delicate drafts of our excavation units. Mohamed Alilou, a conservator at the archaeological site of Volubilis, provided superb drawings of the mosque-madrasa complex and elite residences west of the mosque. Nancy Benco of George Washington University was with us in 1993, and her comparative approach, based on her field excavations at al-Basra, proved extremely useful. Julie Coco, Ron's capable graduate assistant, focused her attention on the Ben Akla site, unveiling the dimensions of that immense market space and transforming her findings into a brilliant master's thesis. Samantha Messier came with a biologist's sense of purpose and worked long lab hours to reveal the nature of the archaeobotanical materials found at the site.

In the broader reconnaissance of the Sijilmasa site, MAPS is grateful for the expertise of Dale Lightfoot, from Oklahoma State University, and Tony Wilkinson and Eleanor Barbanes Wilkinson, now at the University of Durham, who worked with us to determine the nature of the site, the surrounding oasis, and the human redesigning of the Tafilalt over time. My field research assistants, who led me through the exploration of the Tafilalt oasis, merit high recognition: Addi and Youssef Ouadderou, Youssef Qaroui, Rachid Ismaili.

Miller's work in the archives and with the personnel of the regional office of the Ministry of Agriculture, the Office Régional de Mise en Valeur Agricole du Tafilalet in Errachidia, was facilitated by its director, Driss Jellouli. We also thank the several local administrators of Rissani, the *caids* and *gendarmerie* of the Ministry of the Interior, who not only looked out for us but also took our work seriously and offered generous assistance when we needed it. In Rabat, 550 kilometers (342 miles) from Sijilmasa and a world away, we want to mention our university colleague Abdelhay Moudden and his wife, Farah Cherifa d'Ouezzane, always welcoming and eager to discuss the dig and bring us up to date on what was happening in the Morocco of the present. Abdelhay's guidance and encouragement when the project was still in its incubation stage was indispensable in getting it off the ground.

Our work at Sijilmasa would not have been possible without our colleagues at home. At Clemson University, I wish to thank the Department of History and Geography for its support, and the special interest that James Barker, the former dean of the College of Architecture, Art and Humanities and a past president of the university, took in our work in Morocco.

Both of us were awarded Senior Fulbright grants for our work at Sijilmasa, which leads us to thank the administrative support offered by the director, Edward Thomas, of the Moroccan-American Commission for Educational and Cultural Exchange, and his able program assistant, Saadia Maski.

At Middle Tennessee State, I, Ron, thank President James E. Walker and

Provost James Hindman for their endorsement of the project. On every occasion that an extraordinary need arose, they typically responded, "We'll find a way to do that." I owe special recognition to Myra Norman, director of Special Programs, who worked hand in hand with us in administering the many grants that have supported this project, including eight grants from MTSU, four from Earthwatch, three from National Geographic, and one each from the American Institute for Maghrib Studies, the Social Science Research Council, and the Max van Berchem Foundation. We extend our sincere appreciation to all of these granting institutions.

At the University of Texas Press, Jim Burr's patience with us has been extraordinary, and without his calm persistence, this book might not have seen the light of day. Thanks, Jim.

Finally, a word about time. More than twenty-five years have passed since Ron Messier's first exploratory mission to Sijilmasa, in 1986. Ron and James have spent twenty years together engaged in Sijilmasa and other pursuits. It has been a partnership with many highs and some lows. We thank each other for the mutual support that we have shown each other, and we underline that projects like this take time, a commodity we live with, cannot live without, but find increasingly hard to find.

The Last Civilized Place

Ibn Battuta's Sijilmasa Journey

"Welcome to Sijilmasa." While no one can really say that today, over its thousand years of greatness, Sijilmasa welcomed many. It also repelled attackers, and it was—several times—invaded and seized. More than six centuries ago, it was visited by Ibn Battuta—a native of Tangier whom we might call today the most famous Moroccan historical figure of all time. Ibn Battuta's life took him from the Atlantic to the Pacific and through a multitude of lives led as a pilgrim, court scribe, and dozens of other occupations. Most importantly, he was a traveler and a keen observer who set down his observations in his famous book, known in short as the *Rihla*, or "Journey." Inferences based on what Ibn Battuta tells us, what we know from historical texts, and from what we have learned Sijilmasa was like, on and in the ground, allow us to imagine what Ibn Battuta experienced in Sijilmasa. When the worldly traveler went there toward the end of the year 1351, Sijilmasa was no mythical kind of place; it was a kind of global city in premodern times. For Ibn Battuta, this was his last journey, and for him, Sijilmasa was yet another point in his encounter with the world. For others, Sijilmasa was still what al-Bakri had called it some three hundred years before—the "last civilized place."[1]

Our informed imagination allows us to present a picture of his journey, illuminating not so much Ibn Battuta's world as that of Sijilmasa—connected to Africa to the south, the Mediterranean world to the north, and relaying trade and cultures in a compass rose outward from its corner of Morocco.

As angular morning light strikes from the east across the Sahara, the ruins of the great Islamic city are illuminated in the heart of the Tafilalt oasis. When the harsh sun ends its journey and evening sweeps across the northwestern Sahara, the call to prayer of the muezzin peals through the air at Sijilmasa. Standing in the ruins of the mosque in the heart of the city, the clear human voice reminds the faithful of their duty, just as other muezzins did in Muslim communities hours earlier far to the east in Cairo, Baghdad, and beyond. Prayer occupied the moment at this place centuries ago as it does today in Rissani, the modern town adjacent to the ruins.

To anyone standing today in the ruins of Sijilmasa, it is difficult to realize that its people helped forge the structure of the modern Moroccan state and that even long before, Sijilmasa was a guiding light in the history of the Islamic West. So it was 650 years ago, 600 years into the history of Sijilmasa, when the man responsible for a remarkable narrative called "A Gift to Onlookers concerning the Curiosities of Cities and the Wonders of Journeys"[2] visited "one the mightiest cities of Morocco" near the end of a lifetime of world travels and remembrances of places.[3] Ibn Battuta was forty-six years old and had seen much of the known world. By the time he arrived in Sijilmasa, he had already logged some 75,000 miles over the course of thirty years. As we begin our own journey to Sijilmasa, we open our imaginations to travel with him, informed both by what he tells us of what he saw and what we have learned through the tools of our trade as archaeologists, historians, geographers, geomorphologists, ceramicists, and architects.

By his mid-forties, Ibn Battuta had made four pilgrimages to Mecca, centerpieces of a kind of continuous journey between 1325 and 1349 that had taken him from his native Tangier to lands from Istanbul to Zanzibar, and from Delhi to Indonesia and the coast of China. In 1351, he visited the south of Morocco for the first time. He called Marrakech "among the prettiest cities," but found that it had been struck by the plague, and described it much as he had Cairo two years before: a "honeycomb without the honey." Indeed, the Black Death was sweeping across the Middle East, Africa, and Europe, devastating numerous places besides Marrakech.[4] While we cannot reconstruct the impact of the Black Death on Ibn Battuta's thinking, we know that from Marrakech he returned north to Salé, on the Atlantic coast, from which he proceeded inland to Meknes and Fez, the capital of the Merinid sultan, who ruled over the "land of the farthest west," as Morocco has always been known to the Arabs. When Ibn Battuta arrived in Fez in the fall of 1351, the city and much of Morocco was under the control of Sultan Abu Inan, the fifth ruler in the Merinid dynasty, which had been the central power in much of Morocco for a century.[5] And in Fez, the stakes were high.

Three years earlier, in 1348, Abu Inan had declared himself sultan when his father, Sultan Abu'l-Hassan, was rumored to be dead. The father, hoping to place the entire rim of the Islamic West within his grasp, had been at war in the far eastern corner of North Africa, in Tunisia (or Ifriqiya as it was known), extending the authority of the Merinids 1,200 miles east of the capital, Fez. It was reported that Abu'l-Hassan had been killed on the field of battle at

Qayrawan in central Tunisia.⁶ He hadn't been, but his son wasted no time in establishing his own rule. Ibn Battuta doesn't tell us about these events, which were unfolding around him. Instead, he set off across the Sahara for Mali, a place he had not seen before. Mali was the land of an important Islamic kingdom on the North African periphery, a place of fabled fortune whose reputation had taken root a generation earlier when the *mansa* (king) of Mali distributed untold wealth in gold in the bazaars of Cairo on his way to Mecca. Mali was due south of Morocco, Ibn Battuta's relationship with the Moroccan sultan was close, and the sultan's intentions, while not clear, were clearly expansionist. And not enough was known about Mali, successor to ancient Ghana, which had been so vividly portrayed by al-Bakri three hundred years earlier. In any case, the caravans that brought gold to Sijilmasa started out in the Kingdom of Mali, and Ibn Battuta was to be a witness to that trade for the next two years.

He was off to see another world. From Fez, he journeyed to the Sudan—the land on the other side of the Sahara. The journey took him south from Fez to Morocco's "port" at the edge of the Sahara, Sijilmasa, where in the winter of 1351–1352 he spent four months at the edge of his native land preparing for his journey.

Much of the Morocco that Ibn Battuta saw in the 1350s might look like the Morocco of today. On his way to Sijilmasa, he traversed the heart of the Middle Atlas Mountains and passed along roads whose landscapes would be familiar to the modern traveler. As he crossed the Saïs plain south of Fez and Meknes, he was struck as he approached the mountains by the "green gardens stretching in every direction." The same would be true today. At the end of the first day of his journey, he might have stayed in Sefrou—traditionally, a predominantly Jewish town of cherry orchards and barley fields at the foot of the mountains. Upon reaching the first upsweep of the Middle Atlas, Ibn Battuta found its slopes covered, as many still are, with dense forests of evergreens and holly oaks crowned by age-old stands of lacy, long-living cedars.⁷ In his day, lions haunted the edges of the woods, as they did until modern times. Lynx and boar were abundant; hawks soared overhead by day, and owls echoed at night. Packs of macaque monkeys would have moved across his path in the sylvan mountain glades. Morocco was a wild place in its many recesses and uninhabited places; indeed, it remains so still. In the higher elevations of the Middle Atlas, where piles of volcanic rock sculpt the surface, small lakes dot the landscape and forest covers the landscape in many places. Farther south, as aridity became more and more apparent, Ibn Battuta crossed some of the highest of the Atlas ranges, the Eastern High Atlas, which projects toward the central Maghrib and where vales of cedar and juniper nestle along the western- and northern-facing slopes. While it could well be that his road cleft well west of today's main thoroughfare, he may have stopped at places, then as now, that are obvious points of rest along the road—towns such as Midelt or Rich—before undertaking the arduous climb upward through the passes of the Eastern High Atlas.

The passage through any part of the Atlas—Middle, Eastern, or High— can be treacherous. Snow is sometimes heavy: the intensity of low-pressure systems over the Atlantic reaching far inland across North Africa varies widely from one year to the next, or from one winter month to another. Later, when returning across these mountains to Fez, Ibn Battuta noted that he set out from Sijilmasa on December 29, 1353, "during a period of fierce cold": "A lot of snow came down on the road. I have seen many rough roads and much snow in Bukhara and Samarkand and in Khurasan [in Persia] and in the land of the Turks, but I have never seen anything more difficult than the road [through the Atlas]."[8] Fold after fold of the Eastern High Atlas, surface projections of the earth's deep tectonic movements, unravels across the landscape toward the south; mountain gorges, the mothers of rivers running east and north to the Mediterranean to form the Oued Moulouya watershed, compete with gouges in the earth carrying waters furiously east and then south into the Sahara, bleak birthplaces of the *oueds* (rivers) Gheris and Ziz.

Out of the mountains, the snow ends quickly in Morocco. The descent from the Atlas is sharp, and the environmental changes are dramatic. The desert beyond the Atlas, the pre-Sahara, is reached quickly: a desert landscape punctuated by Atlas waters rushing outward to their deaths in the true desert beyond. At the modern city of Errachidia, at the foot of the route follow- ing the Oued Ziz out of the Eastern High Atlas, the air is dry; vegetation is thin; springs abound; rivers flow out into the desert; there is no more forest; and the desert is at hand. Elevations decline and temperatures rise. Ibn Bat- tuta continued onward through the deeply incised canyon of the Oued Ziz known as the Rteb, where Berber cultivators tended forests of date palms and irrigated plots of barley and Saharan fruits, pomegranates and almonds, in a sinuous passage leading to the great southern oasis beyond, the Tafilalt and its beacon, Sijilmasa. The surrounding canyon heights are still surmounted by watchtowers from ancient days, perhaps the same as those that ensured the safety of caravans in Ibn Battuta's day.

Ibn Battuta followed the blue waters of the Oued Ziz—literally, the "gazelle river"—flowing like a wave ahead in a landscape of ever-drier propor- tions, south to the oasis of Tafilalt and the port city of the Sahara. The Rteb Canyon opened up into dry country along the riverbank, signaling the great desert to come, and all sense of the Atlas was left behind. The fourteenth-

Figure 0.1. The Rteb Canyon along the Ziz, upstream from the Tafilalt. The valley floor is a forest of date palms whose abundance is due to the local springs entering the Ziz, not to water from the modern dam on the Ziz upstream at Errachidia. The numerous villages in the valley are obvious stopping points for travelers today, just as they were in Ibn Battuta's day.

century traveler passed by an isolated peak (today's Borj Erfoud, a military outpost on an outlying butte of the high desert mesa to the east) towering over a district where the waters of the Oueds Ziz and Gheris nearly join and numerous villages of date farmers dot the landscape along both rivers. Unlike the remote mountain areas, here the rule of central authority was strong, and the shaykh of a walled village, a *qsar* in Arabic, may have invited the illustrious traveler to spend the night. Ibn Battuta, a disciplined man of high learning, would have been happy to be among a society eager to hear news of the court in Fez.

The next morning, he began his last day's journey toward Sijilmasa, in a stretch of open country along the Ziz just downstream from the palm oasis of today's Erfoud. Perhaps Ibn Battuta paused along the river to observe a waterworks. Unlike the Ziz earlier in its course, the river now jutted off straight ahead, deflected by a low mortared dam, a *sed*, such as he had seen years before in Mesopotamia and along the Indus, far distant but still within the *dar al-Islam*. Behind the dam, a diversion stuck in the river course like a big brick, an empty channel running to the southeast loomed under the rising desert sun. While he had undoubtedly been impressed by the intricate nature of waterworks in Granada and the underground horizontal wells, the *khettara*, surrounding Marrakech, he had seen nothing this massive in all his journeys west of the Nile. "These people know how to make water work in the desert," he may have mused. He picked up speed, following the course of the Ziz to the first palms of the Tafilalt. By nightfall, he would be in Sijilmasa.

As Ibn Battuta entered the northern edge of the Tafilalt, he was still a few hours' ride away from his destination. The shallow waters of the Ziz coursed ahead toward a horizon of dark green palm trees. We do not know how the main road through the Tafilalt was then arranged, but surveys in the oasis have led us to believe the obvious: it went through the center of the oasis, connecting the greatest number of *qsur* (plural of *qsar*) and their irrigation works, which spread outward from the Oued Ziz into ever-smaller canals emptying into the oasis fields. Ibn Battuta saw a well-ordered agricultural scene, like the fields in the north, but this was an oasis landscape, dominated by date palms. He was undoubtedly eagerly anticipating getting to Sijilmasa by nightfall. Friends awaited him there, relatives of merchants he had known from trade networks and would see again in Africa across the Sahara: he had a list of Sijilmasa folk in his head to look up and knew that they and people in the Sudan would form connections with many places he had been before. This journey was a culmination of all his travels for over a quarter of a century throughout the world of Islam. What other Moroccan knew the world so well? What he did not know was how much Sijilmasa mattered in Africa, how many merchants and slaves knew Sijilmasa as home and a passage to other worlds. Sijilmasa was their point of departure, a necessary waypoint in the convergence of Africa north and south.

But now, his thoughts focused on the world around him. Looking right and left along the road through the palm oasis from the nimble mount that had carried him through the Atlas Mountains, he was again confirmed in his view that Morocco "surpasses . . . all other countries"[9] and is the best governed. As he passed through orchards of dates being harvested, we imagine him coming across the people of Terrist, a *qsar* on the right bank of the Ziz. He would have been invited to sample their dates, which were being brought to their village to be sorted on a stone platform alongside their solid, rectangular *qsar* topped with crenellations reminiscent, in their own mud-brick way, of the architecture he had seen emerge in Fez under the Merinids during his generation away from home. *Asr* (afternoon) prayers would be at hand. He would be just a few miles from Sijilmasa, and his desire to continue moving forward before nightfall would be great. But it was only *asr*; there was still travel time left before sunset, and he and his party would be invited to pray

Figure 0.2. Rsif Dam and Qsar Terrist. In the heart of the Tafilalt oasis and upstream along the Ziz from Rissani and the Sijilmasa site, the Rsif dam may be the oldest of the many dams on this oued. Twelve dams have been found, but elusive vestiges of others remain in the bed of the Ziz. The village of Terrist lies on the western side of the Ziz. A new road built across the Ziz in 2010 fundamentally altered this 1996 view.

and to take nourishment along the road. Ibn Battuta would have found the same strength in prayer in the simple mosque just inside the gate that he had experienced in so many places elsewhere in the world. As the men of Terrist welcomed the travelers, their humble prayer room held all the attributes needed to accomplish the most fundamental of Muslim duties. The delicately scalloped, arched niche in the side of the mosque, a *mihrab* pointing ideally toward Mecca, directed the bowed heads of the assembled in prayer. A *minbar*, a small stepped wooden pulpit from which the local shaykh would deliver his message during Friday prayers, lay alongside the *mihrab*; like others in the region, it could be rolled out farther out into the room on wooden rails for the Friday sermon. After prayer, Ibn Battuta and his small band of travelers would commune with the elders over sage tea and fresh dates. He found that their dates, a "kind called *irar*, has no like anywhere," and compared them to the next best he had known, those of Basra, in Mesopotamia.[10] He might have asked the men about their *sed*, known as the Rsif, running across the Ziz right in front of them, built to impound water from the Oued Ziz so that their date palms could be well watered throughout the year. The top of the dam, rising ten meters (thirty-three feet) above the waters of the shallow Ziz, was broad enough to constitute a road across the river, part of the labyrinth of roads and trails forging the entire Tafilalt into one communicative environment. He was curious, full of questions, seeking views and information to add to what he already knew from the rest of the world.

"Shukran, barrak Allahufik," words of thanks, and then Ibn Battuta was back on the road, across the dam and onto the road that would bring him into Sijilmasa on the east bank of the Ziz. The road followed one of the canals that drew water from the Rsif and was named for Sijilmasa's founding dynasty, the Bani Midrar. The canal was the Midrariya, and it and its waters formed a district in the oasis, also called the Midrariya. He reflected on the fact that a full six hundred years of Islam had moved through this place: the Midrar had founded Sijilmasa as a religious refuge and commercial center in 757 and ruled over it for the next two hundred years, and their reign had ended four hundred years ago. Ibn Battuta, who knew his history well, might have thought of the curious emergence of the Fatimids, the people who first unsettled the Midrarids' steady reign over Sijilmasa. He knew the story of how the founder of the Shi'ite Fatimid dynasty, which was later to rule over Tunisia and then eventually found Cairo and reign over the eastern Mediterranean, had come to Sijilmasa to await a miracle signaling their greatness—which eventually came in the form of a geyser spouting from the land. "That was over 450 years earlier, and now here I am in that same land!" he may have thought to himself. Suddenly, the canal ended; its waters delivered. The road continued, and the landscape opened up to a broad plain along the Ziz.

He stopped at a gate. As invariably happens, children would have come up to him and his party; they might have asked, "Oh *sidi*, are you the emissary from Fez and our master, the sultan?" To his amazement, Ibn Battuta was in front of the first piece of imperial architecture he had seen since departing from Sefrou weeks earlier, and it was magnificent: a majestic city gate in the style of Fez. He smiled in joy at this fragment of urban splendor, reminding him firmly that he was in Morocco, a land of God different from all the rest. Oddly, he thought, they have already heard of my coming; word travels fast in this land of dates and the Ziz, the Tafilalt. Indeed, this part of Morocco was its own country.

Ibn Battuta had arrived at one of the few large structures of Sijilmasa still standing today, a gate now known as Bab Fez, the Gate of Fez, but also more forlornly as Bab al-Rih, the Gate of the Wind.[11] It was named, as city gates in premodern societies often were, for the next most important place; in this case, between Sijilmasa and the north—Fez was the next stop in the world. Bab al-Rih was a Merinid version of earlier gates leading into the Moroccan

Figure 0.3. Bab al-Rih (Gate of the Wind), also known as the Bab Fez.

capital of the Saharan world. The *haris al-bab*, or guardian of the gate, would have approached the riders, looking for the man whose fame had preceded him, a man reckoned to have seen the corners of the earth.

"The shaykh Abu Abdallah awaits you, and I am ordered to escort you there," announced the gatekeeper. Ibn Battuta bid farewell to the companions he had made along the long road from Fez. They would see one another again in the bustling town. As he rode through the pointed arch, he looked up at the graceful scalloped frame and a herringbone pattern carved in the adobe above the portal. Once inside the gate, he found himself in a covered patio with arches opening in several directions. He was not really in a city; he was not really in the country. In the words of al-Bakri, written in 1055: "The town of Sijilmasa is situated on a plain the soil of which is salty. Around the town are numerous suburbs with lofty mansions and other splendid buildings. There are also many gardens. The lower section of the wall surrounding the town is made of stone, but the upper one is brick . . . There are twelve gates, eight of which are of iron."[12] Ibn Battuta may have read this description in manuscript and now recognized the place, as would travelers and archaeologists in ages to come.

Next, Ibn Battuta and his new guide passed through one of those "numerous suburbs," an open land of houses and gardens, each, it seemed, watered by a different small canal. His guide led him to the main road going south to the center of town, taking him past a number of villas, walled houses with interior gardens and fountains. These could have been the houses of some of the wealthier farmers in the oasis.[13] This neighborhood was very unlike the Midrariya, where large orchards of date palms shaded understories of pomegranate and plum trees, and where barley, alfalfa, and vegetables—beans and *wargiya* (kale)—were watered by the irrigated ditches. Here was a sense of wealthy citizens organizing land and life at the edge of town. If it was at all like it is today, donkeys and their riders passed Ibn Battuta, hurrying home to their *qsur* as the lowering sun made long shadows against their paths.

Ibn Battuta and his guide rode on, and buildings on a jutting rise came into view. "What is here?" he inquired. "The *dar al-imara*," the governor's palace, was the answer. At the northern end of Sijilmasa, a dense mass of structures emerged before them. A wall some forty feet above them surrounded the heights of the promontory, enclosing a citadel—a fortress consisting of a palace and barracks. "This is the home of the *wali* of Sijilmasa and his soldiers," Ibn Battuta's guide might have announced.[14] Some of the soldiers, serious-looking young men, were members of an Arab tribe relatively new to the region, the Ma'qil, whose loyalties were being sealed to the Merinid regime through their work as scouts and soldiers throughout the southern periphery.

They moved on, entering the heart of town. The main street was flanked on the left by the western wall of the citadel, made of thick adobe, isolating the seat of government from the rest of the city. Past the citadel, both sides of the street were lined with walls of houses and shops, some with their wares jutting out into the thoroughfare. As in Fez, houses of the rich and the poor alike lay behind unremarkable walls that came right to the street (unlike the houses just outside of town). Inside, Ibn Battuta would find that Sijilmasa houses were decorated with geometric designs, ceramic tiles, and carved stucco in floral patterns that continued the simple styles set by the city's founders, the Bani Midrar. A few might have been like the "shops where wine was sold" that had been smashed during the prohibitions of the Almoravid era but had found

Figure 0.4. The Sijilmasa citadel, approached from the north.

Figure 0.5. Typical street in the Rissani *mellah*, perhaps resembling what streets in medieval Sijilmasa looked like.

their way back into the thread of Sijilmasan life in Merinid days.[15] It was a wealthy place: Ibn Battuta later recorded that every inhabitant of Sijilmasa had a house and a garden.[16]

Throughout his four-month sojourn in Sijilmasa, Ibn Battuta stayed in one such house: "I stayed there with the *faqih* Abu Muhammad al-Bishri, whose brother I had met in the city of Qanjanfu of the land of China. How far apart they are!"[17] Ibn Battuta knew the al-Bishri family (as he did so many other people) from several directions, including, besides the brother he had met in China, relatives he had met just a year earlier in Sebta (Ceuta).

Continuing along the main north-south city street, Ibn Battuta passed through an elaborate gate complex, "a real city gate," he might have noted, and the street, clearly an urban thoroughfare, took a sharp turn to the left, passing public baths and latrines. He recalled al-Bakri's claim that the baths were not well built, but there could have been much improvement in three hundred years![18] Just beyond the baths, he arrived at the heart of the city, the Mosque of Ibn Abd Allah, the most magnificent structure he had seen since leaving Fez. It was nearly dark, and the *maghrib* prayer would be called, so he dismounted his horse to enter the mosque and pray. In the dimly lit interior, twenty-four columns divided the space into four bays and nine aisles. While not nearly as large or ornate as many of the mosques he had known in the East, this one had a long tradition as a place of religious refuge. He was among the powerful fellowship of the dar al-Islam once more: Fez, Granada, Tunis, Cairo, Damascus, Bukhara, Delhi, and now Sijilmasa. All reached to the matter at hand: prayer among the believers. As he stood shoulder to shoulder with the pious of Sijilmasa, he gave thanks for his safe arrival in this famous caravan city. At the end of prayer, he would not be able to hide his presence, his selflessness, in this place. His guide, who had also bowed his head in prayer, spoke to the congregation, and the word spread that this great man was in Sijilmasa.

The rest of the city, where clay oil lamps were being lit to illuminate supper on a warm winter evening, lay below him: a hive of dwellings, large and small, sweeping downward toward the Oued Ziz just below.

What did Ibn Battuta do in Sijilmasa for four months? On market days, he would have gone to the city market along the east-west thoroughfare, the road that entered from the irrigated fields, the *gamaman*, at Bab al-Sharq, the eastern gate, and led directly to the market gate to form a walled enclosure about the size of two standard football pitches.[19] There were no permanent structures in the market, only wooden stalls with thatched roofs to shelter the merchants and their goods. The bargaining, then as now, must have been intense. Sellers enticed prospective buyers to their stalls as they hawked their merchandise and assured people that their wares were the best. Goods in the Sijilmasa market came from all compass points. Ibn Battuta would have recognized almonds, candied fruit, figs, and raisins from Malaga and Almeria in the Andalus; pistachios from Gafsa in Tunisia; and distinctive olive oils from as far away as Seville and Sfax in Tunisia. Fine cotton, silks, and brocades woven with gold and silver thread came from Egypt and Yemen. Cop-

Figure 0.6. Suq Ben Akla Drive.

per, bronze, and iron utensils, even Coptic bronze lamps from Egypt, could be had. Enameled pottery from Cordoba and sculpted marble stelae from Almeria might have been in the market. At the spice merchants, cinnamon and cloves from Zanzibar vied with saffron, ginger, and sugar from the Sus Valley to the west. Cone-shape mounds of spices in brown, red, and yellow were accented by the bright sun, stimulating the eye much as their scents did the nose. The spice merchants were at the same time apothecaries and healers, selling medicinal herbs and drugs, dried animal skins, skulls, and bones for magic potions. Here, like everywhere he went on the continent, what Ibn Battuta was really doing was learning about Africa.

The journey south demanded serious preparations, many of which took him to a place outside town and across the river on the western edge of the oasis, the Oued Gheris. This was a marketplace as well, but a very different mercantile world. This was the Suq Ben Akla. To get there, he passed out through the western gate, Bab al-Gharb, crossed the Ziz, and rode past the noria, the waterwheel on the riverbank, and went west some five kilometers (three miles). Crossing the Gheris meant leaving the oasis, and on the west bank of the Gheris, Ibn Battuta found himself at an enormous global crossroads.

Many of the merchants at Suq Ben Akla were international traders. Their capital was locked up in large, highly organized caravans moving goods north and south. Security was at a premium, since the desert and the long distances to be covered held all kinds of risk. Top traders banded together. They would often come with seventy, eighty, or a hundred camels laden with goods, and yet would still make up only part of a caravan numbering hundreds or even thousands of camels.[20] For them, it was not practical to go to the city market in Sijilmasa; they went instead to Suq Ben Akla. In its seasons, Ben Akla was a huge camp and a market. Its service community that catered to the caravan trade lived in permanent residences, and there were many facilities for the trade. It was a kind of open-air caravansary where traders could find lodging and the space to trade, tend their camels, and store their goods. On its northern edge, Suq Ben Akla had a mosque and a cemetery.[21]

Ibn Battuta mingled with the caravaners and listened to their tales of Saharan perils, profit, and plunder. Few places would have piqued this world traveler's imagination as much as this as he mapped Suq Ben Akla and its stories onto the grid of his own global crossings. The tales were told and retold. One was the story of how a caravan was guided by a blind man who rode the lead camel and commanded a handful of sand to be given to him at standard intervals. He would raise the sand to his nose, smell it, and sense the direction to take even in the midst of blinding sandstorms. The problem of transporting enough water, carried in skin bags, and of having decent clean water across the Sahara, was overwhelming. A favorite story told of the evildoer who climbed down a prized well along the desert trail and cut the ropes of the buckets as the caravaners dropped them down to fetch water. They would eventually run out of buckets, and without water they would die of thirst. The man would then climb out of the well and claim their treasures. But a slave of the caravaners climbed down into the well and killed the thief, saving the traders.

Other stories dealt with the gold trade that made this market and, indeed, Sijilmasa a global trading center. They described how, in the upper reaches of the streams flowing down from the Guinea Highlands, partners in the gold trade from such places as Timbuktu engaged in silent barter for gold.[22] Merchants from Mali would lay down their merchandise and clothing on their bank of the river and then disappear into the forest. The people from places such as Bambuk and Buré in the Highlands, where gold was panned in the rivers, would then come across the river to see what the merchants had left. If they found it suitable, they would leave the quantity of gold they were willing to pay for the merchandise, take the goods, and leave in turn. When the traders returned to see what the natives had left, if they were satisfied with the amount of gold left for their goods, they would take it and leave, deal done. If not, the process would be repeated, sellers and buyers increasing their quantities until both sides were satisfied and the transaction complete.[23] What

Figure 0.7. Date pounder. Smooth river stones fashioned into hand-held hammers are scattered on the ground at Suq Ben Akla. Eroded, transported from the Atlas Mountains in earlier, rainier times, stones of a convenient size for people to clench in their fists were used to smash date pits, an essential fodder for camels and other animals corralled at the site. Thousands of pack animals would have been at Suq Ben Akla during high points of the caravan trade.

fascinated Ibn Battuta was the recognition that the goods in the market, both here and in town, were some of the very trade goods that would travel south, stop at Timbuktu and other cities in Mali, and then be transported again to the third point in this global supply chain of the gold trade, to the unknown people who lived in the source of the gold itself.

Suq Ben Akla was a thrilling experience. Ibn Battuta needed camels for the next leg of his journey, and so he went to the staging area at the southern edge of Suq Ben Akla to negotiate with merchants who were forming a large caravan. He found women and men pounding mounds of date pits into camel feed and marveled at the date pounders fashioned from local rock. He noted: "[I] bought camels there and fed them for four months," indicating that he must have visited the Suq frequently during his time in Sijilmasa.

We know little of what he saw in those four months. But when he left, in February 1352, there is little doubt that he had seen much: "Then I set off at

the beginning of God's month of Muharram in the year [7]53/18 February
1352 with a caravan whose leader was Abu Mohammed Yaandakan al-Masufi,
may God have mercy on him. In the caravan was a company of merchants of
Sijilmasa and others. After 25 days we arrived at Teghaza. This is a village
with nothing good about it."[24]

Over the course of two years, from February 1352 until January 1354, Ibn
Battuta made his final daring journey, during which he crossed the Sahara
down and back, voyaging to the empire of Mali along the upper and middle
reaches of the Niger River.[25] He crossed the desert in an organized caravan,
describing a ten-day stay midway in a salt-mine town, Teghaza, which he
called the "most fly-ridden of places," where even the houses were fashioned
from slabs of salt. He moved on to the southern edge of the desert, to Oualata, a town within the sphere of the Malian Empire, where he began to ac-
custom himself to the ways of people new to him.[26] By the end of July 1352,
he was in the seat of government of Mansa Suleiman, the sultan on the other
side of the Sahara.

He stayed seven months exactly in the capital of a people whose Islamic
practices he found quite different from his own and from those carried out by
all the peoples he had visited far and wide in the dar al-Islam. His descriptions of the court of Suleiman, "a lofty pavilion . . . where he sits for most
of the time," speckled with adornments and ornaments of gold, are indications of the links forged between North African traders and Mali, as are the
numerous transactions in gold elucidated by him along the way. His mixed
feelings about what he found good and bad in Mali, mostly along the lines of
how Islam was followed—or not—in Malian culture, led him to outline the
brief "Account of What I Found Good Amongst the Blacks and of What I
Disliked"—a list unique in his manuscript. His sojourn in the Malian capital in the upper reaches of the Niger River, a place, curiously, that he never
named and whose name and location is still not known, came to an end as he
pushed onward, at the end of February 1353, through modern Mali to Timbuktu and Gao, and then farther east and north through the northern Niger
of today, meeting Moroccan traders everywhere he went.[27]

From Gao, Ibn Battuta had joined a "big caravan" bound north for Ghadamès, an eastern North African port of the Sahara (near the southern tip of
modern Tunisia, in Libya) much like Sijilmasa, at the juncture of trade with
the "Land of the Blacks," the *sudan*, from which the traditional name of West
Africa, "Sudan," is taken in Arabic. He recrossed the Sahara, accompanying
the caravan in the summer of 1353 as far as the oasis of Takadda (in modern
Niger), a separate Berber "statelet" beyond the Malian realm. Takadda was a
copper-mining crossroads where fleets of camels laden with slaves, ivory, and

gold converged and then diverged to ports on the northern edge of the trade—Nul in the far west of the Anti-Atlas Mountains, Darʿa (modern Zagora) in the Draa Valley, and Sijilmasa in the Ziz, all in Morocco today; Ouargla in east-central Algeria; Ghadamès.[28] At Takadda, his world caught up with him, and his reverie ended. To use an anachronistic image, the telephone rang. Sultan Abu Inan was on the line from Fez.

We shall never know why. What we do know is that Ibn Battuta had to hurry home to Fez. He described the moment: "The young slave of al-Haj Muhammad Ibn Saʿid of Sijilmasa arrived with a command from our master the commander of the faithful, the supporter of the faith, the depender on the Lord of the worlds, commanding me to appear in his sublime presence. I kissed the order and complied with it immediately."[29] Ibn Battuta bought two camels and took sufficient provisions for seventy nights, enough to allow him to reach Touat, in today's northern Algerian Sahara. He left Takadda on September 11 in a caravan—with some six hundred slave women—and reached Sijilmasa in mid-December, spending two weeks there. At the end of December 1353, he set out from Sijilmasa in a "period of fierce cold" and traveled through deep snow in the Atlas. He arrived in Fez a month later.

Back in Fez, over the next year or two, Ibn Battuta must have rubbed shoulders with a rising star in the Moroccan intellectual community.[30] Ibn Battuta had come home to compile his travelogue at the behest of the sultan; Ibn Khaldun was a bright young clerk in the service of the court, eager to hear the tales told by one who had traveled to the ends of the earth. Ibn Battuta must have told Ibn Khaldun of all the wonders he had seen, feeding the mind of one who would develop a universal outlook and put it down in his systematic history, the *Muqaddimah*. Ibn Battuta's most recent journey might have been the first he told the man who is by any measure today known as the most famous Tunisian of the fourteenth century.

For two years in Fez, Ibn Battuta dictated his book of travels to the court scribe Ibn Juzayy. His complete description of Sijilmasa is as follows, with the introductory line announcing his arrival at Fez late in the summer of 1351, just before setting out for Sijilmasa and the land across the Sahara:

> Then we arrived at the capital, Fez (may God protect it!) and there they took leave of our Lord [the sultan] (may God support him!) and set off *bi-rasm al-safar* [with the purpose of traveling] to the land of the Sudan. I arrived at Sijilmasa. It is one of the finest of cities where there is an abundance of excellent dates. In its abundance of dates, it resembles the city of Basra, but the dates of Sijilmasa are better; the *irar* kind has no like in all the lands. I stayed there with the *faqih* Abu Muhammad al-Bishri, whose

brother I had met in the city of Qanjanfu of the land of China. How far apart they are! He treated me with great hospitality. I bought camels there and fed them for four months.[31]

In later years Ibn Battuta apparently served as a *qadi* (judge) in a Moroccan town or two, much as he had in Delhi and the Maldives a generation earlier. When he was received by the sultan in Fez, he wrote: "[I] kissed his noble hand and deemed myself fortunate to see his blessed face," words that end, more or less, the immense narrative of one who had truly traveled to the ends of the earth.[32]

Ibn Battuta's life ended in the 770th year of Islam, 1368–1369, or perhaps as late as 1377, of what cause and where we do not know. In the Tangier medina today, his small white tomb, a saint's shrine, a typical North African *qubba*, doesn't figure among the tourist attractions.[33] Abu Inan ruled until 1358, strangled by his own vizier, and the Merinid dynasty fell into bloody dissension among competing viziers, regents, and family members, leading Morocco into a state of complete civil war by the end of the fourteenth century. Disorder reigned for a full hundred years, and Sijilmasa was among its victims. But in the age of Ibn Battuta, Sijilmasa was strong; it was secure.

CHAPTER I

Approaches to Sijilmasa

Sijilmasa is an African El Dorado. Most people who have heard of it know it as the legendary City of Gold. Medieval Arabic texts describe it that way. Writing in the third quarter of the ninth century, al-Yaʿqubi, one of the earliest Arabic writers to mention Sijilmasa by name, said of it, "Around it [Sijilmasa] there are deposits of gold and silver. It [the gold] is found like plants and it is said that the wind blows it away."[1] Al-Masʿudi, in the mid-tenth century, wrote: "All that gold which the merchants obtain is minted in the town of Sijilmasa."[2] At about the same time, al-Istakhri wrote: "It is said that no other mine [the one between Sijilmasa and the land of the Sudan] is known to have more abundant or purer gold, but the road there is difficult and the necessary preparations are laborious."[3] Sijilmasa became a mythic place veiled by a sense of auric mystery. The legacy of Sijilmasa, the "City of Gold," became cloudy as the physical reality of the city became lost to the sediments of time.

In 1992, as we were beginning our second season of archeological research, a Moroccan journalist interviewed members of MAPS, the Moroccan-American Project at Sijilmasa. He was well aware of the reputation of Sijilmasa. Still, he asked whether it was a real place. The Moroccan minister of cultural affairs, who was certainly better informed, asked a similar question: "We know that Sijilmasa was a real city—but is there anything of it left for us to see?" The answer to both of those questions is an emphatic yes.

Our mission was guided by a desire to know how the archaeology of Sijilmasa could illuminate the descriptions of a city found in nearly twenty notable medieval Islamic manuscripts, and vice versa: how archaeology could enlighten our understanding of the texts. Many of these manuscripts are histories and geographies in the vein of cosmographies, compendia of everything known about all places, a type of literature written from the 900s to the 1500s. Authors such as al-Istakhri (flourished 950), Ibn Hawqal (wrote 988), al-Muqaddasi (wrote 985–990), al-Bakri (wrote 1068), Ibn al-Athir (died 1233), Ibn Idhari (wrote 1312), Ibn Abi Zar (died 1315), al-ʿUmari (wrote 1337–1338), Ibn Khaldun (died 1406), and Leo Africanus (died c. 1554) give us the history of Sijilmasa in broad brushstrokes.[4] Of all these, al-Bakri's mid-eleventh-century *Kitab al-Masalik waʾl-Mamalik* (The book of routes and realms) is a constant guide to the site of Sijilmasa. No other work is so suggestive of the social and morphological organization of Sijilmasa. But the *Kitab al-Masalik* is no city street plan, and many of its descriptions are as elusive as they are exquisitely enticing. Al-Bakri is of high interest for the archaeology of Sijilmasa also because he repeated all known information about the city, garnered from many sources, as writers did in those days. He wrote his description at the end of one epoch in the city's life—just before the astounding conquests by the Almoravids, who appeared out of the desert in the 1050s and went on to conquer Morocco, al-Andalus, and much of the rest of North Africa. After nearly three hundred years in its first iteration, Sijilmasa was about to become a linchpin in the Almoravids' new empire as they emerged out of the western Sahara to unite the Maghrib and reconquer a faltering Iberia in the name of an Islam reborn in a desert milieu.[5] Al-Bakri provides a benchmark for the end of one Sijilmasa and the beginning of another.

Al-Bakri's and others' accounts provide pictures of the past, useful but uncertain guides for our quest. Sijilmasa was a name with little content. What was its extent? How did it change over time? How did the city organize the oasis to sustain not only itself but also fleets of caravans? There are questions about Sijilmasa's relations with ancient Ghana and, even in al-Bakri's time, about the origins of Sijilmasa's wealth in gold and the tandem development of Islam in Ghana. What broader relationships did Sijilmasa establish with the gold-rich African societies with which it traded dates, brass, and glass? Did Islam travel hand in hand with the trade across the Sahara?[6] Many questions about Islamic urban form, such a constant element in Islamic social history, were also present from the onset of our work in the field. Altogether, these questions led us to this place, which in turn led us outward in many directions—the Maghrib to the north, Iberia and farther abroad in Europe, Islam in the East, Africa across the Sahara to the south. Pulled in by these questions and others, we began work at the site in earnest in 1988. Studies in the structure and form (morphology) and the function of cities throughout the world of Islam guided our approach to excavating Sijilmasa. Gleanings from historical texts, the minutiae of the archaeological pits at the site itself, the broad realm of Sijilmasa's morphology, and geography all combine to form a comprehensive picture of Sijilmasa and its place in history. That is what is new about this book.

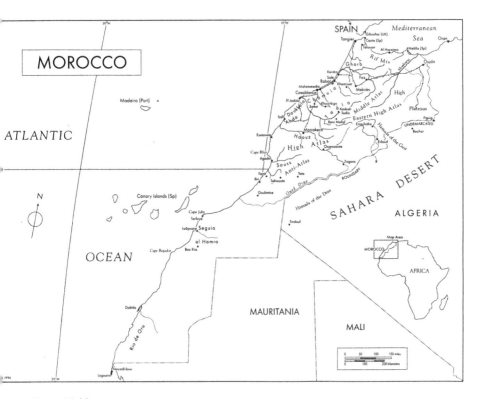

Figure 1.1. Morocco.

Themes

Sijilmasa was both remote and central. It was, and still is, geographically remote within the world of Islam and within Morocco itself. On the Michelin
road map, it is at the end of the line representing the highway going south
from Meknes or Fez. It is in the Tafilalt oasis on the edge of the Sahara. When
most Moroccans talk about it, either by its medieval name of Sijilmasa, or by
the name of the new town, Rissani, adjacent to the medieval ruins, they think
of it as "very far away." Once, when we rented a car in Marrakech and asked
the agent whether we could return it at another location, he said yes, but then
quickly added, "Except Rissani!" If it seems remote today, it must have been
even more so in the Middle Ages. It was a place of refuge for a group of Kharijite Muslims who fled there from Qayrawan in the mid-eighth century, the
second century of Islam. They were Sufriya Kharijites, very much in conflict
with Ibadi Kharijites as well as with Sunni and Shi'ite Muslims. When the

Ibadis gained control of Qayrawan, the Sufriyas had to flee as fast and as far as possible. They fled to the frontier, to the very edge of the Islamic world; they fled to Sijilmasa.

Besides being at the end of the road from Fez, so to speak, Sijilmasa was also at the beginning of another road. It was the jumping-off point for caravans going south, across the Sahara, to far off places such as Ghana, Awdaghust, and Timbuktu. It is in that sense that it was central; it was the link to sub-Saharan West Africa. Through Sijilmasa, Islam made its way south. But merchants, not missionaries, were the agents who brought Islam to the Sudan.[7] (Reminder: "the Sudan" refers here to West Africa, not to the modern country of Sudan.) The thought of crossing the Sahara for any reason, a forty- to fifty-day journey across a vast emptiness, was daunting at best. What might make it less so? Knowing what the rules would be at the other end of the journey. Islam would provide, at least in part, some of that assurance. The other motivator was gold.

We believe that gold was carried across the Sahara from West Africa to the Mediterranean world as early as the fourth century.[8] West Africa, what the Arabs called *bilad al-sudan*, the "Land of the Blacks," was the most important source of gold for the medieval Mediterranean world until a new, more productive source was discovered across the Atlantic Ocean in the sixteenth

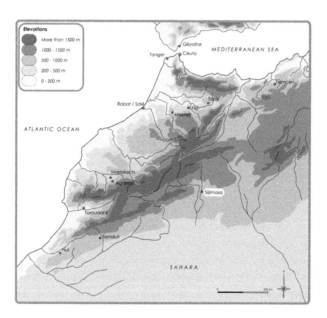

Figure I.2. Northern Morocco showing the location of Sijilmasa.

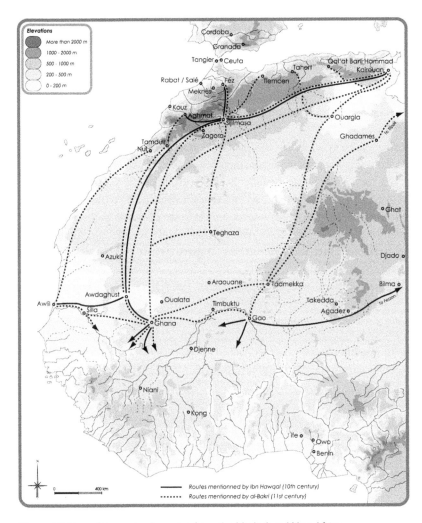

Figure I.3. Trans-Saharan trade routes from the Maghrib to West Africa.

century. We argue that the gold that passed through Sijilmasa was, in large part, what gave Iberian kingdoms their taste for gold on the eve of and during the era of the Crusades. We go as far as to suggest that it was a contributing cause of the Crusades, and among the means used to pay for them. Sijilmasa was central to the story of the medieval global economy.

The story of Sijilmasa is a mirror of Moroccan dynastic history. It was an independent Amazigh (Berber) city-state at a time when most of Morocco was ruled by independent Amazigh tribal rulers. Many of these tribal rulers became vassals to either the Umayyad rulers of Cordoba (Spain) or the Fatimid rulers of Mahdiya (modern Tunisia) when those two regimes competed with each other to control the gold routes going south. Sijilmasa was the first Moroccan city to be conquered by the Almoravids, who came from the central Sahara in the mid-eleventh century, and it became the springboard for their conquest for the rest of Morocco. In 1147, it was among the last strongholds to fall to the Almohad dynasty, which then ruled there for another century. During the reign of the Merinids, who ruled Morocco from their capital in Fez, Sijilmasa both reached its economic apogee and began its road to decline.

The traditional date for the "collapse" of Sijilmasa as a city is 1393, when a civil war broke out among Merinid rivals, a disastrous conflict that saw the extensive destruction of structures and infrastructure in Sijilmasa. We say "traditional" date because we offer a significantly revised interpretation of Sijilmasa's collapse. The civil war was followed by a period of salutary neglect during which Sijilmasa was only intermittently controlled by the successive Wattasid and Saadian rulers of Morocco. The Alaouites, the current ruling dynasty, ushered in the most recent phase of Sijilmasa's dynastic history. Each of these successive regimes left a distinctive mark on the city's development. To facilitate the reading of this dynastic history, a chart of the dynasties, their rulers, and their dates appears as an appendix.

Methodologies

Our approach is necessarily interdisciplinary. We began as historians do, by reading texts. Those texts gave us the broad outlines of Sijilmasa's history. They did not tell us very much about Sijilmasa's morphology, its "mortar and bricks," its environment. For that, we had to look on the ground. We examined aerial photographs of the central city and of the entire oasis of the Tafilalt. We analyzed multispectral satellite images of these same areas. The combination enabled us to project the existence of subsurface structures, mainly walls; we could see how water channels had shifted over time. Of course, what we saw in these remote-sensing images had to be confirmed by extensive ground truthing. Concurrent with the reconnaissance on the ground, we talked to the people who live in the Tafilalt. We quizzed them about agriculture, patterns of water distribution (current and traditional), stories about Sijilmasa's heyday, and its demise as the City of Gold. They directed us to fragments of the ancient circuit wall of the city, to some of its principal gates, and to a peripheral site, Suq Ben Akla, that turned out to be the staging area for the great caravans that crossed the Sahara hundreds of years ago.

As archaeologists, we looked at objects. We excavated sixty-five units over an area of approximately 1.5 square kilometers (370.7 acres). We identified several architectural remains, city walls, domestic architecture, public baths and latrines, and, most especially, the Grand Mosque and madrasa. We could discern distinct levels of occupation (stratigraphy). From latest to earliest, they were as follows: a level contemporaneous with the Alaouite dynasty, a level that dates from the Merinid dynasty through the Filalian period (mid-fourteenth to mid-seventeenth century), a level contemporaneous with the great imperial dynasties (Almoravid, Almohads, and Merinids—eleventh through the mid-fourteenth centuries), and a pre-Almoravid level (pre-1050).

As in most excavations, the most abundant objects found were ceramics. We catalogued over 15,400 sherds, which form the basis of a useful typology of Sijilmasa pottery. Ceramic forms allow us to form judgments about prevalent functions that occurred in parts of the site, for example, public space versus private space, or residential space versus commercial space. The typology is time sensitive, that is, it shows how forms changed over time, and thus it can help determine the relative dating of the levels mentioned above. Some ceramics, imported as well as exported, provide insight into Sijilmasa's far-reaching commercial network. A description of the Sijilmasa ceramics typology appears as an appendix.

Our time-sensitive ceramics typology allows us to determine whether a particular object or a particular level is older or newer than another one. It does not give a specific date for an object or a level. We have relatively few absolute dates in our archaeological data. We do have forty-five carbon-14 dates for the levels mentioned above. There are very few historical events that we can date with some precision by texts *and* that we can see evidence for in the archaeological record. These relatively few "absolute" dates, when visible in the stratigraphy, allow us to move down or up in the levels, backward or forward in the chronology of Sijilmasa.

Coins can be useful for establishing chronology. Many Islamic coins bear the name of the ruler of the regime that issued the coin, the date of issue, and the name of the mint. Unfortunately, we found very few coins in our excavations at Sijilmasa; most of those were Alaouite coins of the eighteenth and nineteenth centuries. But vast quantities of Sijilmasa coins exist in collections all over the world. We have done qualitative and quantitative analyses of dinars (gold coins) struck in Sijilmasa. Neutron activation analysis allowed us to determine the mineral content of the coins. We estimated the relative production of the Sijilmasa mint from year to year based on a count of all the coins published in museum catalogues, collectors' catalogues, dealers' catalogues, and scholarly numismatic articles.[9] Whenever possible, monetary historians have used the die-count method to quantify coin production. That method consists of comparing coins of the same issue to determine whether they were struck from the same or from different dies. The theory is that if we have two coins, we can conclude that two coins were struck in a particular year at a particular mint. But if we can determine that two different dies were used, knowing that each die could produce hundreds or even thousands of coins, we would have a more accurate impression of the volume of production. The die-count method requires firsthand analysis of the actual coins or good-quality photographs of the coins. We used both approaches in our analysis.[10]

Anthropologists and sociologists make extensive use of theoretical models. The model of the "Islamic city" has proved to be an extremely useful tool in our attempt to understand the morphology of Sijilmasa. No one would question that Sijilmasa was an Islamic city. After all, it was founded in the middle of the eighth century by Muslim refugees. The vast majority of its inhabitants from the very beginning and throughout its history have been Muslims. But how does it compare with other Muslim cities or with some prototypical Islamic city? The question is hard to answer because there is no consensus about exactly what constitutes the Islamic city, even though much has been written about the subject since the time of Ibn Khaldun in the four-teenth century. In recent times, Janet Abu-Lughod traces two separate isnads (chains of authority) that try to describe the Islamic city.[11] The first starts with an article by William Marçais in 1928 and runs through George Mar-çais, Robert Brunschvig, Gustave von Grunebaum, Roger Le Tourneau, and Jacques Berque.[12] These scholars base their generalizations on French North African sources and studies particularly focusing on Fez, that is, a series of studies looking back on one another. But there is, according to Abu-Lughod, a second isnad consisting of the works of Jean Sauvaget and, more recently, Ira Lapidus. These studies concentrate on Damascus and Aleppo; Lapidus adds supporting material on the Mamluk capital of Cairo.[13] Thus, one reason for the lack of consensus is that scholars are sampling different groups of cities, looking at either the Maghrib (Islamic West) or the Mashriq (Islamic East). Lapidus's work expresses concern about the validity of an Islamic city model. His work differs from earlier ones in an important way. Rather than describing features seen in a particular Islamic city or a particular selection of Islamic cities, at a particular time, he examines those social processes that make a city a city. He suggests that cities are Muslim because of the predominance of sub-communities that embody a Muslim way of life. Looking at cities as processes rather than products is a major methodological breakthrough.

To these two isnads, we add a third, Middle Eastern–North African schol-ars, beginning with perhaps the very first attempt to define the Islamic city, the work of Ibn Khaldun in the late fourteenth and early fifteenth centuries. One model that has greatly guided the formation of our own is that of Frej Stambouli and Abdelkader Zghal, who in 1976 outlined four discernible patterns of spatial order in precolonial North African cities.[14] The debate about the validity of an Islamic city model seemed to peak in the 1990s. Nezar al-Sayyad examined those processes that shaped early caliphal garrison and capital cities, namely, Basra, Kufa, Damascus, Aleppo, Baghdad, Cordoba, and Cairo.[15] He argues for a more geographically and chronologically grounded approach, focusing on what he describes as Arab-Muslim cities in the first Islamic centuries.[16]

Discussion of the validity of the Islamic city model continues apace. Amira K. Bennison and Alison L. Gascoigne offer a series of articles to illustrate three themes: "urban transformations occasioned by the rise of Islam and their conceptualization by Muslims; the impact of Muslim regimes on urban development; and the ways in which religion may have affected the functioning of public amenities."[17] The long discussion has culminated (to date) with the publication of *The City in the Islamic World*, edited by Salma K. Jayyusi, which she "visualized as a voluminous, comprehensive account of the Islamic City," but noted also: "We have chosen to title this volume 'City in the Islamic World' specifically to circumvent the no longer productive discourse on the 'Islamic City.'"[18]

Let us be clear about how the discussion of "the Islamic city model" or "the city in the Islamic World" has been productive for our study. There are many models out there, some more valid than others, some justifiably questioned and criticized. And although no model can encompass all cities in the Islamic world, the models do point to certain characteristics common to many Islamic cities. Awareness of those characteristics helped us recognize those present in Sijilmasa. We developed a model of our own by reading the literature on the Islamic city, by looking at several theoretical models described by both Eastern and Western scholars, and by looking at many Islamic cities on the ground. In some cases, what we found confirmed our model; in other cases, we saw significant differences. Either way, the process helped us recognize or understand what we were looking at on the ground, and also helped us refine our evolving model. We became especially sensitive to how Sijilmasa changed over time, how it was in a constant process of changing throughout its history. We can demonstrate how we understand a "city" to be not so much a product to be looked at as a process to be observed. Finally, we offer the archaeological data that we have collected as a data set that should be useful to others who are engaged in the ongoing discussion about Islamic cities and models of Islamic cities. Where large portions of the urban landscape of cities past can be examined firsthand, archaeology offers a way of looking at the material fabric of those cities as they existed in the past rather than at how they morphed into something else in the twentieth or twenty-first century. The ruins of medieval Sijilmasa, west of modern Rissani, offer such an advantage.

Organization of MAPS

It was the lure of the City of Gold that first attracted us to Sijilmasa. The subject of Ron Messier's PhD dissertation was the circulation of gold currency in the Mediterranean world during the tenth through twelfth centuries. Gold coins, dinars, a significant percentage of which were struck in the mint of Sijilmasa, were a major source of documentation in that study. From 1969 to 1971, he examined Islamic dinars in major museum collections in New York, London, Paris, Casablanca, and Tunis. Neutron activation analysis determined that most of the gold used in the coins circulating in the Mediterranean world came from south of the Sahara, in West Africa. Most of that gold passed through Sijilmasa. Much of it was struck into dinars in the Sijilmasa mint.

It was not until 1986, when Messier was again in Morocco doing archival research on the Almoravid dynasty, that he made his first pilgrimage to the City of Gold. There was not very much of the medieval city to see on the surface, on the outskirts of Rissani—only a few broken mud walls and the partial remains of one structure that local residents identified as the "mosque." The latter was the only ruin that even remotely looked like a building: two rectangular rooms, much of the walls missing, square holes in the floor where pillars once stood to support a roof. The pillars and roof were gone. But there was an abundance of potsherds, many recognizably medieval, strewn all over the ground.

Over the next year and a half, Messier negotiated with officials in the Moroccan Ministry of Cultural Affairs and the Moroccan National Museum of Archaeology to launch MAPS, the Moroccan-American Project at Sijilmasa. In 1987, Messier and Neil MacKenzie, one of his graduate school classmates with long experience in medieval Islamic archaeology in the Middle East, made an exploratory mission to Sijilmasa to develop strategies for the excavation. MacKenzie served as field director for the six seasons of excavation that followed.

MAPS was not the first archaeological project in Sijilmasa in the twentieth century. In the early 1970s, the Ludwig Keimer Foundation organized two archaeological and ethnological missions to the region of the Tafilalt.[19]

The excavations were done approximately three kilometers north-northwest of Rissani. According to a summary of the report, the first mission uncovered a network of underground canals with associated water mains in glazed terracotta, as well as a bridge and a dam near a large reservoir, which was located by Inspector Ben Shemsi of Meknes.[20] The second season uncovered the remains of walls, a fountain, plant fossils, and human bones. In addition, the excavations produced fragments of fine glass, jewelry, and small tiles in faience. Stratigraphic information from these two seasons is unpublished. In 1974, Inspector Ben Shemsi conducted an excavation in "the Mosque Area." The mud walls exposed in that excavation contain sherds that suggest the walls are unlikely to predate the seventeenth century, meaning that they are Alaouite walls. There are numerous sherds of ceramics in storage in the National Museum of Archaeology in Rabat from the Keimer Foundation excavations, but stratigraphic information was not available.

The "Convention de Coopération" between the newly established Institut National des Sciences d'Archéologie et du Patrimoine (INSAP) and Messier's university, Middle Tennessee State University, was signed in the spring of 1988. Mme. Houdia Benslimane, the director of INSAP, and Messier were the signatories. Professor Abdulaziz Touri, the associate director of INSAP at the time, later described it this way: "We had many requests for projects at Sijilmasa, but the time seemed right to launch this Moroccan-American project."[21]

Excavations began in June 1988. That summer, James Miller was continuing his work in the Draa Valley, investigating the effects on downstream users of the construction of the dam on the Oued Draa at Ouarzazate. He knew that Messier had organized a team from Tennessee and INSAP to begin digging at Sijilmasa, and he was curious about how they were faring in the Tafilalt, where a dam had been constructed on the Oueds Ziz and Gheris, which flow into the Sahara. As a geographer, he found his interest piqued. His university, Clemson, had provided him some funding for that summer's research, and after visiting Messier and company, he vowed to return. Together, they forged ahead, returning to Sijilmasa for five more seasons: 1992, 1993, 1994, 1996, and 1998. In addition, Miller returned to Rissani in 1999 to organize the shipment of artifacts for a traveling exhibition of the results of our efforts, *The Sijilmasa Caravan*, which was shown in Birmingham, Memphis, and Nashville in that same year.

Between 1988 and 1998, MAPS excavated and explored in and around the Sijilmasa site. Sijilmasa's larger home, the Tafilalt oasis and the magnificent landscapes of desert mesas, plains, and dunes speckling the Moroccan Saharan periphery, became its field of examination. Over the years, many others joined the MAPS team: Stephen Brown, a historic preservationist, and John Runkle, an architectural draftsman, both from Nashville; Dale Lightfoot, a remote-sensing specialist from the University of Oklahoma; James Knudstadt, a free-lance archaeologist from England; Tony Wilkinson, a geomorphologist then at the University of Chicago, now at Durham University in England; and Samantha Messier, a biologist from the University of Colorado—all made up the interdisciplinary professional staff. The agreement between INSAP and Middle Tennessee State University called for an equal number of Moroccan and American students. Six to ten students from each country participated each season. Beginning in the second season, the Earthwatch organization supplied eighteen volunteers each year, totaling ninety volunteers in all over the next five seasons of the project. Last but by no means least, an indispensable foundation of the team was a corps of dedicated, local Moroccan workers.

As a team, we calculated where to dig, then excavated, sifted, washed, drew, photographed, and catalogued. We explored by using contemporary techniques that expose and develop the past in ways unavailable to earlier scholars. Our work was supported by the Centre d'Études et de Recherches Alaouites (CERA) in Rissani, the local office of the Ministry of Culture, which graciously housed our laboratory and storage facilities. We also lived in Rissani off and on over a ten-year span. When newcomers came to join us, arriving in town by bus or by car, all they had to do is ask, "Where are the archaeologists?" And they would be immediately taken to us. When we walk the streets of Rissani now, more than a decade after we last dug, people recognize and greet us as warmly as they ever did. It seems that we became, in our own special way, a noticeable part of this Tafilalt community, enough to learn much about it from the inside. Our Tafilalt friends taught us to cook recipes that we had read about in early texts. Food that needed to be baked, including our Thanksgiving turkey and apple pies, we took to the local public oven. We visited craftsmen in their shops and watched them craft pottery, new but in forms like those we saw in all the levels of our excavations. These potters taught us much about how many of these plates and bowls were used and what they were called. We bathed in the local hammam, no different from hammams of centuries ago. Three days a week, on Tuesday, Thursday, and Sunday, we enjoyed market day. Rissani is now the regional market for dozens of villages in the oasis. Sunday, our day off, was the most important of the three market days. It was not difficult for us to allow our minds to travel back in time several centuries to when, just a few hundred yards away, Sijilmasa's market functioned in much the same way. After generations of silence from Sijilmasa, we can now open a new chapter in the history of this place. Sijilmasa can now speak.

Our intention is to present more than an archaeological report. We want to tell what we know of Sijilmasa's history, its legends, its material existence, the role that it played in the international economy of northwest Africa, and the role that it played in the formation of Morocco's national identity. Our goal is to present our historical, geographic, and archaeological data as a story in lively prose, the story of the city and the story of the dig. MAPS's presence in the Tafilalt is an important, integral part of the narrative. In the prologue, we allowed our imaginations to engage in the narrative. We tried to imagine how a famous fourteenth-century Muslim traveler, Ibn Battuta, saw Sijilmasa. We know that he spent over four months there. He told us so, and he told us some of what he saw. From our own research, we know much of what was actually there when he was there in the fourteenth century. So it was not hard to imagine. Chapter 2 establishes the geographic and chronological scope of the story. The four chapters after that move through four distinct periods in Sijilmasa's history, telling the story in the order that a historian would tell it. Woven into that story is the material evidence that traces how the city and its environment changed over those periods of time. Chapter 7 compares the theoretical city models to what we found Sijilmasa to be on the ground. Finally, Chapter 8, the conclusion, describes our (Messier and Miller's) return visit to the site in October 2011. It reflects on what we found in Sijilmasa and the Tafilalt in the late 1980s and 1990s. It describes a picture of the past better understood and a present beset by rapid change. The mid-eleventh-century Arab writer al-Bakri described Sijilmasa as "the last civilized place." In the pages that follow, we explain what that means.[22]

CHAPTER 2

Confluence of Time and Space in Morocco's Desert Land

At Sijilmasa, the frame of human life meets the immensity of the greatest desert, the Sahara. Sijilmasa is "an excellent frontier town," noted al-Muqaddasi in his compendium of geography, which appeared in 985. And indeed, Sijilmasa's setting near Rissani in the Tafilalt oasis still is.[1] Sijilmasa is in the desert foreland of North Africa, the fringe of what Arab geographers have called *al-jazirat al-maghrib*, "the island of the West."[2] "Sijilmasa is situated at the beginning of the desert and no inhabited places are known to the south and west of it," wrote al-Bakri in the century following al-Muqaddasi.[3] Sijilmasa is at once in the Maghrib and at the edge of it.[4] From a geographic perspective, arriving from the desert or leaving the Maghrib, Sijilmasa is in the pre-Sahara, a transition zone where the Maghrib to the north contacts the Sahara to the south.[5] Sijilmasa, in the farthest southeastern corner of the modern map of Morocco, ruled over a broad area encompassing the land at the southern foot the Atlas Mountains, marking the edge of a different land and life to the north, a more human realm, and running out to the Great Western Erg, a more physical realm, a vast sandy sea that begins in eastern Morocco, extends across much of western Algeria, and is one of the predominant features of the northern Sahara. As al-Mas'udi, the great geographer of the tenth century, tells us: "The province of Sijilmasa [is] on the desert fringe [*sahil*]."[6]

At Sijilmasa, we are concerned with its pre-Saharan hearth, the Tafilalt, where Atlas-born rivers run parallel in an oasis and where Sijilmasa was born. In this intermediate zone, pre-Sahara and post-Atlas, Sijilmasa reigned supreme for over a thousand years. Here, where the Sahara and all its features begin and become ever more intense, several key environmental characteristics etch Sijilmasa's setting and, indeed, its destiny: mountains, rivers, sands, and other desert features. High mountains lie to the back of the Tafilalt, toward the rest of Morocco. The Tafilalt basin and the waters of the two rivers stream-

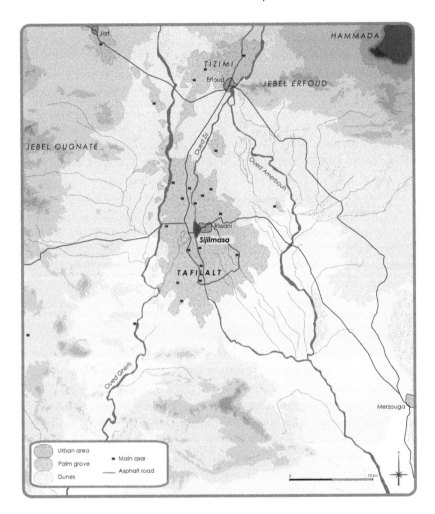

Figure 2.1. Map of the Tafilalt oasis.

ing down from the Atlas, the Ziz and the Gheris, frame the beneficent site of Sijilmasa, its geographic present. Desert features surround it and lead into the Sahara, a seemingly endless space beyond Sijilmasa. The Tafilalt is Sijilmasa's home. Our quest is to understand the nature of this special realm.

The Atlas Mountains to the north form a high environmental divide separating the Morocco of the two seas, the Atlantic and the Mediterranean, from the Morocco of the Sahara, the desert sea that spreads like an apron south of Sijilmasa and the Maghrib. From many peaks ranging higher than 3,000 meters (9,800 feet), elevations drop steadily southward from the Eastern

High Atlas down its pre-Saharan piedmont and on into the desert. Streams from these mountains, such as the Oueds Ziz and the Gheris leading to the Tafilalt, or the Oued Draa coming out of the Central High Atlas, carry snowmelt from the southern flanks of the Atlas's many peaks and valleys and course south into the desert, wrongheadedly, it would seem. But along all these, the Ziz and the Gheris, the Draa to the west or the Guir farther east, people have expanded life in the oases along the desert margins. The waters of these rivers gradually disappear, flowing out beyond the pre-Sahara with no renewal and ending as the full desert emerges. The Ziz, the Gheris, and the other desert streams are destined to die on land, victims of the desert, never reaching the sea. Flowing into the Sahara, they run slowly and then not at all in summer as their mountain sources of water dry up; they charge furiously in flood, common in spring and fall, when they can be powerful, turbulent streams. But normally, as mountain snows melt in the Atlas and the long, dry Mediterranean summer begins in Morocco, they flow tranquilly to their deaths in the desert.[7] Eroded sediments brought down from the Atlas Mountains have been deposited in pockets along these streams, forming the basis for human life and agriculture in an otherwise desolate region.

One such pocket is the broad Tafilalt plain, where the Ziz and the Gheris nearly converge and create Morocco's largest oasis. From an environmental point of view, Sijilmasa is the creature of the Oued Ziz. From its headwaters in the very heart of the Atlas mountains, the Ziz moves first eastward and then, from a point near modern Rich, flows generally southward toward its ultimate desert confluence with the Oued Gheris to the south of the Tafilalt basin. Below Errachidia (elevation 1,031 meters; 3,383 feet), the Ziz flows through a spectacular canyon, the Rteb, which runs southeast some 50 kilometers (31 miles). Here, encased in the impressive walls of the Rteb, which reach heights of some 200 meters (650 feet), the Ziz is fed by springs that rejuvenate it and create an extensive forest of date palms on the canyon floor. The Ziz drops southward, coursing along the eastern side of the Tizimi oasis as it reaches Erfoud, where the river, nearing the Tafilalt, takes on an entirely different character.[8] Our findings point to a major reconstruction of the Oued Ziz at Erfoud at some point in the Almoravid dynasty. Here, the Ziz takes on the character of a braided stream as the river flows into several channels over relatively flat terrain. This naturally braided nature of the Ziz below Erfoud was transformed into one main channel. This is what we know as the Ziz in the Tafilalt, which runs down the center of the oasis in what we believe to be an improved bed, more or less straight, plunging due south from Erfoud and running through the center of the Tafilalt toward Rissani (750 meters; 2,460 feet) and onward. The eastern channel, known as the Oued Amerbouh, is blocked off by massive rock dam structures, built and rebuilt over time, empty except during times of exceptionally high water. The channels of the Ziz and Amerbouh then meet at the southern end of the Tafilalt some 20 kilometers (12.4 miles) southeast of Rissani. The Tafilalt basin warps gently downward and is enclosed at its southern end by a perimeter of low hills. Here, both the Ziz and the Gheris, which wraps along the western edge of the Tafilalt in parallel to its cousin, slip through gaps in the hills into the desert of nomads beyond, toward the undefined confines of the Moroccan-Algerian border.

The western-framing Gheris then joins the Ziz farther downstream, south of the Taouz Massif, where the combined rivers take the name of the Oued Daoura.[9] As we shall see, fundamental adjustments to the Ziz were made in the 1970s through the construction of a dam, the Hassan ad-Dakhil, which impounds its waters just above Errachidia, the former Ksar es Souk. Before the construction of the dam, the oasis fields and date palms of the Tafilalt were fed by the high waters of the Ziz and Gheris in spring, replenishing the oasis through myriad canals, ever smaller, that brought water to every square inch of arable land in the Tafilalt. The flow of water diminished, bit by bit, in the summer and fall as dates matured. Flash floods, often arising in the pre-Sahara as the season changes from winter into summer in March, and from summer into fall in October and November, could bring great and sudden amounts of water—beneficial up to a point, disastrous after that point—to the Tafilalt.

Mountains, water, and then that most elemental feature of the desert—sand and barren rock. The desert is not flat. Here and there, all around the Tafilalt, winds form huge mounds of sand as they sweep across the Tafilalt, gather loose surface materials, carry them into the air, and deposit them at the foot of the escarpments (*kreb*) and barren plateaus (*hammada*) that rise above the Tafilalt and contain it to the south, east, and west. The Erg Chebbi dunes, a major tourist attraction just east of Rissani at Merzouga, are the best known of these. These mountainous dunes rise symmetrically to form peaks in pyramidal mounds with arms stemming outward from their tops. From above, they look like twirling stars. Trapped by the cliffs of the *hammada*, the dunes build upward rather than spread across the landscape. This, then, is Sijilmasa's regional formula: mountains, rivers, and desert. It is worth pausing to ask how this environmental formula developed over geologic time to become the Tafilalt of today.

Underlying the environmental basis of Sijilmasa are very active and diverse events in the recent geologic history of the northern Sahara. For the last several thousand years, the Sahara has been nearly equal in size to its maximum during the Pleistocene epoch, so often called simply the ice age but in reality a long and diverse geologic time stretching from 2.5 million years ago to the near present.[10] During the Pleistocene, the proto-Sahara experienced a great diversity of climates, but during the peak of the last glaciation, which began some 110,000 years ago (YA) and reached its maximum characteristics in what is called the last glacial maximum (between 26,500 and 19,000 YA), the Sahara was even larger than it is today.[11] In this period, much of Europe was cold steppe and tundra, and the Alps, Scandinavia, and most of Britain were solid fields of ice. To the west of the continent, a thick sheet of ice projected into the North Atlantic, depriving North Africa of its most important source of moisture.[12] The Maghrib was cold and dry. The Sahara reached its known maximum size.[13]

By then, people had already long been living in this land. Hominids (*Homo erectus*) inhabited North Africa and the Sahara from some 200,000 YA, maybe longer. *Homo sapiens* appeared, as the archaic species, at 50,000 YA. By 30,000 YA, Paleolithic descendants of these early people were at a stage of advanced toolmaking, engaging *Homo sapiens sapiens*, modern humans, in a North African culture known as Aterian. Aterian culture vanished from the Maghrib as the climate became colder and drier toward the end of the last glacial maximum. Then, as continental glaciation retreated to the north and the geologic present, the Holocene epoch, began, people called Iberomaurusians (of "both Iberia and North Africa") appear in the paleontological record of the Maghrib at about 16,000 YA.

Analysis of pollens and animal bones at Iberomaurusian sites indicates the beginning of a new, warmer and much wetter era across North Africa.[14] Iberomaurusians hunted Barbary sheep, wild cattle, gazelle, zebra, and deer; their diet included freshwater snails and wild plants. The Maghrib had greened up with the retreat of the ice and the return of free waters to the North Atlantic. But further dramatic changes lay ahead for the Maghrib during the first half of the Holocene.[15]

Between 12,800 and 11,500 YA, a sudden climatic shift known as the Younger Dryas event swept over the world, interrupting the progression of warmth experienced since the retreat of the last glacial maximum.[16] Average temperatures in North Africa and throughout the planet plunged. Glacial conditions returned in the Northern Hemisphere. After at least 4,000 years of warm and relatively wet conditions, North Africa became, again, colder and more arid for 2,000 years.[17] Then, and for reasons not yet known, the Younger Dryas ended, the Sahara again greened, and greened again, to the degree that much of what is today desert went up the biological scale to become grassland and woodland for the next 6,000 years.[18] Seasonal freshwater ponds and lakes and their associated flora and fauna—collectively known as "lacustrine conditions"—dotted much of the northern Sahara along the Atlas in what is now the pre-Sahara and the Sahara itself.[19] Water flowed in abundance southward from the Atlas; the combined waters of the Gheris and the Ziz created the Oued Daoura, which flowed deep into the Sahara.[20] To the east of the Tafilalt, the Oued Saoura, which combines the flow of the Oueds Guir and Zousfana, created a massive system drawing water from the Eastern High Atlas and the southern flanks of the Saharan Atlas in modern Algeria and infiltrating the substratum of the western portion of perhaps the world's largest groundwater system, known as the Continental Intercalaire.[21] In parallel, in the Tafilalt, strata in road cuts today reveal lake terraces, indicating the presence and recession of shallow lakes that periodically covered the basin.

Flints and burial mounds, Paleolithic and Neolithic, are commonplace throughout the region. We do not know whether these were produced by descendants of the Iberomaurusians or by settlers from the Nile Valley or by Africans following these rivers northward into the Sahara; all can be suspected. In any case, it is clear that the entire Saharan fringe from Morocco to Egypt was well populated in prehistoric times. By 9,000–8,000 YA, these people were herding sheep and goats, following the early lead of peoples in the Middle East and the diffusion of Neolithic culture throughout the northern Sahara. A culture identified as "Capsian" (from Gafsa, Roman Capsa, in Tunisia) developed in the eastern Maghrib. Fine microliths, anthropomorphic stone and clay figures, and other cultural elements found at sites recognized as Capsian allowed Gabriel Camps, among the most dedicated of scholars of the prehistory of the Maghrib, to argue that the Capsian culture was generated by migration from the Levant.[22] Cultural similarities stretching to the Nile furthered Camps's speculation that Capsian culture represented the origins of the Berber peoples of northern Africa—a hypothesis proposed earlier by the American anthropologist Carleton Coon—and indeed it may be so.[23] As Capsian culture became more pervasive across the Maghrib, proto-Berber peoples spread with it, diffusing it, perhaps absorbing earlier peoples; we do not know. In any case, the Maghrib flourished, environmentally and socially.

By 7,500 YA, cattle herding was widespread in the Sahara, and the region became the first in Africa to exhibit domesticated crops and animals. Rock carvings (petroglyphs) and rock painting (parietal art) found throughout the Sahara depict scenes of wild game being hunted and cattle being herded.[24] Rock art at the openings of valleys all along the Moroccan pre-Sahara indicate that the area was fully part of a new and abundant human life during this fascinating period, known as the Neolithic, Saharan, or post-Pleistocene subpluvial, and increasingly known simply as the Green Sahara.[25]

For at least 6,000 years, the North African environment was significantly different from what was to come, just over the horizon toward the present; there are some reasonable suggestions but no sure answers why the Green Sahara prevailed through most of the first half of the Holocene, the current geologic epoch.[26] The entire North African–Saharan biosystem was more abundant; forests were denser and broader; woodland and steppe vegetation ranged deep into what is today desert; the desert itself was less extensive and less harsh.[27] Faunal life was equally richer, especially, and large savanna mammals are depicted everywhere in rock art throughout the Sahara.

But the climate shifted. Sometime after 5,400 YA (3400 BC), the Sahara and the Maghrib became drier, and people retreated from environments that had been humanized for several thousand years; they, like the fauna and flora that supported them, dispersed north and south. The desert grew again. Aridification may have begun in the east and moved west, where a wetter climate persisted longer. There remain many difficulties in identifying the end of this golden era for the Sahara as evidence mounts from many disciplines about its global significance.

A new Sahara took hold, without doubt in jagged climatic shifts, and human populations adapted. Petroglyphs datable to 3,200 YA (1200 BC) provide visual evidence for North African cultures that crossed the Sahara in horse-drawn chariots. The Maghrib and, for that matter, the Sahara stood at the brink of prehistory being overtaken by history. The civilization of the antique Libyan Garamantes people and their Saharan chariots, recorded by Herodotus, is being revealed.[28] Saharan rock carvings of horsemen are found in locations as far away as the Niger River. Chariots are not found that far west. Finally, by AD 300, when signs of trans-Saharan connectivity as represented in petroglyph art end, Saharan rock carvings record a literate Berber culture in which the Tifinagh alphabet is used.[29] The Sahara as we know it had arrived.

Sijilmasa was founded in 757. What urban settlement, if any, had been in the Tafilalt before its founding is discussed in the next chapter. Sijilmasa's function as a trading center was shaped by its location as a caravan port set between the green lands to the north, where there were cities such as Fez and Sebta, and the lure of the other *sahil*, the other shore, the African lands on the other edge of the Sahara, to its south. Sijilmasa was part of a network of places that renewed the trans-Saharan connections from the prehistoric past. Sijilmasa, "a great city to the south of the outer cities of Morocco adjoining the desert," was at once deeply Saharan and North African.[30] It had direct connections to distant sites; the human places in between were few. Sijilmasans used their few but key environmental attributes—river water, alluvial soils, a relatively enclosed basin—to build an oasis that became the infrastructural backbone of the caravan trade. Water usage was refined, expanded, and ever refashioned, since the primary local concern was to increase irrigation capacity. Let us look more closely at those environmental resources to grasp the materials from which Sijilmasans developed the Tafilalt into their storehouse of local treasure.

Over the long life of Sijilmasa, from the mid-700s to the near present, there were wetter and drier periods, but overall there has been great stability in the climate. "Sijilmasa also belongs to this desert region," wrote al-Dimashqi in the early fourteenth century, the Merinid age in Moroccan history. "It is a town on a salty plain with groves of palms and a river called the Ziz, which has a flood like the Nile. Rivers descending from the mountains of Daran (the Atlas mountains) feed the Ziz."[31] The pre-Saharan environment is defined by a climatic regime of low but highly variable precipitation and high average annual temperatures in a modified Mediterranean-type model of hot, dry summers, brief transitional seasons, and cool winters with occasional precipitation. Average annual precipitation in the watersheds of the Oueds Ziz and Gheris averages 250 millimeters (9.8 inches) in the Eastern High Atlas Mountains, declining to 122 millimeters (4.8 inches) at Errachidia, and 50 millimeters (2 inches) at Rissani, the site of Sijilmasa itself.[32] There is high interannual variability. At Errachidia, annual precipitation over the period 1973–2009 ranged from 1.15 millimeters (.04 inches) in 1983–1984 to 297.4 millimeters (11.7 inches) in 2008–2009. Virtually no rain falls during the summer months, and any precipitation is likely to be a brief, dust-laden burst of rain at the end of the sharp easterly winds, the *chergui*, which can bring dust storms for days at a time, especially in June and July. Sudden bursts of rain, sometimes in surprising amounts, allow very little infiltration into the soil, and over 90 percent of rainfall becomes runoff. Brusque autumn and spring rains are common in the region, and flash floods are most frequent at the turn of the seasons—early October, when the immense heat of summer suddenly dissipates, and late March, when it begins to return.

When the Sijilmasa project began in the mid-1980s, the region's hydrologic infrastructure had been recently and fundamentally transformed. A massive flood on the Ziz in November 1965 sent a wall of water through the Tafilalt, destroying fields, farms, and lives.[33] King Hassan II, dusting off plans first conceived by the French colonial authorities, began the policy of dam building, *la politique des grands barrages*, for which he became famous. The Tafilalt's age-old irrigation system, derived from channelizing water locally out of the Ziz and the Gheris, was overridden by a modern system of canals bringing water downstream from the reservoir at the Hassan ad-Dakhil dam. The hydrologic infrastructure of the Tafilalt became a mix of large, modern features and small, traditional irrigation installations; the two systems, which were often incompatible, competed with each other. Most importantly for the Tafilalt, the waters of the Ziz were gathered in the reservoir at Errachidia, and the downstream Ziz, in large part, went dry. Farmers became dependent on the waters of the dam, delivered through agricultural and hydrologic engineering that was dependent, in turn, on the precipitation that fell on the Ziz watershed and was held in the reservoir.

The dam had the unintended consequence of encouraging the growth of Errachidia and its concomitant urban needs, in part because the water supply was now entirely spatially concentrated there and not distributed by the natural flow of the Ziz and the ability of local users to spread its waters over their fields. Several factors have made the problem of irrigation in the Tafilalt more complex, not less, after the development of a modern dam, reservoir, and irrigation network. First, the dam generally receives less water than it can hold: Hassan ad-Dakhil is an "underfit" dam.[34] Second, putting the Ziz in a reservoir in the high desert above Errachidia has resulted in significant loss of water due to evaporation. Third, downstream users, who had constructed and reconstructed, elaborated and modified, their own systems of water distribution out of the Ziz and Gheris over the entire period of human habitation in the Tafilalt, had been led to expect a new system of regular and adequate flows through the modern irrigation system. But that system, engineered to bring water to central points in the oasis, did not connect with the micro-landscape inside the oasis, leading to a multitude of disjunctures between the new system and traditional irrigation. Previously distributed via intricate systems of timing and social labor organization, the water supply became centralized and subject to being turned on and off like a spigot by remote and sometimes unknowing and uncaring officials. Perhaps even more importantly, water was appropriated in blocks of time over which individual farmers had no control and between which, for long stretches, no water was available. And most important was that generally not enough water was available overall.

One could contradict these statements by saying that all the *qsur*, the adobe villages of the region, were now connected to a system of clean piped-in drinking water, and that health conditions improved immediately as a result. True, and miraculous. But the river ran dry, and the date palms and crops of the oasis withered. The ecology of the Tafilalt was sharply altered. As the new system of water distribution settled in, Tafilalt farmers developed alternative and adaptive strategies to cope with the changes. Knowing that a water table lay beneath them, Tafilalt farmers purchased diesel pumps (known as *moto-pompes*), built wells, and pumped their own water from under their fields, connecting the pumped water to the old irrigation system. Farmers sometimes

Figure 2.2. The Murqni canal from the Slaoua dam on the Oued Ziz. The modern irrigation canal from the Hassan Ad-Dakhil dam is dry even as the traditional irrigation system canal continues to function. Here the Murqni canal runs full after local rains in April 1996. The modern canal has been broken at various times, rendering it useless. The great push in the Tafilalt oasis today is to recover its agricultural heritage, which has been damaged through modern engineering miscalculations and high-handed development projects made without local input.

broke the new canals and connected the water from the dam to the old system, paying the occasional price in fines. The few years when sufficient water collected in the reservoir to send adequate and regular flows downstream gave some reprieve to the new, hybrid water regime. On the other hand, when the reservoir behind Hassan ad-Dakhil seemed full to overflowing in late 2009, the authorities released a vast amount of water without warning, flooding the southern portion of the Tafilalt with a meter of water that worked its way through the broken system, lapped up into houses, and washed out parts of the macadam road that circles the oasis.[35] The effect of the *moto-pompes* has been a regular and general lowering of the water table throughout the Tafilalt; farmers now incur energy costs where none previously existed; age-old social systems that were rooted in part in the distribution of water and were responsible for the location of the *qsur* themselves have fallen apart; labor out-migration has increased; populations of the *qsur* have decreased. Since the beginning of the Sijilmasa project, in the mid-1980s, it has become apparent to the authors that the general human ecology of the Tafilalt has deteriorated considerably. The negative factors resulting from misguided irrigation systems have combined to create a steady downward spiral of rural life in the region.

Perhaps the most significant intrusive additional factor subtracting from the quality of life in the Tafilalt has been the spread of a type of date palm wilt, *bayyoud*, in the period following the construction of the dam. The disease, caused by a soilborne fungus (*Fusarium oxysporum f.sp. albedinis*), spreads through the intertwined root systems of the palm orchards, rises up through the xylem (water tubes) of the palm, and slowly kills the tree through wilting. It often attacks one side of the tree, whitening its fronds with powdery mold, and then chokes the tree to death.[36] Detected as early as 1870 in Algeria, fusarium has become endemic in the oases of Morocco and western Algeria and represents the most dangerous disease attacking the date palm, which is the lifeblood of the oasis. In the past, the fungus was occasionally washed out of the upper layers of the soil by flooding—the mitigation of which was the motivation for building the dam in the first place. In the absence of flood, *bayyoud* has spread and intensified throughout the Tafilalt and beyond. Without the occasional flood, *bayyoud* and the other enemy that builds up in oasis soils, mineral salts, are not flushed out; the fungus and the salt buildup create a deadly threat against which there is no remedy and no reprieve. While the Tafilalt still produces dates—and in a good year with adequate water, as in 2011, an excellent crop—the date palms of the Tafilalt have shortened lifespans, many areas have been abandoned because of salt- and *bayyoud*-contaminated soils, and the overall productivity of the region is far less than it could be.

Four Levels of Spatial Analysis

A useful spatial framework for organizing our work at Sijilmasa, leading us to be able to place Sijilmasa in context over time and space, is to conceive of the city as set within a series of nested spaces reaching outward from the debris of Sijilmasa's core, the city's site; through the local region, the Tafilalt, the city's oasis setting in the pre-Sahara; across Sijilmasa's Maghrib domain in western Islam; to a broad sphere across which Sijilmasa's influence played: the wide world of the Arab cosmographers, the distinctive geography of the Saharan gold trade, and the routes of the political and social movements of Islam as a whole. Together, these form a framework for the spatial analysis of Sijilmasa from the micro to the macro level.

Core

At Sijilmasa's core, we have primarily been archaeologists, working in the ruins of the abandoned and destroyed city, looking for clues in the relatively small area we call the central site. As we can determine from texts and site reconnaissance, Sijilmasa was, at any time, a narrowly shaped settlement contoured along the Oued Ziz in the middle of the Tafilalt oasis. While our archaeological efforts have penetrated but a fragment of the site's total area, it is here where the scale of our efforts has been greatest. We dug sixty-five trenches during six seasons over a ten-year span. In reality, while it is fair to call this area small, the Sijilmasa core forms a relatively large area, since it is the footprint of the entire city.

The conclusions we can make about Sijilmasa from archaeology, substantiated by known history, derive from a dense and intensive analysis of place that accumulated into evidence, which then became focused in two ways. First, out of the strata in which artifacts are found, sequential pictures emerge of Sijilmasa at different times in the course of its millennium-long urban life. Second, we put the frames together, attempting to see the course of change over time. So it is that the Sijilmasa core, small in size and dense in information, has been our constant point of repair. Our work at Sijilmasa was pervaded by an archaeological focus, and the techniques of modern science, along with the travails of archaeology in modern Morocco, permeate the work. Sijilmasa is many holes in the ground.

Oral traditions, constructed out of dozens of formal interviews and an equal number of informal pieces of knowledge relayed to us over more than ten years of work in the field, portray a single, longitudinal-shaped city extending from the Qsar al-Mansuriya in the north to the village of Tabouassamt in the south, a distance of approximately eight kilometers (five miles), along the Oued Ziz. Architectural features dating back at least to the fourteenth century are still visible in both of these *qsur*. Just outside the walls of al-Mansuriya lies the Bab al-Rih (Gate of the Wind), and inside the *qsar* there are several Merinid-era scalloped arches. In Tabouassamt, a fourteenth-century mosque still stands. Historical descriptions of Sijilmasa as a single long narrow city containing most or all the population of the Tafilalt include that of al-Idrisi, who described Sijilmasa in the middle of the twelfth century, early Almohad times, as consisting of a series of palaces or houses and cultivated fields stretched out along the Ziz.[37] The view of Sijilmasa as a city divided between villas and a central district comes primarily from al-Bakri's description of Sijilmasa at the beginning of the Almoravid period (mid-eleventh century) as being "surrounded by numerous suburbs" (*rabad*, plural: *arbad*), as described in chapter 1.[38] A 1994 MAPS geomorphological survey concluded that the heart of medieval Sijilmasa was restricted to a mounded area of about 1 square kilometer (247 acres) in the central site, a "downtown" that extended from the large standing wall of the citadel on the northern edge of the site to Qsar Qusaibah beyond Rissani's modern tarmac road on the southern edge of the site, a distance of about 1.7 kilometers (about 1 mile).[39] This city center is where we found the Grand Mosque, the citadel, the central market, vari-

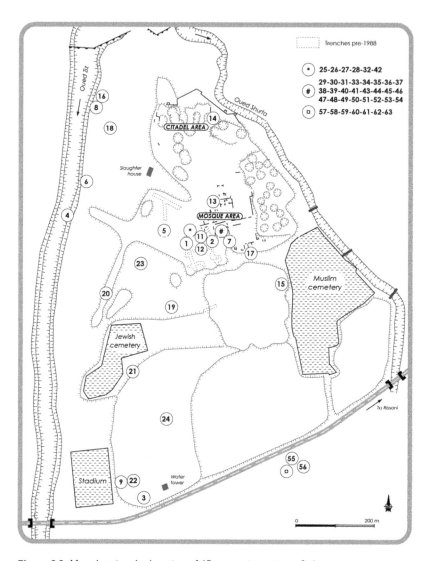

Figure 2.3. Map showing the location of 65 excavation units in Sijilmasa.

ous industries, and residences, both common and elite. Yet another description comes from the tenth-century historian al-Mas'udi, who describes Sijilmasa as having a great main artery a half-day's walk long.[40] Oral traditions in the Tafilalt repeat that description. During the 1996 season, we outlined major near-subsurface wall systems by using a combination of aerial photos and satellite imagery. The pattern of walls suggested that major walls sepa-

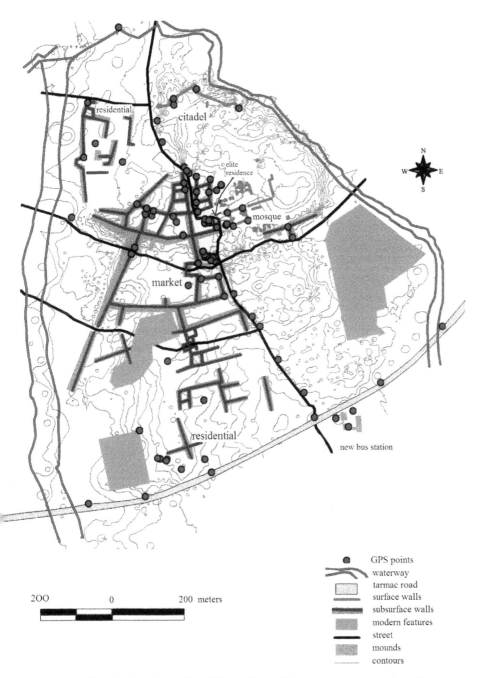

Figure 2.4. Map of subsurface walls in Sijilmasa detected by remote sensing, projected streets, and quarters.

rated quarters within the city and that a north-south central axis ran just to the west of the area of the Grand Mosque. Freestanding villas stretched more or less equidistantly northward from the citadel wall to Bab Fez and southward to Tabouassamt, 3.3 kilometers (2 miles), composing at least some of the "suburbs" described by al-Bakri. The central city lay between, making the total north-south urban extent 8 kilometers (5 miles); it was S-shaped, following the broad curve made by the Oued Ziz at the site.

Region

The Sijilmasa project was more than the sixty-five trenches we dug in the earth at Sijilmasa's core. Our radius of activities had broad local reach, extending throughout the Tafilalt oasis and its setting in the Tafilalt basin, into which the oasis fits as a small but key region. Knowing that Sijilmasa was a city set in an oasis set within a basin in the broad downward outwash sweep of the Atlas Mountains and at the edge of the desert, we dealt with Sijilmasa's immediate geographic environment as its region. Sijilmasa's everyday field of interactions was set within a network of desert streams, the Oueds Gheris, Ziz, and Amerbouh, that flow into the Tafilalt, itself comparable to a "little Mesopotamia," as the hydrologist Jean Margat aptly described it.[41]

Oral traditions have provided us with accounts of the past, sometimes astounding snapshots of a Sijilmasa frozen in time and relayed through the memory of a people to the present. That memory has perhaps served best to describe the biggest features of Sijilmasa—walls and markets. Perhaps what we have heard, recorded, and tried to tie to literature and the landscape may be wrong. But perhaps it isn't, and in an environment where there has been a steady recounting of the past and where the nature of place has shifted subtly over time, human memory, too, must serve as a guidebook to the past. The trick is to talk and walk with people in those places that they know as the totality of their lives.

One set of oral traditions in the region recount that Sijilmasa's fields (*gamaman*) directly outside the city, and not just the city itself, were enclosed by a circuit wall some four meters high during the reign of the oppressive Sultan al-Khal, or the "Black Sultan."[42] The wall was designed to "keep the people in Sijilmasa," as people say, and it had four gates: the east gate, originally called Bab al-Sharq, near today's Qsar Amsifi; the south gate, originally called Bab Sahil, between the *qsur* Mtara and Gaouz; the west gate, Bab al-Gharb, near Qsar Moulay Abd al-Moumen; and the north gate, which, as we have seen, was originally called Bab Fez (because it lay in the direction of Fez), and is located still just outside Qsar al-Mansuriya. Local residents today call

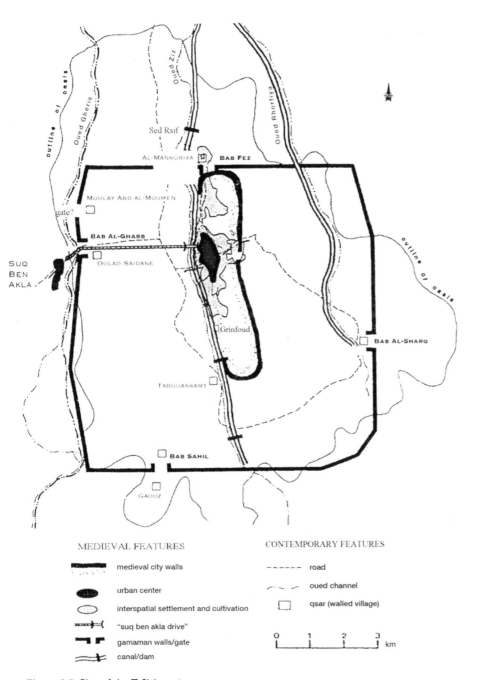

Figure 2.5. Plan of the Tafilalt oasis.

MEDIEVAL FEATURES

- medieval city walls
- urban center
- interspatial settlement and cultivation
- "suq ben akla drive"
- gamaman walls/gate
- canal/dam

CONTEMPORARY FEATURES

- road
- oued channel
- qsar (walled village)

0 1 2 3 km

Sed Rsif

AL-MANSURIYA BAB FEZ

MOULAY ABD AL-MOUMEN

gate?

BAB AL-GHARB

OULAD SAIDANE

SUQ BEN AKLA

Grinfoud

TABOUASSAMT

BAB AL-SHARQ

BAB SAHIL

GAOUZ

Oued Ziz

Oued Gheris

Oued Rhorfiya

outline of oasis

it Bab al-Rih and identify it as the northern gate of Sijilmasa. These points help determine the boundaries of the Sijilmasa *gamaman* and constitute a lasting mental picture of Sijilmasa enduring until today. Portions of the walls connecting these gates are observable in aerial photographs and have been confirmed by field survey. Two long segments of an eroded wall, described by local folk as part of the presumed oasis wall and conforming to an older channel of the Gheris, were located by field reconnaissance along the east bank of the Gheris. Another part of this circuit wall, nearly six kilometers (3.7 miles) long, emerges from aerial photos of the southeast quadrant of the oasis.[43] The field area enclosed within this circuit wall is 11.5 kilometers by 10 kilometers, or 115 square kilometers (44 square miles). Oral history, combined with the geographic survey, we may conclude, points to a late Merinid landscape that survives as a memory among local people.

An earlier Sijilmasa wall is presented to us as a puzzle by al-Bakri, who says that the city was surrounded by a wall built in 814/815 by al-Yas'a. This wall had twelve gates, eight made of iron.[44] MAPS's excavations tend to confirm al-Bakri's description. Later medieval historians, on the other hand, notably al-Dimashqi (d. 1327) and Leo Africanus (early fifteenth century), describe what seems to be a circuit wall resembling that of the oral tradition.[45] Al-Dimashqi describes a wall 70–80 kilometers (43–50 miles) long—apparently, an exaggeration. One explanation for these discrepancies could be that when al-Bakri wrote, only the central city itself was within the circuit wall, and then, at some later point, perhaps toward the end of Merinid Sijilmasa, the entire field area was enclosed, perhaps for reasons of security.

Another area of high interest for the study of Sijilmasa is the strong possibility that the city had an exterior market—a vast commercial zone removed from the central city and devoted to the caravan trade. In 1992, an interested resident of Qsar Ouled Saïdane (just west of Rissani) led the team's geographers to a site across the Oued Gheris called Suq Ben Akla, approximately four kilometers (two and a half miles) due west of central Sijilmasa. He described this place on the Gheris's west bank as Sijilmasa's market and a *diwan*, or customs point. Analysis of aerial photographs subsequently revealed a faint geometric patterning of ruined walls over an area of 0.5 square kilometers (123 acres). Field reconnaissance with the man and others from the village led to the discovery of a nearly straight footpath crossing much of the field area between Ben Akla and the noria along the western wall of Sijilmasa, described by local people as a road that remains in the same place as in ancient times. A survey of the site done in the 1994 season by Tony Wilkinson revealed two rectangular enclosures north of the modern tarmac road, bordered on their north by a cemetery.[46] South of the road he noted a roughly square mound,

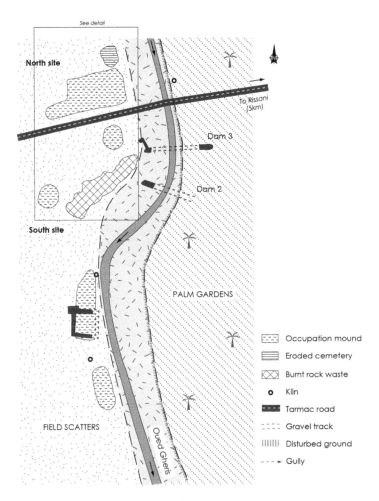

Figure 2.6. Sketch map of Suq Ben Akla, west of central Sijilmasa.

perhaps fortified, extending 90 meters east-west and 80 meters north-south for a total of 7,200 square meters (1.8 acres), that could be conceived of as the site of a caravansary or a fort. West and north of the Ben Akla site are extensive scatters of small battered sherds. These may be remaining bits of settlement-derived refuse—household waste originally containing remnants of pottery and brick, for example, that was applied to fields as manure or compost. The pottery and brick, weathered and shifted around through low-level saltation (skipping through the source of wind), remains on the surface. This suggests that the Ben Akla settlement was surrounded by cultivated gar-

Figure 2.7.
Satellite image of
the Tafilalt oasis;
data purchased from
SPOT, processed by
MAPS.

dens and formed a self-contained extension of the main city, or what al-Bakri might have described as a "suburb."

A desert basin and its oasis: these form the Sijilmasa region. The oasis, surrounded by desert and steppe and created by streams flowing into and around it, was the heartland of Sijilmasa's local career. City dwellers, farmers, and nomads created a checkerboard of local interrelationships whose dynamics figured strongly throughout the life of Sijilmasa and figure among those who live there still. The pattern of relations among the city, the oasis villages set among the waters and fields of the Tafilalt focused on the cultivation of dates and barley, and the interlacing patterns of nomads was the most central feature of Sijilmasa's regional life. The management of water, the motor of oasis life, has been the framework for life in the Tafilalt. The earliest textual reference to water management in the Tafilalt is found in al-Bakri, who tells us: "The water one drinks is brackish, as is that which comes from all the wells. The water that irrigates the planted fields comes from the river and is collected in basins as is done elsewhere in agricultural production."[47] The modern author Mahmud Isma'il says that the first ruler of Sijilmasa, Isa Ibn Mazid, "undertook the channelization of water for each garden."[48] The earliest indication that we have on the ground is the construction of a *seguia*, an irrigation canal, called the *seguia midrariya*, and a bridge, also known as the Midrariya, crossing it. The *seguia midrariya*, immediately upstream from Sijilmasa along the Ziz, gave its name to a district in the oasis; the canal irrigates a broad sector of fields just north of the city. The name "Midrariya" refers to the first dynasty to rule the Sijilmasa city-state, the Bani Midrar. At the point of the Rsif dam, the waters of the Ziz were, and still are, resupplied by springs where the underlying strata of conglomerate lies at the surface. Oral histories relate that during medieval times, a spring at Rsif known as the Timedrine was famous for its abundance and reliability. Today, eight springs in the same general area resupply the Ziz, though local people note that the Timedrine springs are far less abundant today than they were in medieval times.[49]

Field reconnaissance and regional aerial and satellite imagery have given us surprises. By living in the Tafilalt and learning the lay of the land, one realizes that the channel of the Ziz beginning just south of Erfoud and then running through the remainder of the oasis is unusually straight along most of its course. This is in sharp contrast to the broad meanders of the Amerbouh and Gheris. One conclusion is that in all likelihood, this stretch of the Ziz is an artificial stream—a great central irrigation canal—within the confines of the oasis. At the point where the Ziz and the Gheris nearly meet and then diverge, at modern Erfoud, massive stone works, refashioned many times over, lead the Ziz into a man-made channel. The stream's natural channel, known today and perhaps always as the Amerbouh, leads on to the east and is dry except in unusually wet periods. The Ziz was diverted out of its natural channel at the head of the Tafilalt and redirected through an engineered riverbed, essentially a ditch, in the center of the oasis. When did this diversion take place? Jean Margat speculated that it occurred in the 900s or 1000s.[50]

We tend to believe that the renewed and expanded commercial needs of Almoravid Sijilmasa, which was suddenly part of an empire, were underpinned by the agricultural production of the oasis and met through a massive hydraulic project.[51]

Oral tradition provides us with different—and sometimes irreconcilable—frames of view. Consistent accounts point to three low dams (*sudud*) and an associated network of canals (*seguiat*) that diverted the Ziz's water into irrigated fields during the medieval period. One, the Rsif, as we have just noted, is in the northern half of the Tafilalt oasis; another, the Batha, is located in the southern half; and the third, the Shamoukh, lay at the southern margins of the city. In medieval times, again according to local tradition, two major canals led off the Ziz: the Shurfa, which lay just north of the central part of the city and led to the district known as Oued Shurfa, and the Rhorfiya, which branched off from the Ziz just north of the oasis and provided water for the eastern fields. From these larger canals, ever-smaller ones branched off, and in addition there were then, as now, canals that flow directly from the Ziz and Gheris.[52]

What is remarkable in any case is the presence of dams on the Gheris

Figure 2.8. Bridge over the *seguia midrariya* irrigation canal.

Figure 2.9. Downstream side of the Rsif dam. Beginning in Almoravid times, the waters of the Tafilalt were managed to feed its people and to provide ecological resources for the trans-Saharan trade, which was focused on gold. Dams such as Rsif were built and rebuilt. They remained in use until the USAID-sponsored Hassan ad-Dakhil dam at Errachidia began operations in the mid-1970s.

Figure 2.10. View of the Rhorfiya canal alongside Qsar Khella. Observers through the ages have remarked on the Tafilalt being its own Moroccan country, a fortunate oasis laced with ever-smaller canals branching off from the remarkable dams built along the Oued Ziz and its western companion, the Gheris.

and the Ziz—their number, their dimensions, and, even in their state of ruin today, their stupendous beauty. In all, twenty-two dams have been explored, ten on the Gheris and twelve on the Ziz. The most prominent of these are numbered 1–13 on figure 2.12. It is significant that by the mid-twentieth century, only one dam on the Gheris remained in operation, in contrast to the dams on the Ziz, all of which functioned to one degree or another. Also noteworthy is that most of the Ziz dams show evidence of earlier dams lying beneath or adjacent to later refurbishments, whereas dams on the Gheris that were breached by periodic major floods were not replaced in situ; rather, a new dam would be built up- or downstream, often near the wrecked dam. This suggests that the Ziz dams were more stable features and less likely to suffer catastrophic failure than the dams on the Gheris. The Gheris is subject to wide swings in its flow and potential for torrential flood. The Ziz, on the other hand, is a relatively mild-mannered stream whose periods of high water can be managed by using the Amerbouh as a safety valve.[53]

As we have seen, the Ziz was dammed in the early 1970s when Hassan ad-Dakhil was constructed just upstream from Errachidia, then still known as Ksar es Souk. The new reservoir, just over 100 kilometers (62 miles) upstream

Figure 2.II. Architecture along the Ziz: Bou Himara dam. At least a dozen dams were constructed on the Ziz to support the intricately irrigated agricultural production that undergirded the commercial resilience of Sijilmasa over the millennium of its existence as a world trading center. This dam exhibits some of the architectural magnificence still apparent in other Ziz dams.

from the Tafilalt, held the waters of the impounded desert stream. The dam was built as a USAID project, and the downstream irrigation network was constructed with eastern European assistance. During MAPS' first season of research in the Tafilalt, in 1988, we assigned two students from INSAP the task of interviewing farmers in the region about their agricultural practices and water resource concerns.

The students asked to be reassigned after two days. They found that the farmers were sharply critical of water management policies and ORMVAT (Office Régional de Mise en Valeur Agricole du Tafilalet; located in Errachidia) agents, and the entire dam project in general. "Government water" and "the dam" were akin to curse words. To offset the lack of sufficient water released from the dam into the new irrigation system, itself contentious, ORMVAT had built local pumping stations to tap groundwater supplies, and then charged farmers for the water. As mentioned above, farmers bought diesel pumps (*moto-pompes*) and pumped their own water from the water table beneath their fields, paying for the fuel and delivering the water in irrigation ditches old and new, to their satisfaction. One ORMVAT field engineer con-

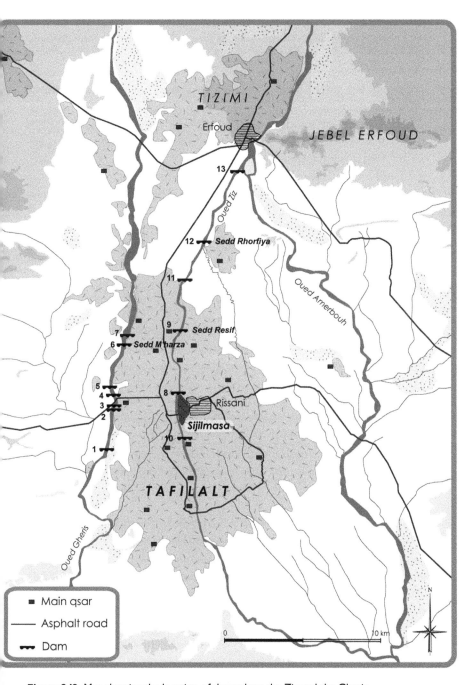

Figure 2.12. Map showing the location of dams along the Ziz and the Gheris.

fessed: "Water from the dam is supplementary—it's always insufficient. So we encourage people to fix the *khettara* [underground horizontal wells] and put in *moto-pompes*. Even though they know that will lower the water table. We have to help people get more water. We limit their [*moto-pompes*] spacing and depth. But never a limit on the number of *moto-pompes* or the amount of water they can pump."[54]

The technocratic solution to the problems of agriculture in the Tafilalt, rooted in preventing flood, has led to a system of declining water supplies, anarchic stopgap solutions, and extensive, expensive infrastructural investments, both public and private. Groundwater levels have dropped far below what they were when the transformation began. Laws of unintended consequences have worked inexorably. The changes set in place in the 1970s were abrupt and profound, but given what has happened to the Tafilalt in the past, perhaps not so different from what oasis dwellers have experienced over the centuries. It has always been a region in change.

In the mid-1000s, Al-Bakri described the agriculture of Sijilmasa and its region as abundant: "They sow in the land of Sijilmasa in one year and they harvest from that sowing for three years. The reason for this is that it is an extremely hot country with severe summer heat, so when the grain is dry it gets scattered during harvesting, and as the ground is cracked the scattered grain falls into those cracks. In the second year they plow without sowing, and so [again] in the third year . . . there are many date-palms, grapes, and all sorts of fruits."[55]

Our geomorphological study confirms al-Bakri's account; it shows that Sijilmasa was surrounded by good agricultural land. During the 1993 and 1994 excavation seasons, we collected archaeobotanical material through a flotation process. We extracted samples from a variety of trenches: numbers 21 and 22, representing residences in the southwest quarter of the city; 25–28, elite residences and latrines west of the mosque; and 31, 32, and 38, an elite residence below the Grand Mosque (see figure 2.3). Analysis of that material shows that dates (*Phoenix dactylifera*—116 specimens) were present in al-Bakri's time.[56] Under the shade of the date palms, oasis cultivators grew winter grains and an assortment of vegetables. The most abundant grain was barley (*Hordeum*—483 specimens), which, being more resistant to heat, drought, and salty soils than wheat, became the bread, porridge, and couscous of Sijilmasa. We found grains of wheat (*Triticum*—46 specimens) in much smaller quantities.[57] Grape pips (*Vitis vinifera*—715 specimens) were, surprisingly, the most abundant plant remains in the macrobotanical sample. Such large quantities of grapes posed questions that would have to be answered later.[58]

Genius was employed to secure all of these tasks, and Sijilmasa rendered

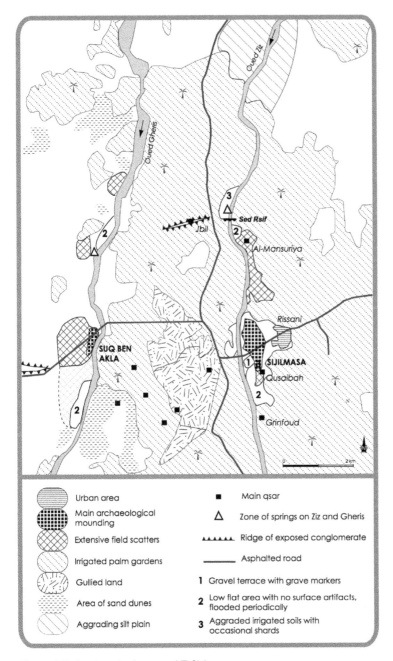

Figure 2.13. Land use in the central Tafilalt.

the region, the Tafilalt, better over time: it was engineered and reengineered to create an ever-more productive environment. There were failures and successes. Flood was a constant danger. Sijilmasa moved with the times, and new technologies entered the oasis. The Tafilalt was a dynamic setting for economic forces, and regional success was largely due to Sijilmasa's prosperity. The city generally grew in size over time, and that is its most significant regional measurement: an indicator of the wealth of its regional environment. The intensity of the exploitation of the Tafilalt environment increased generally, sometimes in fits and starts, depending on war and peace.

Domain

The Sijilmasa domain places the caravan capital in an interactive spatial network of political and spiritual relations: the rectangle of western Islam. Located on one edge of this rectangle, Sijilmasa lived within the context of broad historical events in the world of Islam, North Africa, Iberia, the Sahara, and Africa beyond. Islam's earliest debate—who should lead the faith—led to Sijilmasa's founding early in the second century of Islam. But it was the whole of the Maghrib and Iberia—a realm framed by the desert on the south, Libya's Jebel Nefusa in the east, the Mediterranean coast, and Morocco and Iberia in the west—that was Sijilmasa's constant companion. Along the southwestern edge of this frame, Sijilmasa had the advantage of being removed from the main lines of commerce and communication across the Maghrib while still being connected to it. One can conceive of Sijilmasa as a funnel, gathering in caravans from across the Maghrib and then sending them far beyond, to the Sudan in tropical Africa.

Maintaining good relations with the rest of the Maghrib and with Spain was essential to Sijilmasa: Islamic ideologies created the city and underpinned its dynastic rule, and all the political movements directed toward and against Sijilmasa emanated from other points equally interested in the rule of Islamic authority over the Maghrib and Andalusia. Sijilmasa reveals the full extent of the politically possible in the Maghrib—its founding Kharijite ideology, emanating from Mesopotamia; the indigenous Berber Midrarid political founders; the incursion of the Fatimids, again from Mesopotamia; the arrival of the Almoravids from deep in the Saharan south; the reign of the Almohads, Moroccan iconoclasts who reinvented and reinterpreted the Almoravid political landscape they conquered; the rise of successive Moroccan regimes—the Merinids and Wattasids; the emergence of the Alaouites, spiritual imports from Arabia, somnolent in the Tafilalt for nearly 400 years and then emerging across Morocco in two short generations 400 years ago. Sijilmasa was a great and enduring Maghribi city, interacting spiritually and politically with other cities in the Islamic West, including Fez, Marrakech, Tahert, Tunis, Sebta, Cordoba, and Seville, as an equal, a partner, a rival, a threat, an object of conquest, a node in the trade routes of everyday commerce—whatever impinged on human life in this region at any time after Sijilmasa's founding in 757. For us, working at the site of Sijilmasa, the connections across its domain have been the substance of events and movements that reveal much of the city's significance over time.

Sphere

At the top end of this nested set of Sijilmasa's relations lays the Sijilmasa sphere, where the city's relations were narrow but rich, vastly larger in space but far more unidimensional in commerce and human relations. Here, Sijilmasa's realm of influence extended into the Sahara and beyond to the Sudan, to one or two or a handful of places. The most important of these was across the Sahara, what Arabs called *bilad al-Sudan*, the "Land of the Blacks," and what we know today as the African Sahil. The most significant place in the Sudan was ancient Ghana, a locus of trade from a time before the founding of Sijilmasa until early modern times. Ghana and others—the Takrur state to the west (in modern Senegal), the Songhai Empire to the east (north-central Niger at its easternmost point)—were the trading partners of Sijilmasa in its most important commodity, gold. Much of what we know about the gold trade comes from the sometimes concrete, (almost) always repetitive, and often fragmented passages of medieval Arab histories. While the focus was on gold, other commodities—salt, slaves, ivory, ambergris—accompanied that trade and may have been more significant from time to time. But gold made Sijilmasa rich. And once Sijilmasa slipped from view in world history, it was gold that made the place a mystery.

Sijilmasa's influence extended not only to the distant south. Like the rest of the Maghrib, Sijilmasa was engaged with Andalusia, Islamic Iberia, and the Mashriq, the Islamic East. Its trade influence extended still farther to the non-Islamic world in Europe and even as far as China.[59]

Sijilmasa: An Urban Historical Trilogy

As archaeology alone can reveal, Sijilmasa performed different roles through the ages, having been in effect several cities over its more than a millennium on the world stage. Three distinct periods emerge in Sijilmasa's long life, along with several significant minor detours. First, Sijilmasa was an independent Islamic city-state, rooted in its Kharijite personality and its Midrarid dynastic rulers; second, Sijilmasa was subsumed in successive Moroccan empires, Almoravid and Almohad first, and then the Merinid. Sijilmasa's imperial period began with the Almoravids, who emerged from the western Sahara to Sijilmasa's south, and continued under the Almohads, who came from the Anti-Atlas Mountains. Both established vast empires ruling over all of western Islam, and both sustained the growth and influence of Sijilmasa. Third, Sijilmasa and the Tafilalt were the springboard for the creation of the modern Moroccan state under the Alaouites, a force emanating from the Tafilalt itself. Between the imperial and Alaouite periods, Sijilmasa languished in what we call the Filalian period, a historical "intermission" when Sijilmasa reverted to local rule during the wobbly Wattasid period (1472–1540s) and the subsequent Saadian dynasty (1540s–1640s).[60] So it is that an initial three centuries of functional independence as a city-state were followed by three hundred years as part of successive North African empires, followed by three hundred years when Sijilmasa was not nearly the city it had been but was more than a memory and a ceremonial center, as has been previously suspected. Each period had its own relationship with the sphere, Africa across the Sahara plus the larger Islamic world; each period had its own relationship with the domain, Morocco and the Maghrib surrounding it; the region, too, was differently modeled in each period as the Tafilalt oasis was called upon to support Sijilmasa's everyday ecological needs of water, labor, and food; and each period exhibited a different core, the city site itself. The story of each period is told in the following chapters. Let us take a moment to outline them here.

Independent Sijilmasa

Sijilmasa was initially a small independent city-state, a Kharijite refuge separate from the rest of Islamic society. This Sijilmasa, guided by the Bani Midrar dynasty of Kharijite amirs and their legacy, prevailed from the city's establishment until the second half of the 1000s. It was a private kingdom, wealthy beyond imagination, with an economy rooted in the trade in gold with the peoples of the region of the upper Niger River across the vast desert. As whenever gold and a distant, poorly known place intersect, Sijilmasa's greatness became legendary shortly after the city's founding around AD 757. The how and why of Sijilmasa's founding remain intriguing questions in the context of early Islam in North Africa; however, Sijilmasa fit within a string of Kharijite settlements strewn along the desert margins of North Africa, removed and isolated from the mainstream of the emerging Islamic world.[61]

Sijilmasa entered the global geographic record within one hundred years of its foundation, and historical narratives composed during Sijilmasa's long period of independence provide some clues to its history, in part corroborated by MAPS excavations and surveys.[62] Distinctive variations within Sijilmasa's independent period began in the 900s as the city attracted the attention of, first, the Fatimids, a schismatic movement originating in Mesopotamia, and then of the Umayyads of Cordoba and their Moroccan allies. Both came to rule over the City of Gold. Whatever the sectarian affiliation of Sijilmasa's rulers, most of its people, it seemed, remained largely Kharijite, and its specific religious nature and distinctive urban and social qualities were conserved throughout its first three hundred years.[63] From the perspective of what was to come, Sijilmasa led one life until the Almoravids knocked down their door and created another.

Sijilmasa in Empire

The second period in the Sijilmasa record was ushered in by the Almoravids, and while it was relatively short in duration, the Almoravid inheritance was powerful and persistent; it was altered and reconfigured by the Almohad and Merinid empires that followed, but the Almoravid city laid down essential urban patterns for what was to follow. The Saharan Almoravids, conquering in the name of a refashioned, rejuvenated Islam, seized Sijilmasa, first of all places in the Maghrib, as they established a territorial empire spanning two continents.[64] Sijilmasa's capacities were enlarged as the underlying hydraulic infrastructure of the Tafilalt was, as we have seen, altered to expand the agricultural basis of local society. New technologies harnessed the Oued Ziz to tap its potential, and the city grew in size as greater wealth converged on Sijilmasa through an enlarged gold trade moving through the routes and realms of the Almoravid Empire. Besides creating Marrakech in the Haouz plain just over the Atlas Mountains, the Almoravids had a plan for Sijilmasa, as the environmental record of the Tafilalt oasis, its sediments and dams, testifies. As the Almoravids' abbreviated century ended, the city continued to grow under the equally religiously imbued Atlas Berbers, the Almohads, so much so that the new regime had to expand the city's Grand Mosque. Sijilmasa grew still more under the artistically inspired Merinids (the Bani Marin), whose origins lay in today's western Algeria, in the area near Tiaret (Tahert in Berber). Sijilmasa flourished anew each time it was reorganized, by empires focused first on Marrakech and then on Fez, reaching a population estimated at 30,000 by the end of the 1300s.[65] Each dynasty redesigned the city in its own image, in processes clear to us from excavations at the Grand Mosque, the persistent focus of urbanism at Sijilmasa's core. By Ibn Battuta's time in the first six decades of the 1300s, it was a normal and reliable human experience to start and end a journey across the Sahara from Sijilmasa; that Moroccan world, however, was about to fall apart.

At the end of the 1300s, in the second half of the Merinid dynasty, Sijilmasa seemed to disappear from the map. Arabic manuscripts speak less and less of the city. The judgments of several scholars, including earlier conceptions held by members of the MAPS team, initially concluded that Sijilmasa came to an end in 1393 as a result of troubles in the Merinid dynasty.[66] But as we subsequently learned at the site, events were not so clear-cut, and Sijilmasa led yet another, last life.

Filalian Sijilmasa

Leo Africanus, the Granada-born Arab observer of the North African scene, painted a dismal portrait of Sijilmasa in 1515 after his visit early in the Saadian period. From him we learn of the end, or at least something of the end, of imperial Sijilmasa. Among other factors, perhaps, the city had been largely abandoned by its own people, provoked by the mistreatment they had endured at the hands of the bloodily divided Merinid dynasty. Rival Merinid princes in Fez and Marrakech used Sijilmasa as a bargaining chip in their bids for domination over Morocco, and the city had been repeatedly occupied, sacked, and traded between warring parties. We believe that the Tafilalt oasis then began to take on its present aspect of walled, crenellated villages (*qsur*; Leo's "fortified houses") dotting a landscape forested by date palms. The Sijilmasa region reverted back to control by the people of the Tafilalt, the Filalians.

The Alaouites

Significant events emanating from within the Tafilalt bracket this last era of Sijilmasa with the previous imperial era and once again connect Sijilmasa with the main lines of Islamic history. Descendants of the Prophet Mohammed's son-in-law, Ali, living in Yanbu on the Red Sea coast of Arabia, settled in the Tafilalt in the 1200s. Sijilmasa's leaders who were on pilgrimage to Mecca invited the Alaouite *shurfa* (holy people descended from Ali) to come settle in the Tafilalt. They carried with them the spiritual mantle of the Prophet and infused Sijilmasa with a renewed sense of holiness. As they settled into the fabric of life at Sijilmasa, and as imperial Sijilmasa declined in the aftermath of the Merinid dynasty, the Alaouites defined leadership in ways the region had not seen before. As security and trade declined and the fortunes of the Tafilalt ebbed, the Alaouites began to make their mark on Morocco. The inhabitants of the Tafilalt pledged their fealty (*bay'a*) to the Alaouites in 1641, who then began a campaign of territorial conquest focused on safeguarding and enlarging the trade routes to and from the Tafilalt. In a series of dramatic moves, the Alaouites became the undisputed masters of Morocco within a generation and developed the lineaments of the modern Moroccan state.

We have found that the Alaouites, far more than their imperial predecessors but undoubtedly taking their cue from them, rebuilt the environmental infrastructure of the oasis, expanding large-scale irrigation through an intricate network of dams and canals off the Ziz and the Gheris. They had long since become Filalian, and used the term "Filalian" in new and powerful ways. Their Filali identity and their uninterrupted chain of rule over Morocco ever since may have served to keep alive the memory of Sijilmasa and its lure in history, but the reality is that under them, Sijilmasa, their original home in the Tafilalt, barely survived in its fundamental spiritual and economic elements. From these essential events, a new Morocco—the parent of the Moroccan state today—took form.

CHAPTER 3

Founding the Oasis City

What history tells us runs in the opposite direction of what archaeology reveals. The historical narrative normally moves in a linear, chronological fashion from earlier to later. Archaeology, on the other hand, moves stratigraphically from later to earlier, from the most recent occupation at the top to the earliest at the bottom. How to tell the story of Sijilmasa from both historical and archaeological perspectives poses a quandary. Should the historical narrative set the stage, followed by the story of the discovery of Sijilmasa's strata as we found them? Or vice versa? In answer to this question, we have woven both elements together, allowing the warp of history to be embellished by the patterns of archaeological evidence. By necessity, we will move back and forth from texts to material evidence and from historical narrative to archaeology.

Pre-Islamic Origins?

Sijilmasa's founding is noted in many medieval Arabic sources with the precise date of 140/757–758. But there are some records hinting that Sijilmasa was founded in pre-Islamic times. We begin with two local traditions recorded by Leo Africanus from his visit to the Tafilalt in the mid-1510s.[1] The first of these, generally dismissed by Leo, says that Dhu'l-Qarnain, "he with two horns," who is often taken to be Alexander the Great in Islamic traditions, founded the town.[2] In this version, Sijilmasa was established as a rest home for the sick and crippled in Alexander's army, but we, like Leo, discount this idea: Sijilmasa is so far from the westernmost point that Alexander is supposed to have traveled, namely, the oasis of Siwa in Egypt's Western Desert and Cyrenaica in Libya of today, that there is no likelihood of an Alexander connection.

The second tradition, considered seriously by Leo and one that trails across the centuries in references to Sijilmasa, attributes the city's founding to the Romans in the middle of the first century AD. Leo wrote: "Some are of the opinion that this town was built by a certain Roman Army captaine, who having conducted his troupes foorth of Mauritania, conquered all Numidia, marching westward, built a town, and called it Sijillummesse, because it stood on the borders of Messa, by a coorupt worde it began to be called Segelmesse."[3] Weighing this possibility takes us deep into the diverse sociocultural world of northern Africa over the course of three generations in the time of the Great (or Caesar's) Roman Civil War, 49–45 BC, and its aftermath, which resulted in the end of the Roman Republic and the emergence of Rome as an empire. It opens a window into the economic and social relationships between Rome and North Africa, particularly along the fringes of Roman North Africa—precisely where Sijilmasa lies. Perhaps most interesting of all is that it is the death of Cleopatra's grandson Ptolemy, himself king of what is today essentially Morocco, that leads us into the question of whether Sijilmasa became a place in antiquity.

Following Rome's conquest of Carthage in 146 BC and its reformulation as the Roman province of Africa Proconsularis, Rome developed close relations with the Berber kingdoms to the west. Mauretania, the land of the Mauri, lay in the far west; Numidia occupied the central Maghrib.[4] A century later, Julius Caesar emerged as all-powerful. He was in Africa from late 47 BC until mid-46 as he vanquished his Republican enemies Scipio and Pompey in the last phases of the Great Civil War. One of Caesar's culminating victories came at the Battle of Thapsus, following which the Republican allies and friends Marcus Petreius and the Numidian king Juba I died in a suicide pact.[5] Juba's four-year-old son, the man who would later become King Juba II of Mauretania (ca. 50 BC–AD 23), was brought to Rome by Caesar and raised in the heart of Roman social and intellectual life by him and then, following his assassination, by his nephew, Octavian—the future Caesar Augustus.[6]

In a Roman twist of fate, Juba II married Cleopatra Selene, the daughter of Mark Antony and Cleopatra of Egypt. Cleopatra Selene had also arrived in Rome as a prize of war and was raised in the household of Octavia, Augustus's sister.

Augustus placed Juba on the throne of Numidia sometime between 29 and 27 BC. But not for long, since after going to Spain to serve in the last of the Republican Wars, Juba came home to a kingdom that had never quite existed, at least not in its new reformulation at the end of the war. Numidia was divided in two, and the western part was joined with Mauretania to create a large Roman ally, a frontier client state. Juba II had his work cut out for him: a stranger to the place and a stranger to the native Berber language, he soon faced revolt—perhaps because he was too foreign, too Roman. Grain supplies to Rome from North Africa were threatened in 22 BC, and there were revolts in Rome.[7]

Revolt put down, Juba and his bride, Cleopatra Selene, returned to North Africa. Their child, Ptolemy, like his father and mother, was sent to Rome for his upbringing, returning to Mauretania to rule jointly with his father for a few years in the early twenties AD.[8] Ptolemy continued his father's success as a popular monarch of his far-flung kingdom. Ptolemy's Mauretania was known for its wealth in grain, olive oil, specialty woods (citrus, olive, cedar), animals for Roman amphitheatrical spectacles, *garum* (a type of fish sauce), and purple dye.[9] This last commodity, made from the secretions of the murex sea snail found on the Atlantic coast of Mauretania, was the basis of an ancient and wealthy trade developed especially at Mogador, today's Essaouira, and it forms the basis of the legend of Ptolemy's death and could have brought the Roman commander Suetonius Paulinus to a place to be called Sijilmasa.

When Ptolemy was 49 years old in AD 40, his second cousin the Emperor Caligula invited him to Rome. In the capital, Mauretania's wealth was obvious: the animals in the coliseum, the grain that flowed to Latium, the *garum* used to flavor the foods on the Roman table. Exceptionally remarkable and probably especially galling to the emperor was the purple raiment his cousin wore to the amphitheatre. As the story goes, and befitting Caligula's enduring reputation, he had Ptolemy assassinated after becoming jealous of the admiration he attracted. Rome's western ally was dead. In turn, Mauretania lost its freedom when Caligula was assassinated two years later and his successor Claudius annexed Mauretania as an imperial province.

The murder of Ptolemy and the Roman annexation of Mauretania precipitated a popular revolt. Within the first three years of the conflict, Rome committed 20,000 troops to its suppression under the praetor Suetonius Paulinus, and it is in his campaign that we find, perhaps, the seeds of the myth of a Roman founding of Sijilmasa.[10] Suetonius moved quickly to protect Mauretania's west-east roads from Saharan nomads who migrated north in summer and typically raided these strategic routes that funneled trade to Rome. There are important clues to the nature of Suetonius's route across Mauretania: he saw snow-capped mountains and cedar forests, and experienced at least one freezing winter and a broiling hot summer. Following the suggestions outlined by La Chapelle in 1934, we imagine that his army entered from the northeast and quickly moved up the Moulouya River valley, marching along the eastern Middle Atlas and the foot of Jebel Ayachi, and then pushing onward across the pre-Saharan plains as far as the Oued Guir. Like the Oued Ziz, its cousin, the Guir flows out of the Eastern High Atlas and runs into the Sahara, some

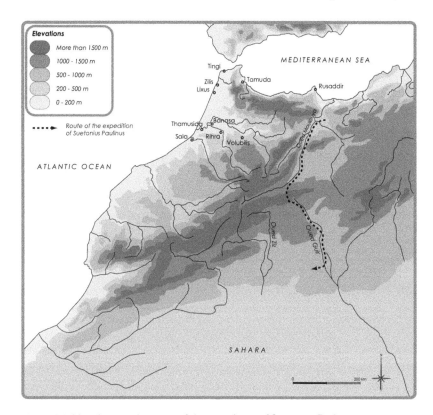

Figure 3.1. Map showing the route of the expedition of Suetonius Paulinus.

150 kilometers (93 miles) east of the Tafilalt. Of the Ziz, where Sijilmasa sits on a small bluff above the river, an excellent natural setting for a Roman encampment, we have no Roman reference.

In any case, Suetonius's mission did not quell the rebels. Rome dispatched an expedition under Gnaeus Hosidius Geta the following year, but again we have no details of its route. We do know that Geta specifically targeted the tribal chief Sabalus. And having learned of the difficulties presented by the desert, his army took as much water as it could but nevertheless suffered from great thirst. The Berbers, who knew where the sources of water were located, maintained their resistance. Berber resistance was so intense, in fact, that Roman control of Mauretania was generally limited to a triangle between Tangier, Fez (Volubilis), and Rabat (Sala).[11] Although Sabalus and his people surrendered, difficulty in keeping the east-west trade routes open may explain the division of Mauretania by Claudius into two parts, Mauretania Tingitana (west; more or less the Morocco of today) and Mauretania Caesariensis (east;

Figure 3.2. Upper Moulouya River.

western Algeria today). We do not read about any more expeditions to secure the routes against attack by nomads until the middle of the second century, during the reign of Antonius Pius.

Rome, the Tafilalt, and the Ancient Gold Trade

Like every great civilization, Rome was concerned about the problem of gold. Evidence strongly suggests that as early as the fourth century, Rome enjoyed the benefits of the gold trade that passed through the Tafilalt. That Rome was rich in gold is undeniable. Where did it come from? We can be fairly certain that Romans were striking coins from gold mined in West Africa and transported across the Sahara in the early fourth century. The Roman solidus, a coin first issued in 312, provided the standard used for weighing gold in the trans-Saharan trade. It was retained as the standard by Arabs issuing their own coinage in the medieval period, but then it was dropped when new systems of coinage were introduced. Standards of weight north of the Sahara changed a number of times as monetary systems changed.[12] But south of the Sahara, local gold currency was not minted. The gold standard weighed gold dust rather than coins.[13] Since gold dust could be apportioned in any quantity, it could always be weighed with the same set of weights. Therefore, there was no compelling reason to change the standard from the time that the coins were first introduced in the region (in the fourth century) until the nineteenth century in the Sudan (modern West Africa). Much more convincing than the argument of units of weight is the fact that beginning in the fourth century, Rome increasingly demanded that payment of taxes from North African provinces be made in gold.[14] Coincidentally, this occurred when camels were first introduced to the Saharan landscape, which made significant long-distance trade across the Sahara possible.[15] As it turned out, Rome did not need to occupy the Tafilalt to benefit from the trade to the south.

Over the years we worked in the Tafilalt, friends in Erfoud told us that Roman coins have been found in the area. Daniel McCall provides a reference to two Roman coins found "in the desert a good way south of Sijilmasa."[16] Interesting as that is, Roman coins traveled as objects of trade and are not evidence of Roman settlement.

In addition, McCall states that a doctor in the hospital at Erfoud told him that there were Roman ruins nearby. Twenty-five years later, the Moroccan scholar Mohammed el-Mellouki refers to this same physician.[17] That, too, is very interesting, but no serious archaeological survey of the area has confirmed the presence of Roman ruins. D. Jacques-Meunié explains this by suggesting that climatic conditions were not conducive to the adoption of Roman architectural forms.[18] We found the legends of a Roman founding of Sijilmasa sufficiently intriguing to consider every twist and turn, but in the end we have to consider them only legend. In fact, our archaeological research has found absolutely no evidence of a Roman presence at the Sijilmasa site or in its environs.

A Seasonal Encampment

Although our archaeological research negates the idea of a Roman presence at Sijilmasa, the site provides evidence of temporary settlement that predates the founding of the Islamic city in 757, but it is not Roman. One carbon-14 sample taken from a fire pit in a hard-packed floor level beneath the lowest level of the mosque, i.e., in the very center of ancient Sijilmasa, is dated to 370, unquestionably before the founding of the Muslim city and much later than the Roman military campaigns mentioned above.[19] At least a half dozen other carbon-14 samples from the southern residential sector of Sijilmasa have a date range that overlaps the sixth through eighth centuries, so they also could predate the Muslim city. These samples point to a temporary, pre-urban

Figure 3.3. Earliest fire pit, located on the lowest level under the mosque, dated by carbon-14 analysis to the late Roman period.

settlement that could well have been a seasonal camp for Berber herdsmen and traders, exactly as al-Bakri describes it.[20]

Before there was a city of Sijilmasa, the site was an uncultivated plain where Berber tribes came at a certain time every year to trade. One of the early founders of Sijilmasa, according to some accounts, was a blacksmith, and he brought iron utensils to this annual market. He set up a tent to serve as his dwelling, and other Berbers settled around him.[21] Al-Bakri does not tell us what time of year they came, but it was probably in the fall, when the date palms were laden with fruit and the river swelled with water from the north. Archaeology confirms the possibility of al-Bakri's assessment of pre-urban Sijilmasa. The earliest occupation that we have been able to document is located on the elevated plateau in the very center of the site, under the Grand Mosque and in the area immediately to the west of it. As mentioned above, we found fragments of charcoal through carbon-14 analysis dated to 370. Another fragment from under the mosque dates from 640, and in excavation units to the west of the mosque, we found a fire pit dating back to between 590 and 800.[22] This last fire could have burned out just after the founding of the city in the mid-eighth century. More likely, though, it occurred shortly before the founding of the city. Even then, it would have been logical to camp on the elevated plateau, since the lower plains are underwater when the Ziz overflows its banks. Apparently, that had been the pattern for centuries before Abu'l-Qasim settled in the Tafilalt in the mid-eighth century. And it must be precisely here where Abu'l-Qasim settled and where al-Yas'a built Sijilmasa's first mosque.

From Seasonal Encampment to Religious Refuge

The Bani Midrar governed Sijilmasa for 160 years. The first of them was Abu'l-Qasim ibn Samgu ibn Wasul al-Miknasi. . . . He had met, in Ifriqiya, Ikrima the freedman (mawla) of Ibn Abbas and heard [hadith] from him. He was possessed of flocks and often used to seek pasture on the site of Sijilmasa. A group of Sufriya joined him, and when they had reached 40 men [in number] they made Isa ibn Mazid the Black their leader and put him in charge of their affairs and began to build Sijilmasa. This was in 140/757–758.[23]

Al-Bakri further states that Sijilmasa's growth "caused the depopulation of the town of Targha, which is two days distant." It also caused "the depopulation of the town of Ziz."[24]

Right from the start, Sijilmasa was a refuge for religious dissidents. Abu'l-Qasim Samgu was a Kharijite Muslim of the Sufriya sect. He was in Qayrawan when Sufriya Kharijites seized power from the descendents of Uqba Ibn Nafi, the Muslim conqueror who had ruled the city as an independent Arab enclave after an earlier failed attempt by the Kharijites to take the city. According to al-Bakri, Abu'l-Qasim was studying Sufriya doctrine with a Kharijite scholar named Ikrima, who had come from Basra with his master, Ibn Abbas, both of them riding on the same camel bearing their provisions.[25] Ikrima is said to have started a school there, where he taught the principles of the new sect along with other theological subjects such as *tafsir al-Quran* (exegesis of the Quran), hadith (the sayings of Mohammed and his companions), and *usul al-fiqh* (sources of the law). Picture Ikrima sitting cross-legged on the floor of the Great Mosque of Qayrawan and teaching his students,

Abu'l-Qasim among them, and through his students spreading the Sufriya doctrine of Kharijite Islam among the Berbers of North Africa.

Kharijism is one of the three sects of Islam that traces its origin back to the time of the "great schism" following the last of the Rashidun (first four) caliphs in the mid-seventh century. The story is well known. Those Muslims who supported the last Rashidun caliph, Ali, and believed that the caliphate belonged to the bloodline of the Prophet through his daughter Fatima and her husband, Ali, became Shi'a. Those who supported Ali's cousin Mu'awiya believed that any member of the family of the Prophet could succeed; they became Sunni. But there was a third alternative: those who rejected Ali's decision to submit the issue of legitimacy to arbitration claimed instead that "judgment belongs to God alone." They literally walked out (*kha-ra-ja*—third person singular of the verb "to walk out") on Ali. They believed that merit was the sole criterion of a person's status, including succession to positions of authority. They were, at the very core of their being, dissenters. They settled first in Mesopotamia and then fled to North Africa following the general direction of Islamic conquest, but only after sowing ample anarchy in the heartland of the Umayyad dynasty, thereby allowing the rival Abbasids to revolt and rise to power.

The Kharijite attitude toward central authority was perfectly suited to the Berbers of North Africa because of their general resistance to any form of foreign rule. An early Arab historian, Ibn Abi Zayd, notes that the Berbers revolted twelve times before they accepted Islam. Ibn Khaldun adds that even after Berbers converted, "They went on revolting and seceding, and they adopted dissident (Kharijite) religious opinions." That is what Ibn Khaldun meant when he said that Ifriqiya (the medieval name for what is now Tunisia and eastern Algeria) divides the hearts of its inhabitants. The statement is a play on words connecting *Ifriqiya* with the Arabic root *f-r-q*, "to divide."[26]

The Arab conquerors of North Africa certainly looked down on Berbers, somehow, as second-class beings. Ibn Khaldun claims that Berbers lack "taste," which he defines as "the tongue's possession of the *habit* of eloquence" or "the conformity of speech to the meaning intended"—in other words, language. He meant that since the language of culture and authority in the Islamic world is Arabic, and Berbers did not speak Arabic as a native language, they lacked taste. And Arabs looked at them disparagingly for that. These "rebellious" Berbers rejected the idea of dynastic legitimacy. They thought that every believer who was religiously and morally irreproachable should be eligible for the position of imam by the vote of the community, "even if he were a black slave."[27] Indeed, if the chroniclers are correct, the first ruler chosen in Sijil-masa was Isa Ibn Mazid al-Aswad; the last part of his name means "black."[28]

The same rigor that characterizes the Kharijite view of central authority is found in its ethical principles. It demands purity of both the body and the conscience in order for acts of worship to be valid. Kharijites push their moral strictness to the point of refusing the title of believer to anyone who has com-mitted apostasy. Kharijite extremists say that apostates can never reenter the faith and should be killed for their sin. Sufriya Kharijites were generally more lenient on this particular point, but they still placed ultimate responsibility for an individual's actions on the soul of the individual, all while offering the promise of God's forgiveness.[29]

In 756, the Sufriya sect of Kharijites gained ascendency in Qayrawan. But that ascendency was short-lived. The very next year, the Ibadi leader of Basra, Abu Ubayda, proclaimed an Ibadi imamate in Tripolitania, with Abd al-Khattab as imam. The latter led the Ibadi tribes of Tripolitania into Qayra-wan and expelled the Sufriya leadership. Abu'l-Qasim became an outcast, and was forced to flee from Qayrawan as fast and as far as possible. He fled to the frontier, to the edge of the world of Islam, to the oasis of the Tafilalt, where, according to al-Bakri, he gathered enough of a following of Sufriya Kharij-ites to found the city of Sijilmasa as the first Islamic city in the hinterland of Morocco.[30] This was almost a full century after the Muslim conquest of Morocco in 681–682. Archaeology tells us that Muslims settled in Moroccan cities such as Volubilis right after the conquest, but they did not establish new cities until they built Sijilmasa in 758.

The First Islamic City

The city must have grown quickly under the Bani Midrar. Within fifty years of its founding, the walls and principal buildings were built. Al-Bakri tells us: "The lower section of the wall surrounding the town is made of stone, but the upper one is of mud. This wall was built by al-Yas'a Abu Mansur Ibn Abu'l-Qasim at his own expense, without anyone else sharing the cost . . . Al-Yas'a built the wall in the year 199 (AH = AD 814–1515) . . . The following year, he divided the quarters of the city among the various tribes."[31] When al-Mas'udi wrote in the tenth century that "the city had a main artery the length of which was equal to a half day's march," it was an exaggeration to be sure.[32] But sev-eral carbon-14 samples from our excavations at the Sijilmasa site clearly show that during the early Midrarid period, heavily concentrated occupation ex-

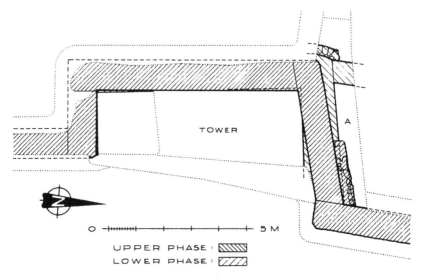

Figure 3.4. Plan of a guard tower along the Ziz.

tended from the Grand Mosque and the *dar al-imara* (governor's palace) on the northern edge of town to the modern water tower on the edge of the tarmac road that cuts through the southern edge of the archaeological site just before reaching the modern town of Rissani. One has to wonder whether the location of today's tarmac road marked some kind of urban limit during the Midrarid era. It was only during the last phase of the Midrarid era or even during the reign of the Bani Khazrun, i.e., the late tenth or early eleventh century, that residential occupation spread to the area south of the tarmac.

In 1992, MAPS successfully delineated the perimeter wall on the western side of Sijilmasa, the side that borders the Oued Ziz. Portions of that wall are visible here and there above the surface all along the riverbed. But is it the wall built by al-Yas'a? We excavated a guard tower along that wall that clearly has two phases of construction, both built of a concrete-like mix of mud and river pebbles and a lime hardener poured between form board panels in a series of sectioned layers one upon the other, with putlog holes through the wall at the edges of each of the mud panels. The upper phase of construction and occupation dates to the refortification of this part of town by the Alaouites in the mid-seventeenth century (described later). But the foundation of the lower phase, which we initially and tentatively dated to the period between the eleventh and fourteenth centuries, is built on a stone foundation, just as al-Bakri describes. The foundation could well have been built as early as the ninth century.

The earliest mosque (*jama'a*), al-Bakri tells us, was strongly built. But we had a very hard time finding it. What tradition describes as the mosque of Sijilmasa, and what our local hosts showed us when we first asked them to take us to the "mosque," was certainly not the mosque built in 814–815 by al-Yas'a. It was several degrees off the correct orientation, and in fact we had no archaeological proof that it was a mosque at all. One feature that would have proved it to be a mosque is a *mihrab* (prayer niche) indicating the direction of Mecca from Sijilmasa, east-southeast. The wall pointing closest to that direction was a solid, massive adobe wall. There was absolutely no evidence of a *mihrab* along that wall. But then we learned that most early, pre-sixteenth-century mosques in Morocco were incorrectly oriented by almost sixty-five degrees to south-southeast.[33] This was the first clue to help us reconcile what we saw on the ground and what we thought the mosque should be. We were looking for the *mihrab* along the wrong wall. We started looking elsewhere for it. Digging a trench across a break in what remained of the south wall of the building revealed what could have been the foundation and two floor levels of a *mihrab*. We were not satisfied. We had to excavate more within the "mosque" itself. We found the stratigraphy within the mosque to be the cleanest on the entire site. Levels there could be excavated like the layers of an onion, giving us a clear picture of the chronological sequence of the structure and of the site as a whole, period by period, dynasty by dynasty. Again, because of the nature

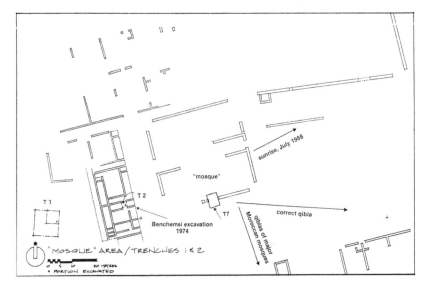

Figure 3.5. Plan of the mosque area showing the correct *qibla*.

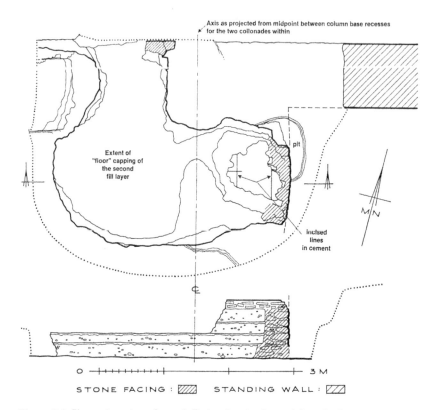

Figure 3.6. Plan and section of trench 7, showing the floor of the *mihrab*.

of the evidence, we had to read the story backward. But we will skip to the beginning of the story and come back to the end later.

The lowest level within the "mosque," dated by carbon-14 to the period 785–875, when earliest Sijilmasa was being built, was beyond a doubt an elite residence that encompassed virtually the entire area of the surface structure. That residence is under the "mosque." So the structure above it is clearly not the earliest mosque, the one built by al-Yasʿa in 814–815. That mosque had to be somewhere else. We needed to go back to the texts for the next clue. El-Mellouki, citing al-Muqaddasi, places it next to the palace of the amir, which would have allowed the prince to easily go to the mosque without having to pass through the city.[34] It is tempting to think that the residence we found is the palace of the amir, the *dar al-imara*. It fits al-Muqaddasi's description. If indeed it is, one should look for al-Yasʿa's mosque immediately adjacent to this structure. But on which side? Here is a perfect example of how the theoretical model of the Islamic city helped us define the morphology of Sijilmasa.

The model of early Islamic garrison cities such as Kufa and Basra provides the clue. In those cities, the *dar al-imara* is located on the *qibla* (facing the direction toward Mecca) side of the mosque. If this model holds true for Sijilmasa, since the *qibla* of most early mosques in Morocco face almost due south, then the earliest mosque would be to the immediate north of the structure we just described. Indeed, during our last season of excavation, in 1998, we found evidence there of a major structure with circular column bases, one of the features of the hypostyle halls of eighth-century mosques. Oleg Grabar says that once mosques began to take on a definable architectural form, between 650 and 750, "they were all hypostyle constructions with columns or piers as the main units of construction and bays framed by two or four columns or piers as the module which allowed an almost infinite growth of the building."[35] The best evidence we have says that the structure we uncovered must be al-Yas'a's mosque. That is how archaeology works. We found the earliest mosque in our last season of excavation.

Let us return for a moment to the *dar al-imara*. After each of our first four

Figure 3.7.
Emplacement for
wooden *minbar* rails.

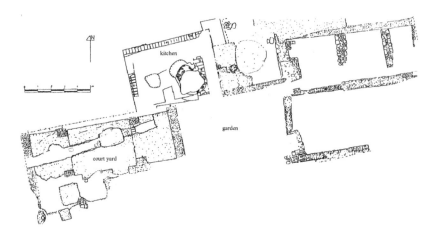

Figure 3.8. Plan of the elite residence under the mosque.

Figure 3.9. Circular column base north of the elite residence.

seasons, our friend and colleague B. G. Martin asked, "Have you found any-thing yet of the Bani Midrar?" Finally, after the 1996 season we could say conclusively yes. In the elite residential complex under the Grand Mosque we found fragments of plaster and wood veneer painted in simple black geometric designs, along with some stylized plant figures, on a white background. We did not have anything that we could effectively compare it to. As far as we know, the patterns are unknown in the history of Islamic art. It can be described as prototypical Midrarid art, and is seen here for the first time anywhere in close to a thousand years. The western portion of the house consisted of a square courtyard with a well-made plaster floor. Through archways to the east and west of the courtyard, one stepped up into rooms on either side. In the eastern part of the complex, we excavated several rooms, more than likely the private rooms of the complex, with stone foundations. More frag-

Figure 3.10. Wood veneer with prototypical Midrarid art.

ments of painted and carved stucco were found there, but most importantly, a piece of plaster was discovered, bearing the words "wusʿaha . . . kasabat . . . ʿalayha" written in square Kufic script, words from the Quran, Sura 2:286. The entire verse reads "la yukalifu Allahu nafsan illa wusʿaha laha ma kasabat wa ʿalayha ma-ktasabat," which translates as "On no soul doth God place a burden greater than it can bear. It gets every good that it earns, and it suffers every ill that it earns."[36] This is an oft-recited verse in all sects of Islam. But it is not an especially popular monumental inscription. On the other hand, the idea that it expresses reflects the Kharijite rejection of the doctrine of justification by faith without good works. This idea would have been especially popular among the Sufriya Kharijite founders of Sijilmasa, popular enough to be inscribed on a wall in one of the halls of the *dar al-imara*. There are no dots above or below the letters, suggesting that the script is an early form of Arabic writing, contemporaneous with the early years of Sijilmasa's history.

Between the eastern and western portions of this complex was an area in which we found no artifacts, only fragments of branches. This could well have been a garden in an interior courtyard, perhaps another of the "many gardens" described by al-Bakri. The kitchen was on the north side of the house and was enclosed by mud brick walls. Here we found several fire pits and trash pits filled with ceramic cooking utensils, a beautifully crafted wooden serving spoon, and a mass of animal bones, evidence of the rich diet of the home's inhabitants.

Figure 3.11. Quranic inscription found in the elite residence.

Figure 3.12. Wooden spoon found in the kitchen of the elite residence.

Residential Quarters

There are other elite residences of the Midrarid period to the west of the Grand Mosque. At one level, dated by carbon-14 to 855, there were stone pavers that once probably covered the entire floor, and a stone column in a fallen position.[37] There were several fragments of painted plaster with designs similar to those found in the residence under the mosque. In addition to the black on white, some of the designs were painted in red. We found several pieces of glazed tile of a kind not typically seen in Morocco until the late medieval period. Glazed tile is seen, however, among the Fatimids at that time. Those tiles, along with a fragment of a glass plate with a floral design, tentatively identified as Egyptian in origin, seem to document the period of Fatimid involvement in and occupation of Sijilmasa that occurred in the third quarter of the tenth century. In this same unit, we found the only gold that we have discovered to date in the City of Gold, a beautiful gold filigree ring, as well as a beautifully carved piece of ivory—evidence not only of a residence of above-average means, but also of the trans-Saharan trade that contributed to Sijilmasa's wealth.

MAPS has done a systematic study of the ceramics of this earliest period.[38] The predominant forms of pre-Almoravid ceramics consist of cooking pots (*qidr*), casseroles (*tajine*), and large milk jugs (*hallab*). In addition, in this earliest period are forms designed for the transportation and conservation of food and liquid. There are average-size pitchers (*qulla* or *khabiya*) and larger pitchers (*kuz* or *ka*). The most elegant of the latter is a beautiful pitcher bearing the inscription *al-baraka, al-yumn* in Kufic characters incised under a green glaze in the middle of the body. In the category of open forms, there are bowls (*zlafa*) and plates (*ghidar*). There are two plates with diverging rectilinear sides that are particularly interesting because of their decoration. One is completely in green and brown *cuerda seca* decorated with a scene in which an eagle with the paw of an animal, perhaps a lion, attacks the head of a man. The other has diverging rectilinear sides and a lip that inclines toward the inside; it is decorated with the inscription (*al-yumn*) painted five times (once in the center and then on each of the four cardinal points) under a transparent glaze. Sijilmasan homes were lit by lamps (*qandil*) with spouts.

In the earliest period of Sijilmasan ceramics, we see a tradition significantly different from that of the rest of the western Mediterranean in the Middle Ages. For example, the culinary ceramics of Sijilmasa include diffused African ceramic traditions in both form and technique. Surely, Muslim intervention brought its own technological, morphological, and decorative contributions to this tradition, thanks to the unique economic role that the city of Sijilmasa played in bringing together peoples from the Islamic East, Andalusia, and black Africa.

The Islamic city model suggests that most Islamic cities were divided into quarters, and Sijilmasa was no exception. As soon as al-Yasʿa finished building the city walls, al-Bakri says, he divided the city into quarters among the various tribes who settled there, quarters that still hold today (i.e., in al-Bakri's day, c. 1063).[39] The archaeological record supports the existence of quarters. Looking at the composite GIS (geographic information system) map of Sijilmasa, a residential quarter can be seen in the northwestern part of town.

Figure 3.13. Black-on-white Midrarid art found in the residence west of the mosque.

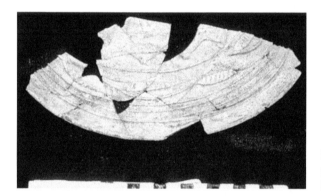

Figure 3.14. Glass plate, likely of Egyptian origin.

Figure 3.15. Gold filigree ring, found in the residence west of the mosque.

Figure 3.16. Vase inscribed *al-baraka, al-yumn.*

There are several residential quarters in the southwestern part of town. The northeast quadrant is where the citadel and mosque-madrasa complex was located, mostly public space, although there were certainly some residences interspersed. We described above evidence of elite residences just to the west of the mosque and south of the citadel, an arrangement described in other Islamic cities by Neil MacKenzie.[40]

Sijilmasa's Independence Is Challenged by Two Competing Regimes

"Wanted, dead or alive!" In 905, the Abbasid caliph in Baghdad put out the word that a dangerous political renegade, Ubayd Allah, the future Fatimid caliph, was on the loose. The Midrarid ruler of Sijilmasa, al-Yas'a Ibn al-Munasir, was warned by the caliph that the fugitive was heading for Sijilmasa. The prediction was correct. Ubayd Allah and his son managed to pass through Egypt in disguise. They arrived in Sijilmasa and managed to remain undetected for four years. When Ubayd Allah's son performed what seemed like a miracle, causing a spring to gush forth, their cover was blown. As the story goes, a local Jew spread the word that these Shi'ite outlaws were plotting to take over the city. The two were found, arrested, and imprisoned. Word got back to Ubayd Allah's partisans in Qayrawan, and they came with an army under the leadership of Abd Allah al-Shi'i, arriving in Sijilmasa in 908–909. They rescued Ubayd Allah, killed al-Yas'a, and treated the Jewish population rather harshly, presumably because of the complicity of the Jews in the capture and arrest of Ubayd Allah. After appointing a new governor of Sijilmasa, Ibrahim Ibn Ghalib, one of their own, the Fatimids returned to Ifriqiya, taking with them 120 camel loads of gold.

The Fatimids held Sijilmasa for only fifty days. In a seesaw battle to control the city-state, the people of Sijilmasa revolted and killed the Fatimid governor and all the soldiers in the Fatimid garrison. The Midrarids were back in power. But the Fatimids sent a second army, retaking Sijilmasa in 922. This time, they did not appoint one of their own, but chose a Midrarid whom they thought they could trust as governor—a wise decision, as it turned out, since Sijilmasa remained loyal to the Fatimids during the reign of the next three Midrarid amirs. And not only loyal, but extremely productive in tax revenues as well.

The fourth amir, though, Mohammed Ibn al-Fath, led a revolt against the Fatimids in 942–943 and reestablished independent Midrarid rule. Ibn al-Fath began to strike gold coins in the name of the Fatimid caliph—not the current caliph, al-Qa'im Ibn Amr Allah, but Ubayd Allah al-Mahdi, who had died nearly a decade earlier. One explanation for this is that it was a political statement midway between refuting Fatimid authority and recognizing the new Fatimid caliph, al-Qa'im.[41] Then, from AH 334 to 340 (944–950), Ibn al-Fath struck coins in his own name as amir. He is said to have been irreproachable in his conduct as ruler and to have seen to it that "justice would prevail."[42]

But then Ibn al-Fath broke with Sijilmasa's religious past. He renounced Kharijism as the religion of the state and adopted the Malikite school of Sunni Islam. He may have done that in recognition of caliphal authority in Baghdad, but soon after, he went even further and took the title *amir al-mu'minin* (commander of the faithful), a title reserved for the caliph himself. And he took yet another caliphal title, *al-shakir lillah* (the grateful toward God), a title that he engraved on his coins.[43]

For sixteen years Ibn al-Fath maintained his independence from the Fatimids. But when he heard that the Fatimids were sending an army under the command of Jawhar to retake Sijilmasa, he fled with his "household, family,

Figure 3.17. Jebel Mudawwar, "Round Mountain."

children, principal officers; he took refuge with them and all of their treasures in Tasagdalt, a stone fortress some twelve miles from Sijilmasa."[44]

We believe that archaeology attests to this place of refuge. We think that Tasagdalt is what Filalians today call Jebel Mudawwar, or "Round Mountain." We have made several excursions to Jebel Mudawwar, a favorite Sunday picnic spot for MAPS, although we have done no excavating there. In 2011, Chloé Capel, the newest member of MAPS, did a detailed survey of the site.[45] It looks very much like other stone forts built roughly a century later by the Almoravids from Sijilmasa to the Atlantic Ocean to protect themselves from the Almohads and other hostile tribes in the High Atlas. There are other Tasagdalts in other places, which leads us to believe that it is a generic medieval Berber term for "fortress."

Ibn al-Fath was captured by Jawhar's troops and taken in chains back to Tunisia. Why were the Fatimids so hell-bent on controlling Sijilmasa? Because of the gold trade. They knew that Sijilmasa was the trailhead for caravans bringing in gold from the south, and that wealth was essential to their imperial plans. They had gathered good intelligence about the city's prosperity. Ibn Hawqal, best known as the geographer whose *Kitab Surat al-Ard* (Configuration of the Earth) describes the Maghrib in considerable detail, focusing especially on its economic productivity and potential, was clearly a Fatimid sympathizer and probably worked for the Fatimids as an intelligence agent.[46] The Fatimids were planning to expand their empire. Preparations to invade Egypt, for example, demanded a large reserve of revenue for military expenditures, for establishing a new capital in a new area, and for propagandizing the venture.[47] Like Ibn Battuta four hundred years later, Ibn Hawqal was among the few writers who based their descriptions of Sijilmasa on first-hand knowledge. He was in the city in 951 or 952, just a few years before Jawhar's campaign. He recorded that the notables of the town were better off than notables of other towns—to the point of living opulently. He saw a statement of debt owed to one of them by another in the sum of 42,000 dinars, a sum, he says, of which he had never heard anything comparable in the East. Most importantly, he reminded the Fatimids of the income that Sijilmasa had produced for the dynasty during the reign of Mu'taz Ibn Mohammed, the Midrarid vassal who had faithfully governed the city for the Fatimids from 922 to 934: "taxes on caravans setting out for the land of the Sudan, as well as tithes, land tax, and old-established dues from what was bought and sold there, such as camels, sheep, cattle and other merchandise going out and coming in from Ifriqiya, Fez, Andalusia, the Sus, and Aghmat, along with other sums due from the mint—to a total of about 400,000 dinars and this from Sijilmasa and its district alone."[48] He pointed out that this amount was fully half of what the Fatimids collected from the whole of the Maghrib. Surely, the Fatimids could not afford to lose such a wealthy province. It was in 958 that Jawhar took Sijilmasa without further resistance.

The mint again struck coins in the name of the Fatimid caliph al-Qa'im. In the meantime, however, the Fatimid caliph al-Mu'izz li-Din Allah introduced a new design, a concentric design radically different from the standard field of horizontal lines—a symbol, perhaps, underscoring the birth of a new world system based on the Isma'ili Shi'ite doctrine. But the Fatimid coins of Sijilmasa did not adopt this new style. Was that a technical matter, that is, did no Fatimid engraver accompany the Fatimid army of Jawhar, or was the decision economic, namely, reflecting a concern that the new design could disturb the well-established reputation of Sijilmasa dinars?[49]

The Midrarids made one last attempt at independence from 963 to 976. Arabic texts make vague references to two sons of al-Fath who ruled successively. By then, though, the Sijilmasa gold trade had become a prize sought by more powerful entities: the Fatimids of Ifriqiya, who had controlled it for brief periods, and the Umayyads of Cordoba, who seized control through their Zanata Berber clients under Khazrun Ibn Falfal al-Maghrawi.

Our quantification of Fatimid and Umayyad dinars dramatically reflects the competition between these two superpowers to dominate the gold trade. A peak in production by one regime most often corresponded to a lapse in the production by the other. A coin count based on all the coins published in museum catalogues, collectors' catalogues, dealers' catalogues, and any other accessible numismatic literature permits the following observations.[50] In AH 316 (928–929), the Spanish Umayyads resumed striking gold coins after a long period of no production at all. In that year, Abd al-Rahman al-Nasir claimed the title of Nasr al-din Allah and presented himself as being in direct competition with the Fatimid caliphate. For the first half of the fourth *hijra* century, there are three peaks in Umayyad production, represented by eight extant dinars from 317, nine from 321, and eleven from 331. In the same years, the number of extant Fatimid dinars is zero, one, and zero. The Umayyads' mint production of gold coinage was high from 331 through 335, precisely when the Fatimids were preoccupied with ridding themselves of the threat of Abu Yazid in the eastern part of the Maghrib, and also when Ibn al-Fath began to defy his Fatimid overlords in Sijilmasa.

For the second half of the fourth *hijra* century, the contrast between the regimes' mint output in gold is even more striking. Three peaks in Umayyad production, represented by twenty-nine dinars from 358, thirty from 363, and thirty-nine from 391, correspond to zero, one, and zero Fatimid dinars from the same years. It seems clear that when one of the two competitors controlled the gold route, it was at the expense of the other.[51] The Umayyads began to strike their coins in the Sijilmasa mint. Dinars were struck in the name of the Umayyad caliph Hisham II in the years AH 378, 381, 383, 384, and 395. When the Umayyad dynasty collapsed in Andalusia, the Bani Khazrun continued to rule Sijilmasa, and they continued to strike both gold and silver currency in the Sijilmasa mint, although extant specimens of these coins are rare. By far the most exciting surface find at the Sijilmasa site during our first season of field work was three dirhams, silver coins, bearing the name of Masʿud Ibn Wanudin, the last Khazrunid ruler of Sijilmasa as an independent city-state, who was killed by the invading Almoravids.

The Sijilmasa Mint

The single most frequently asked question at the Sijilmasa site is "Have you found the mint yet?" The Fatimids established the mint in the early tenth century.[52] We have yet to find it. To the best of our knowledge, no medieval Islamic mint has ever been found in an archaeological context. We do have some idea of what a mint would look like. More than likely, the whole opera-

Figure 3.18.
Dirham of Mas'ud
ibn Wanudin.

tion would have been housed in a small but heavily guarded building. It would have had a small furnace for the melting of metals, an anvil for beating out a flat sheet, a table for cutting the discs to be struck into coins, and yet another anvil for striking the coins themselves, imprinting them with their inscription. The operation would have been overseen by a moneyer, responsible for ensuring the fineness of the metal and the weight of the coins. He might also have been the craftsman who carved the dies.[53] Evidence of a mint could be established by the presence of artifacts used in that industry, like a coin die, yet coin dies are extremely rare. Typically, to prevent counterfeiting, dies were destroyed as soon as a new issue was established.[54]

The Sijilmasa mint not only struck many coins over a long period of time, but also played a crucial role in establishing monetary policy and developing coin-die technology that was later applied in other mints in the western Islamic world. Choukri Heddouchi describes six distinct phases in the development of die-engraving technology.[55] In early Fatimid coins, die engravers punched a series of dots to form square, Kufic-style letters by hitting a pointed punch with vertical strokes. The earlier the coin, the thicker the point. Longer letters were slightly smoother than short letters because the die engraver struck his punch obliquely. In the second phase, that of the independent Midrarid rulers, the die engraver still used a series of dots to form letters, but polished the letters so that they looked smoother. This phase also introduced the *mim* punch, which was used to form the letter *mim*. We see the *mim* punch used from then on. In the third phase, that of the late Fatimids, the mint used cast dies rather than manually engraved ones. The letters are much thicker and lack sharp edges. The fourth phase is that of the Umayyads and the Bani Khazrun. The engravers started to use the *mim* punch for other letters. The Umayyads and their clients were the first to carve "Sijilmasa" as the name of the mint. They used a floral calligraphic style, and they introduced the fleur-de-lis motif, unique to coins struck in this mint. The fifth and sixth stages, which were implemented by the Almoravids and the Almohads, are described later.

Although we have not yet found the mint, we have found what we believe to be the ore washery, the facility used to process the precious metal brought to Sijilmasa in the form of ore. It was located on the east bank of the Ziz River. What has been exposed measures 16.5 meters (54 feet) long by 10.4 meters (34 feet) wide. There are sixteen chambers or basins of various sizes, but most of them are 2 meters (6.5 feet) or less in length and width. These basins are set at different levels and are connected by a series of drains from upper to lower levels. At first we thought that the structure was a tannery or a textile-dyeing plant. Sijilmasa had both tanning and textile industries. But tanneries and textile-dyeing facilities are generally much larger than the structure that we excavated along the Ziz. Our structure looked more like those excavated in Greece, at Laurion and Thorikos, that were described as facilities for washing mineral ores.[56] The minting and mining industry would have required such a

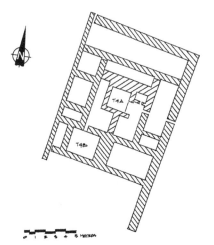

Figure 3.19. Plan of trench 4, the ore washery.

facility. Silver was mined within a 48-kilometer (30-mile) radius of Sijilmasa. And the gold brought to Sijilmasa by camel caravan is described in the literature in almost mythical terms as "the purest of gold."[57]

A Pattern of Political Tension and Religious Dissent

The tenth century and the first half of the eleventh witnessed a seesaw struggle for independence by a local population or its strongest local ruler, on the one hand, and appropriation, exploitation, and domination by an external imperial power, on the other, a pattern that became part of Sijilmasa's history for a long time. As the rulers changed, so did the religious affiliation of the ruling elite. As we have seen, the Midrarids followed the ideology of Sufriya Kharijism. Presumably, Sufriya ideology motivated all the Midrarid rulers. When the Fatimids ruled Sijilmasa, Sevener Shi'ism was the ideology of the state. But Shi'ite rule was short-lived and likely had very little impact on the population of Sijilmasa. The first ruler to adopt Sunni Islam of the Malikite school was Mohammed Ibn al-Fath Ibn Wasul, mid-tenth century. What exactly was his motive is hard to say. We know that he consciously asserted his break from the Fatimids. We know that he asserted his independence, claiming the title *amir al-mu'minin*. But why adopt Malikite Islam rather than revert to the Sufriya Kharijism of the founding fathers of Sijilmasa? Could Sufriya ideology have waned so far that it no longer was an effective rallying point for political identity? Could Ibn al-Fath have followed the model of the Umayyads, who also claimed caliphal authority and professed Malikite Islam? Whatever the religious motivation of any of the rulers of Sijilmasa, we do not know how any particular doctrinal affiliation affected the teaching and learning of Islam in the mosque. Our impression is that Sijilmasa was a center of religious discourse that tolerated a wide range of doctrinal affiliations.

Perhaps it was the emphasis on egalitarianism that attracted scholars to Sijilmasa. One such scholar who came during this early period was Shaykh Abu Rabi Suleiman Ibn Zarqun al-Nafusi. He came with Ibn al-Gham, an Ibadi merchant "from the East." When the latter decided to travel to Sijilmasa, he asked Abu Rabi to accompany him, promising that he could learn everything that he wanted to know. They stayed in Sijilmasa a number of years. When Ibn al-Gham was near the end, he willed all his books to Abu Rabi.[58] Modern Moroccan authors consider Sijilmasa to have been perhaps the earliest center for religious study in Morocco, predating Fez by a half century. El-Mellouki cites three authors who hold this view.[59] Abdulaziz ben Abdallah describes Sijilmasa as "the first hearth of the sciences" (*ulum*, religious learning). Mohamed Haji, writing about centers of learning under the Saadians, says that Sijilmasa was a major center for several centuries, going all the way back to its founding under the Bani Midrar.

We know that the grandson of Abu'l-Qasim married an Ibadi woman, the daughter of Abd al-Rahman Ibn Rustam, ruler of the Ibadi state of Tahert.[60] We also know that an Ibadi merchant sponsored Shaykh Abu Rabi Suleiman Ibn Zarqun al-Nafusi. Qadi Iyad tells us that in the very early years of Sijilmasa, a local scholar traveled to Medina, where he studied with Imam Malik, founder of the Malikite school of Sunni law.[61]

Ibn Hawqal alludes to Sijilmasa as a center of intellectual discourse. He describes the inhabitants as "generous and at ease": "They distinguish themselves from other people in the Maghrib by their comportment. We sense in them a love of science (*ilm*), a sense of modesty, elegance, virtuosity, kindness, and moderation." He adds that he had not seen anywhere in the Maghrib so many shaykhs with such deep knowledge as in Sijilmasa.[62] Al-Muqaddasi echoes this: "The inhabitants of Sijilmasa are excellent people who count among them a number of learned and wise men."[63]

The Bani Khazrun of the Maghrawa confederation, who ruled Sijilmasa in the name of the Umayyads of Cordoba, were Sunni Muslims, as were their Umayyad overlords. After the collapse of the Umayyads, the Maghrawa continued to rule Sijilmasa as an independent city-state, still Sunni. It could be that the religious elite of Sijilmasa were the last of the Sufriya Kharijite ulama to be found anywhere, and that they resisted domination by a Sunni regime. Whatever the reason, it is clear that the ulama of Sijilmasa felt oppressed by their Sunni rulers. The ulama of Sijilmasa wrote to Ibn Yasin, the *faqih*, the spiritual leader of the Almoravid movement in the deep Sahara, as well as to the amir and to the shaykhs of the Almoravids, urging them to come free them from the oppression of the rule of the Bani Khazrun. They told Ibn Yasin of the injustice, contempt, and tyranny suffered specifically by the men of science and religion, as well as by the community of faithful Muslims at the hands of their amir, Mas'ud Ibn Wanudin.[64] The Almoravid response was swift and decisive.

CHAPTER 4

Sijilmasa in Empire

The Almoravids invaded the Tafilalt in 1055. The amir of Sijilmasa, Mas'ud Ibn Wanudin, mounted his defense on the outskirts of the oasis, but to no avail.[1] The Almoravids had adopted new tactics to revolutionize their style of attack. There were three waves of warriors. The first carried long spears and the tall broad shields made of oryx skin, called *lamt*, for which the Almoravids became famous. Standing side by side and shield to shield, soldiers in the first line formed a barrier to protect those in the rear. The second line of warriors carried several javelins each, which they hurled with deadly accuracy. Finally, the cavalry took full advantage of their skills as cameleers, which provided an element of swiftness to their attack. They placed their pack camels in formation behind the charging warriors as a shelter to fall back behind during intervals between charges. This tactic required many camels, which they had. Ibn Abi Zar tells us that the Almoravids had recently seized a herd of fifty thousand Maghrawa camels in the Draa Valley.[2] Even allowing for exaggeration on the part of the chronicler, the Almoravids were capable of this style of attack, and they used it over and over again in the Maghrib and Andalusia.

The Almoravids easily won the day. Mas'ud Ibn Wanudin, the last independent ruler of Sijilmasa, was killed in battle. Ibn Yasin, the Almoravid imam, confiscated the property of the Maghrawa, their mounts and their weapons. He then led his forces into the city itself. It is said that he killed all the surviving Maghrawa. He remained in Sijilmasa long enough to reform the "objectionable practices that he found there," namely, "He chopped up the instruments of music and burned down the shops where wine was sold."[3] We have archaeological evidence to support these contentions.

As mentioned in the previous chapter, the most abundant food crop to appear in the macrobotanical material collected in the 1993 and 1994 seasons was grapes, in quantities great enough to suggest that they were not only consumed on the table but also used in the production of wine. During the 1998 season, we focused on the question of grapes during the collection and analysis of macrobotanical material from every deposit in every trench. Combining the 1998 data with the 1994–1995 data showed that grapes were found in 5 out of 6 deposits dated to the pre-Almoravid period (758–1056), 10 out of 52 deposits within the Merinid-Filalian period (1255–1640), 8 out of 37 deposits from the Alaouite period (1640–present), and only 2 out of 21 deposits from the Almoravid-Almohad period (1056–1255).[4] Where we were able to distinguish between Merinid and Filalian periods, all the samples that contained grapes were in the Merinid deposits.

What does this suggest? Deposits from Almoravid and Almohad periods are almost void of grape pips either because of a breakdown in the central government's ability to maintain the necessary infrastructure to bring water to the oasis or because of prohibition. (Islam prohibits the consumption of alcoholic beverages.) Still, many Islamic societies have been neutral about or supportive of wine production.[5] But this was not the case with the reformist Almoravid and Almohad dynasties. Grapes reappear during the Merinid period, but seem to disappear again during the Filalian period. This second disappearance could have resulted from a collapse of the infrastructure bringing water to the oasis, a collapse coinciding with the civil war that brought Merinid control of Sijilmasa to an end. Grapes reappear yet again under the Alaouites, who resume vast water projects along the Oueds Ziz and Gheris.

What Brought the Almoravids to Sijilmasa?

The Almoravids invaded the Tafilalt because they were invited by the city's religious elite, who complained of the oppressive rule of the Bani Khazrun. As mentioned in chapter 3, the ulama in Sijilmasa had written a letter to Ibn Yasin, the spiritual leader of the Almoravid movement in the deep Sahara. They told him that their ruler treated them unjustly and with contempt.[6] Whatever the real reason might have been, it is clear that the people of the Tafilalt felt oppressed by their rulers. Just what kind of oppression they suffered, we cannot tell from the sources. Was it religious oppression or general social repression? The Maghrawa rulers of Sijilmasa had, in fact, upset the delicate balance between the farmers of the oasis and the nomads in the desert. In earlier times, the Sanhaja Berbers wandered freely with their herds in the whole region in and around the Tafilalt. These nomads were permitted to use the land as pasturage and were given authorized access to cultivated lands after the harvest and to watering places for their herds. They traded some of their wool and hides with the agriculturalists of the oasis for food-stuffs grown among the date palms.[7] The camel herders in the desert supplied the many thousands of camels needed to carry the cargo. They also sold protection to caravans making the long trek across the Sahara. It was this delicate balance of resources and services that the Bani Khazrun disrupted. They restricted nomadic grazing rights. Worse still, they imposed taxes not sanctioned in the Quran. The call for help came from the ulama, the religious scholars who, more than likely, were Sufriya Kharijites resisting the new Sunni Muslim regime.

The Almoravids Bring Religious Reform to Sijilmasa

Ibn Yasin read the letter from Sijilmasa to his advisers and sought their counsel. They said that it was a religious obligation to bring reform to the oasis city; they called for jihad. So it was in the spirit of reform that Ibn Yasin led the Almoravids to Sijilmasa. We have already seen that he imposed a series of "blue laws" on the people of Sijilmasa, abolishing all "objectionable practices." In addition, he "abolished non-Quranic levies such as customs dues and taxes on commodities sold in the marketplace, and left only what the Quran allowed."[8]

The Almoravids came to Sijilmasa very much committed to the Malikite school of Sunni Islam.[9] That commitment went back to the pilgrimage to Mecca of Yahya Ibn Ibrahim, the great chief of the Sanhaja confederation, from which the Almoravids came. Islam was relatively new to the Sanhaja. Traders had brought it to their world a little over a century earlier. At first, these desert dwellers took on material aspects of Islamic culture, such as the wearing of Islamic amulets, ornaments, and dress and the acquisition of food and household habits. Then they adopted elements such as ritual prayer and other religious obligations.

On his journey home from the hajj, Yahya stopped in Fez and was converted to Malikism by Abu Imran al-Fasi, a scholar originally from Fez. He was expelled from there, however, for criticizing the injustice of the rulers of that city, who were from the Bani Maghrawa. The Maghrawa of Fez were Kharijite Muslims, heretics according to Abu Imran. After fleeing Fez and before settling in Qayrawan, Abu Imran studied with some of the great scholars of Muslim law in the East, where he developed a conservative theology and a radical political theory. He saw the caliph in Baghdad as the sole legitimate authority to whom all Muslims owed allegiance. He longed for a way to transcend tribal disunity and rising sectarianism in the Maghrib. He thought that Malikism might be the ideological foundation for a united Maghrib.

Qayrawan had been the center of Malikite Muslim law study since the middle of the ninth century. Malikism based its doctrine on the Quran and on the Sunna, the traditions of the Prophet and his companions, like other *madhahib* (schools of Islamic law). But it was uncompromising in its acceptance of the consensus of the ulama of Medina above all others. Malikite ulama sometimes relied on their own legal opinions more than on the traditions of the Prophet. They were intolerant toward Shi'ites, whom they viewed as corrupt disturbers of the peace. When Yahya Ibn Ibrahim met Abu Imran al-Fasi, Malikite scholars in Qayrawan had become more assertive in public life. They were openly critical of the Zirid representatives of the Shi'ite Fatimids, to the point that some suspect they contributed to provoking riots directed against the Shi'ites, increasing pressure on the Zirids to break from the Fatimids. If Malikism was an effective arm against Shi'ites, thought Abu Imran, why not against Kharijites as well?

Yahya Ibn Ibrahim asked Abu Imran to send a teacher with him back to the western desert. Abu Imran sent Ibn Ibrahim to a former student, Wajjaj Ibn Zalwi, asking him to send a teacher. Wajjaj was originally from that part of the Maghrib known as Sus al-Aqsa. After studying Malikite law with Abu Imran in Qayrawan, he went back home and founded a school of his own for students of science and reciters of the Quran. He called the school the *dar al-murabitin*, "the house of those who were bound together in the cause of God." It was steeped in the teaching of Malikite law. The teacher whom Wajjaj sent was one of his students there, none other than Abd Allah Ibn Yasin.

Almoravid Administration

Ibn Yasin placed the Sijilmasa garrison under the command of a Lamtuna tribesman and then returned to the Sahara. We have no text that says that the Almoravids explicitly built a new *dar al-imara* (seat of government), but circumstances recorded in the chronicles, along with archaeology, suggest that they did. Within a year after Ibn Yasin's departure, the Almoravid garrison in Sijilmasa was attacked by the citizens of the city, and the Lamtuna tribesmen were killed as they tried to take refuge in the Grand Mosque. Later, the people of Sijilmasa regretted what they had done. They blamed it on the Maghrawa and again invited the Almoravids to come and seek vengeance. So in 1056–1057 the Almoravids conquered Sijilmasa a second time. Ibn Yasin and the new amir, Abu Bakr, established their base in Sijilmasa. Although the residents swore an oath of allegiance to the Almoravids, the new rulers were outsiders.[10] They had to protect themselves from the local inhabitants as well as from potential invaders.

We are certain that the *dar al-imara* occupied by the Almoravids was not the one described in chapter 3. By the time Almoravids ruled in Sijilmasa, the original *dar al-imara* had been taken down and replaced by the Grand Mosque. Given their need for defense, they must have built a new one, not only enclosed by a circuit wall to protect it against invaders, but also walled off from the rest of the city, a pattern possibly unique to precolonial North African cities.[11] We believe that they moved the seat of government to a newly constructed citadel on the northern edge of the elevated plateau where we now see the northern walls of the Alaouite citadel. Preliminary analysis of the GIS data that overlays elevation contours of the Sijilmasa landscape, remote sensing of subsurface walls, and surface features on the site suggest that the Almoravid citadel was about 150 meters square (5.6 acres), much smaller than the later Alaouite citadel, its northern walls coinciding with the northern walls of the Alaouite citadel seen on the surface today.

After appointing his cousin Yusuf Ibn Tashfin to command the garrison of Sijilmasa, Abu Bakr went back to the Sahara.[12] Once Yusuf was firmly established in Sijilmasa, he treated the common people well. He abolished non-Quranic taxes and took from them only the *zakat* (the religious tax or tithe required of Muslims as one of the five pillars of the faith). He then set out to consolidate his authority in the rest of the Maghrib. By 1071, he had established himself in his new capital of Marrakech. When Abu Bakr learned how Yusuf had consolidated his personal power in the Maghrib, he decided to return from the Sahara in late fall of 1072. Upon seeing the strength of Yusuf's army, Abu Bakr realized that Yusuf was no longer his lieutenant.[13] Abu Bakr accepted his fate. He prepared to go home with a treasure trove that would greatly enhance his life in the desert. At the parting of Yusuf and Abu Bakr, the two commanders agreed to divide the Almoravid holdings. The Saharan homeland and the newly conquered Maghrib would be ruled as two domains whose tribal connections and interdependence would ensure the prosperity of both. But who would control Sijilmasa?

Some scholars say that Sijilmasa was controlled not by Yusuf but rather by Abu Bakr and his son Ibrahim.[14] Dinars were struck in both Abu Bakr's and Ibrahim's names.[15] A careful reading of the medieval texts suggests exactly the opposite. Ibn al-Athir is very clear: he says that when Abu Bakr appointed Yusuf to the Sijilmasa garrison, he (Abu Bakr) stayed for a while in the desert

Figure 4.I. Contour map showing an elevated plateau on the northern edge of central Sijilmasa.

and then returned to Sijilmasa and stayed there for a year.[16] Later he relieved Yusuf of his duties in Sijilmasa so that the two of them could conduct campaigns in the Sus. Abu Bakr appointed another of his relatives governor of Sijilmasa—his nephew Abu Bakr Ibn Ibrahim. We do not read of this nephew anywhere else except in Ibn al-Athir's account.

Ibn Idhari, on the other hand, says that Yahya, Abu Bakr's brother, had three sons, Mohammed, Isa, and Ali.[17] In 453/1061, a dinar was struck in Sijilmasa bearing the name Ali. He is apparently the nephew (wrongly identified by Ibn al-Athir) who succeeded Yusuf in the position of governor of Sijilmasa. Ibrahim must have been appointed to replace Ali. In the meantime, though, Yusuf had gained control over the entire Maghrib and ruled it from his new capital of Marrakech. After Abu Bakr withdrew to the Sahara for good, Ibrahim marched against Yusuf with a sizable contingent of Lamtuna troops to challenge him for jurisdiction over the Maghrib, which he felt Yusuf had usurped from his father. Yusuf sent his faithful commander Mazdali to intercept Ibrahim with a warning, sweetened by an offer of lavish gifts, the sort of things that would be scarce in the desert but were quite available in the international markets of Sijilmasa. In short, Yusuf called Ibrahim's bluff and bought him off. Ibrahim withdrew to the Sahara as his father had done earlier.

Yusuf Ibn Tashfin learned that governing an empire is hard work.[18] He divided the Almoravid domain into four provinces, each with a provincial capital city, two in the northern part of the Maghrib (Fez and Meknes) and two in the south (Marrakech and Sijilmasa). He relied on his relatives—sons, cousins, and nephews—to serve as military commanders and governors. This had been the custom of his Saharan ancestors for generations before him. Two of Yusuf's sons by his first wife, Zaynab, al-Mu'izz (the oldest) and Tamim, served as viziers in Marrakech. Yusuf's nephew Syr Ibn Abu Bakr was vizier in Meknes, governing the northwestern province, which included Tangier and Ceuta. Umar Ibn Suleiman of the Massufa tribe commanded the garrison of Fez and points east all the way to Algiers. Yusuf's son Da'ud Ibn Aisha became vizier of Sijilmasa.

The garrison of Sijilmasa was of utmost strategic importance for the Almoravids. It was the springboard from which the Almoravids moved from the desert to control the Maghrib. It was the keystone of a string of strongholds that extended along the southern rim of the Atlas into the western Sus, from Sijilmasa to Zagora to Nul Lamta. It served as the *ribat*, a fortified convent of sorts, at the southern frontier of Yusuf's empire. For travelers heading south, Sijilmasa was the last civilized place before they entered the vast Sahara.

Yusuf Ibn Tashfin chose as advisers religious scholars, Malikite *fuqaha* (plural of *faqih*, religious scholar) from Andalusia. These once-powerful men had lost much of their influence under the *muluk al-tawa'if*, the rulers of the Muslim city-states of Andalusia after the fall of the Umayyads. As advisers to the Almoravids, they became more powerful than ever before. Malikism, as practiced by these *fuqaha*, was not characterized so much by its content as by its process of formulating law. Legal texts like the *Risala*, the most complete and authoritative compendium of Malikite law, provided a ready-made system of law for the Almoravids, who were already predisposed to a rudimentary, even arbitrary understanding of Islam.

The famous Muslim theologian al-Ghazzali (late eleventh to early twelfth-century) had denounced the Almoravid *fuqaha* for abandoning the study of the Quran and the Sunna. Still worse, he criticized them for meddling in politics. The *fuqaha* felt threatened by al-Ghazzali's teaching. The *qadi* of Cordoba ruled that any man who read al-Ghazzali's *Ihya Ulum al-Din* (The revival of religious science) was an infidel ripe for damnation. Possession of a copy was likewise a crime, and the *qadi* issued a fatwa to that effect. During the first days of August 1109, in the small square in front of the west portal of the Great Mosque of Cordoba, the *fuqaha* gathered in the presence of the *qadi*. They soaked a bound copy of the *Ihya* in oil and, in a scene that foreshadowed others in history, burned it.[19] Word went out over the empire to burn the works of al-Ghazzali, and similar book burnings occurred in other cities, including Sijilmasa, just outside the Mosque of Ibn Abd Allah.

The Grand Mosque of Ibn Abd Allah

We know the name of the Grand Mosque in Sijilmasa at the time of the Almoravids from the *Tashawwuf ila Rijal at-Tasawwuf*, a biographical dictionary of Moroccan holy men written by Abu Ya'qub Yusuf Ibn Yahya al-Tadili.[20] In the biography of Ibn Nahuwi, al-Tadili writes: "When Abu Fadl arrived in Sijilmasa, he established himself at the Mosque of Ibn Abd Allah where he taught theology and law" (*usul al-din wa usul al-fiq*). MAPS found this mosque in the excavation season of 1994, just below the second level beneath the surface—although it took still another whole season in 1996 to be sure that this is what it was. The building was almost square, 22.5 meters long by 19.5 meters wide (438.75 square meters, or 4,722.7 square feet). It was divided into five aisles, four of equal width and a wider center aisle facing the *mihrab*.

The Mosque of Ibn Abd Allah, in addition to being the Friday mosque, was the equivalent of a university. It attracted scholars and students from all over the western Islamic world to study the books of Malikite law, books of

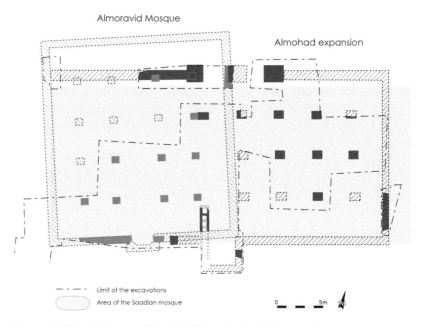

Almoravid Mosque

Almohad expansion

— · — ·   Limit of the excavations
⬭   Area of the Saadian mosque

0 _ _ 5m

Figure 4.2. Plan of Mosque of Ibn Abd Allah, with Almohad expansion.

hadith, and Arabic literature. Medieval biographical dictionaries identify a number of scholars who studied and taught there. From Tlemcen (in northwestern Algeria) came Abu Amr Uthman Ibn Ali Ibn Hassan, a man of scientific and literary mentality. Al-Tadili says that he read the Quran every night and composed poems on religious themes. Bakar Ibn Barhun Ibn al-Ghardia of Fez was an *alim* (scholar of religion) in Sijilmasa during the time of the Almoravids.[21] He was well versed in traditional sciences. He had traveled east to make the pilgrimage to Mecca, but also to study hadith under the famous scholar Abu Dar al-Haraoui. When he came back to the Maghrib, he devoted his life to teaching hadith in the Mosque of Ibn Abd Allah. Among his students was Mohammed Ibn Ali al-Ansari, who had come to Sijilmasa from Andalusia specifically to study with him.[22] Yet another of his students was Abu'l-Qasim Ibn Ward, who, after completing his studies in Sijilmasa, returned to Andalusia.[23]

And there were local students as well. Mohammed al-Daqqaq al-Sijilmasi was celebrated as an accomplished poet and well known as a Sufi (Islamic mystic). His friend Abu'l-Fadl Ibn Ahmed Ibn Mohammed also became a Sufi and a poet, although he was from time to time censored by the local authorities. Once when they were looking for him, al-Tadili tells us, Abu'l-Fadl hid from the authorities in a field on the outskirts of town until he almost died of hunger.[24]

Sijilmasa was known to be a sanctuary for religious dissidents. But even there, religious tolerance was tested during the book-burning days of 1109. Abu'l-Fadl Ibn al-Nahuwi, from whom we learn the name of the Sijilmasa mosque during his day, was a scholar who had immigrated to Sijilmasa from Tozeur (in southwestern Tunisia).[25] He was especially interested in al-Ghazzali's *Ihya Ulum al-Din*, and he refused to comply with the Almoravid edict to burn the book. On the contrary, he had more copies made. One day, Abd Allah Ibn Bassam, the *qadi* appointed by the Almoravid regime to uphold the law in Sijilmasa, came to the mosque to confront Abu'l-Fadl. The *qadi* had the authority to expel from the mosque, even from Sijilmasa itself, anyone who did not conform to the laws of Malikite Islam as defined by the *fuqaha* working for the Almoravids. Ibn Bassam interrogated Abu'l-Fadl, found him to be a threat, and banished the scholar from the mosque. Indignant, Abu'l-Fadl cursed Ibn Bassam, asking God to bring harm to the *qadi*. The next day, so the story goes, the *qadi* was killed by Sanhaja Berbers as he assisted at a marriage in the same mosque. Abu'l-Fadl fled to Fez, but he was also shunned by the *qadi* of that city.

This unfortunate episode suggests that the Almoravids were determined to exercise tight control, even censorship, over religious scholarship. But it also shows that the spirit of free religious inquiry, even if not free religious dissent, was alive and well in Sijilmasa. During the last years of the Almoravid rule in Sijilmasa, yet another scholar was sought by the law. Abu Abd Allah Ibn Umar al-Asam, a well-respected local Sufi shaykh known for his religious knowledge and his poetry, was arrested, along with other shaykhs from the Tafilalt. They were imprisoned in Fez by order of the Almoravid amir Tashfin Ibn Ali.[26] Were they imprisoned for their religious teaching? Or were they considered a political threat? Political opposition to the Almoravids was gaining momentum. During the reign of Tashfin Ibn Ali, the Almoravids struggled to maintain control over the empire; mounting accusations, some based on religious ideology, were being brought against them by another reformist movement, the Almohads.

The Sijilmasa Market

If the mosque was the metaphorical heart of the city, then the market was its belly. In many ways, the market at Sijilmasa was like many markets of the Islamic world. In other ways, it was unique.

We have no direct textual evidence for how the marketplace was organized. But if the Almoravids employed the same model in Sijilmasa that they used in other urban centers of their empire, then we can make certain inferences about the organization of the Sijilmasa market.[27]

According to the *hisba*, a manual for marketplace supervision compiled for the Almoravid regime by the Andalusian secretary Ibn Abdun, the head judge appointed the *muhtasib*, the supervisor of the marketplace. Theoretically, he was responsible for enforcing proper behavior. But in practice, he had jurisdiction only over citizens' behavior in public space. He was the *qadi*'s spokesman in the marketplace. It was his job to license the installation of each commercial enterprise in the city and to regulate the flow of commercial traffic. Ideally, to make a particular trade easier to regulate, he would situate its artisans along the same street. He decided where the hawkers could set up shop. In the vicinity of the Grand Mosque, the law forbade the sale of commodities that would impede traffic or dirty the streets. And on Friday, the shops could not open during the hour of congregational prayer. No beggars, no horses, no armed men, and no children with dirty shoes were allowed around the mosque. Dirty or foul trades like butchering, tanning, and dyeing were relegated to the periphery of the town.[28]

The *muhtasib* and his appointee the *amin* ensured the accuracy of the merchants' weights and measures. The *amin*'s job was to calibrate scales, check the weights and counterweights, and mark with his seal those that were within the margin of tolerance.

There were city building codes. There were regulations against throwing garbage in the streets. Each household was responsible for the upkeep of the street outside its door.[29] The *qadi*'s responsibility extended to the cemetery, which was by custom on the edge of town, never inside the town itself. Overcrowding in the city probably threatened the sacredness of the place, as it still does today. It was a favorite spot for the city's youth to congregate. All that activity impeded the women who came, faces unveiled, to mourn. The Muslim cemetery that occupies the southeastern quadrant of the Sijilmasa site today is relatively recent; it was established after the Alaouite restoration of the northern part of the central city in the late seventeenth century. The medieval cemetery was located south of the tarmac road along the east bank of the Oued Ziz, evidenced by several eroded graves observed on the surface in our field reconnaissance.

Sijilmasa's Open Market

Our archaeological evidence suggests that the Sijilmasa market was located about 60 meters (196 feet) southwest of the mosque. Almost in the center of town, a major east-west axis intersects with the main street. It entered the city from the Bab al-Sharq, north of the modern Muslim cemetery. It then passed through a gate into an enclosed compound about 200 meters square (9.9 acres). Although our archaeological research cannot confirm that this area was indeed the market, it would have been an ideal spot for a weekly open marketplace. Excavations indicate that there were no permanent architectural features within this enclosure. We did find an abundance of ceramic roof tiles in the surface collection. It could be that some of the merchant stalls within the enclosure were covered with permanent tile roofs supported by wooden poles.

This market would have served the needs only of the permanent residents of Sijilmasa. At most, it could have been a regional market for the inhabitants of the Tafilalt. It would have been similar to the thrice-weekly market that now occurs in Rissani every Tuesday, Thursday, and Sunday. The main market for long-distance trade was almost five kilometers (three miles) west of the city. It was called Suq Ben Akla.

Suq Ben Akla

An analysis of surface finds at Suq Ben Akla is the primary basis for interpreting this site.[30] Most of the pottery is from the medieval period. What is conspicuously absent is Bhayr pottery, or pottery of the Alaouite period. Suq Ben Akla functioned when Sijilmasa was at its peak, from the eve of the Almoravid conquest in 1055-1056 through the Merinid period, ending in the late fourteenth century. Local informants describe this place as Sijilmasa's market and as a customs point, or *diwan*. It could be what al-Bakri, writing in 1061, described as one of the suburbs surrounding Sijilmasa. There is no reference to Suq Ben Akla in any medieval text, suggesting that, administratively, it was considered part of the city of Sijilmasa. It was the hub of the North African import-export industry, the intersection of a vast network of trade routes connecting the Islamic world and beyond. It is one feature not found, as a rule, in other Islamic cities. It was not unusual for a secondary market to be near the edge of a city or even just outside a city. That was and is fairly common. But for the secondary market to be larger than the one that served the city itself, to be relatively far from the central city, and to have a permanent resident population of its own was not so common.

Figure 4.3. Subsurface wall at Suq Ben Akla.

Suq Ben Akla was more than just a market. It was the staging area for the large caravans carrying gold and other precious commodities from points south. These caravans were made up of dozens of merchants traveling together, and so a single caravan could easily include thousands of camels. No city center could handle such a flow of traffic, however much wealth it brought. What was needed was a staging area outside town—like Suq Ben Akla. That Sijilmasa had such a market testifies to the scope of its international trade, the size of the caravans that came and went, and their relative frequency.

Today, a nearly straight footpath crosses much of the field between the Ben Akla market and the center of Sijilmasa, terminating at the Oued Ziz precisely where we have identified a housing for a waterwheel (noria). Remnants of mud walls, in some places 3.0–4.6 meters (10–15 feet) high, border the road. At Suq Ben Akla, aerial photographs show a geometric patterning of ruined walls over an area of 0.5 square kilometers (123 acres). In 1994, MAPS did a detailed survey of this site.[31] North of the modern tarmac road, we noted several habitation mounds and the outline of two rectangular enclosures. Within one of these were the remains of two circular brick column bases, suggesting that the structure might have been a mosque. Local informants assure us that there was indeed a mosque in that part of Suq Ben Akla. That area was also where the permanent residents lived. They attended to the service needs of the large caravans. Some permanent residents cultivated the fields surrounding Suq Ben Akla, growing crops to feed the itinerants, both man and beast. Among the items frequently found in our surface collection were date pounders, used to crush date pits into fodder for animals. We know exactly how far north Suq Ben Akla extended because the edge of the settlement is defined by an eroded cemetery where countless of Suq Ben Akla's deceased permanent residents found their final resting place.

Itinerants stayed in the southern part of town. South of the modern road is a roughly square mound, apparently fortified, extending over a total area of 90 meters east-west by 80 meters north-south (1.8 acres). In the northwest corner of the enclosure are a group of rectangular rooms of mud brick and a series of interior rooms in the inner enclosed area. The configuration suggests a large *funduk* or caravansary, a place where caravaners could find temporary lodging and store their goods. Between the caravansary and the habitation area to the north is a large area of burnt rock waste that could be the remains of large cooking areas where heated stones were placed over

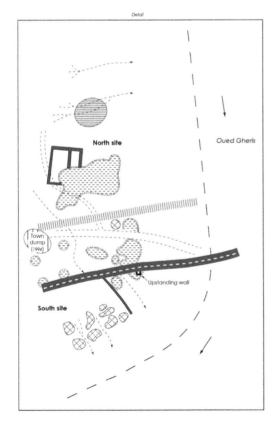

Figure 4.4. Sketch map of Suq Ben Akla, detail of northern area.

meat in pits for a number of hours; an area for heating water for domestic or industrial purposes; or a source for lime, which was used to make mortar (for, among other projects, the construction of dams on the Oued Gheris). The interpretation we find most intriguing is the first. After all, itinerant merchants had to be fed. One can easily imagine a throng of merchants milling among the stalls as meat roasted over charcoal and thick vegetable soup steamed in kettles. Suq Ben Akla provided the first comforts of civilization that merchants coming from south of the Sahara would have encountered after weeks of travel through the desert.

Several kilns along the banks of the river offer evidence in favor of the third suggestion. One of them appears to have been a pottery kiln, but the others produced lime cement used in the construction of the several dams that cross the Gheris. The dams not only were essential to the city's water infrastructure, but also served as bridges for crossing the Gheris to go to Sijilmasa.

Around Suq Ben Akla, as around the city of Sijilmasa and throughout much of the oasis, was good agricultural land. As mentioned earlier, Sijilmasa was renowned for producing a variety of dates. These were in high demand even in places that produced dates of their own. Tafilalt dates are still well known the world over as among the best in the world, a phenomenon celebrated by the annual date festival in the Tafilalt every October. Farmers in the oasis cultivated winter grains, an assortment of vegetables, spring wheat, and, in some periods, grapes. Nomads wandered on the periphery and in parts of the oasis itself between plantings, grazing their livestock among the date palms. Among the products of such a pastoral life were leather and wool, which the herders sold in town, supporting the local industries of tanning and weaving. The long-distance trade that made Sijilmasa famous piggybacked on this local barter.[32] The townspeople traded dates, leather goods, and textiles for a variety of industrial products from the North. That trade made a vast variety of goods available in Sijilmasa, goods from all over the Maghrib, Andalusia, Ifriqiya, Egypt, and places even farther east.

Sijilmasa's Trade

Slaves were an important item of commerce in the Sijilmasa market, second only to gold.[33] The transportation of slaves as commercial commodities across the Sahara was probably linked to the arrival of Islam. Al-Ya'qubi, writing in the ninth century, is the first to mention it. Al-Bakri tells us of the specific culinary skills of black slave women in Awdaghust who prepared *jawzina-qat* (sugared almonds) and *qata'if* (doughnuts); these women, he said, sold for 100 *mathaqil*.[34] That information, with slightly more detail, is repeated by the anonymous author of the *Kitab al-Istibsar* (1191); he adds *lawzinaqat* (almond cakes), *qahiriyyat* (comestibles from Cairo), *kunafat* (semolina with honey and butter), and *mushahhadat* (thin layered pastry) to the list of delicacies that these women prepared. Both al-Bakri and the author of the *Kitab al-Istibsar* recount the sexual attraction of the beautiful slave girls from Awdaghust who were purchased as prostitutes.[35] Ibn Idhari tells us that Yusuf Ibn Tashfin bought two thousand slaves to serve in his new army.[36] Some of the slaves coming from the Sudan were sold in Sijilmasa to work in the fields or to shepherd livestock. Some served the rich as domestic servants, and others became concubines. The most talented became valued assistants to their masters. Some merchants from Aghmat had even entrusted their caravans to their slaves. But most of the slaves were sent north across the Mediterranean world, some to become soldiers in the armies of kings.

Luxury goods from south of the Sahara included ostrich feathers, ebony wood, and ivory, which was carved and crafted into exquisite jewelry boxes, combs, and Quran stands. From the Sus and Awlil to the west and southwest of Sijilmasa near the Atlantic coast came brass, ambergris, alum (used in the dyeing industry), and salt, although Awlil was not the main source for this last precious commodity. During Almoravid times, a highly specialized item from the Sahara was the hide of the oryx (*lamt*), used in making the tall broad shields for which the Almoravids were famous.[37]

From the Maghrib and Andalusia to the north, from Egypt and the Levant in the East, came all sorts of manufactured goods: textiles, leather, metalwork, stonework, glassware, ceramics, and books. A word about the books. We have already established that Sijilmasa had become a place of learning, a "university" of sorts that attracted professors and students from near and far. The presence of scholars meant that books were increasingly in demand in the Sijilmasa marketplace. They were painstakingly copied in the great intellectual centers of the North and the East, cities like Fez, Cordoba, Qayrawan, and, especially, Cairo. Typically, books sold for four or five dinars apiece, almost as much as a fine suit of clothes. Some very rare books sold for twenty dinars or more.[38] Books were among their owners' most prized possessions and were considered a major part of their wealth. Books were highly sought not only in Sijilmasa but also in cities to the south. They were relatively easy to transport and brought good prices in gold in Islamic cities south of the Sahara such as Timbuktu, which was also becoming a major intellectual center in the world of Islam. Many of the manuscripts sold in that commerce are being catalogued, carefully restored, and digitized in Timbuktu today.[39]

Ceuta shipped pearls and coral to Sijilmasa, where local craftsmen made beautiful necklaces of pearl, glass, amber, and other semiprecious stones. They were exported to Mali, where they were in great demand and where coral was used as a form of currency. The jewelers of Sijilmasa refashioned silver from nearby mines and gold from across the great desert. Among the artifacts that we excavated at Sijilmasa were a silver mesh bracelet and a ring of delicate gold filigree (see fig. 23 in chapter 3). We also found a fragment of a beautiful Egyptian glass bowl decorated with a floral motif (see fig. 22 in chapter 3), several examples of Andalusian pottery, and a beautiful marble sundial, also likely from Andalusia.[40] There was fine cotton from Egypt as well as smooth silks and brocades woven with gold and silver thread from Egypt and Yemen. Some of these luxury goods were sold to the wealthy residents of Sijilmasa. The rest were exported to grace the houses of the more affluent in the cities of the Sudan.

Since Sijilmasa's earliest days, dates have been the Tafilalt's most renowned export. Al-Bakri called our attention to dates, Ibn Battuta raved about their quality, and the annual October date festival in the Tafilalt of today inundates the markets of Rissani and Erfoud with a wide variety of dates.

Woolen fabric was apparently an important export from medieval Sijilmasa. Again, al-Bakri provides the details. He says that Sijilmasa bought wool from a *qsar* called Yarara, about three days' journey from Sijilmasa. The sheep there were of a special breed called *kis*, named after a place in Persia famous for its sheep. With this wool of superior quality, the weavers of Sijilmasa produced woolen fabric that sold for "twenty *mathaqil* a piece,"[41] surely an exaggeration, but suggestive of a high price and high quality.

Sijilmasa continued its voluminous ceramics production.[42] The ceramics from this imperial period of Sijilmasa's history, from the mid-eleventh century through the fourteenth, is made from a compact, homogeneous clay, mostly cream colored. The pottery is very thin and of a very fine texture. The typical forms are bowls, plates, jugs, bottles, cups, and lamps. Sijilmasan pottery turns up in archaeological sites south of the Sahara. Denise Robert-Chaleix reports that most of the objects imported to Tegdaoust were household utensils: pitchers, pots, cups, plates, bowls, bottles, and, especially, lamps. These vessels were made from a homogeneous clay with white particles. The color is beige, cream, or white. The glazes used were usually monochrome green, dark metallic, or bluish. These are precisely the characteristics of the medieval Sijilmasan pottery described above, which suggests that Sijilmasa was a probable provenience for much of the pottery found at Tegdaoust.[43] Furthermore, the chemical composition of the clay used in more than half the pottery recovered at Tegdaoust matches that of the clay of Sijilmasan pottery according

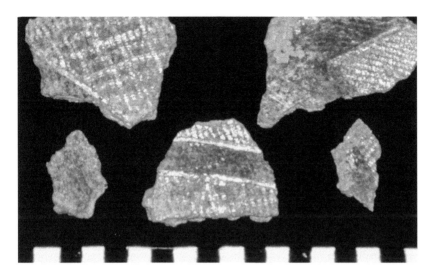

Figure 4.5. Middle Niger pottery.

to analyses done by Maurice Picon, a well-known ceramicist from the Laboratoire de Céramologie in Lyon, France.[44]

Ceramics were also imported to Sijilmasa from every direction. Picon visited the Sijilmasa site in May 1993. As he walked around the site and kicked up surface sherds, he exclaimed, "The entire Mediterranean is represented on the surface of this site!" This bears witness to an extensive network of international commerce that extended from all over the Mediterranean world to West Africa.[45]

The Almoravids and the Gold Trade—
The Saharan "Trade Triangle"

One way to understand the world gold trade is to look outward at it from Sijilmasa, to view Sijilmasa as its hub. Luxury goods and manufactured goods from the North were traded for gold and slaves from the South. But there was a third commodity that made the gold trade work: salt. All the caravans stopped in Teghaza, the city of salt, located about a twenty days' march south of Sijilmasa, within the territory of the Bani Massufa, one of the tribes of the Sanhaja confederation.[46] Teghaza's rise to predominance in the salt trade coincided with the advance of the Almoravids. Until then, much of the salt exported to the Sudan came from Awlil, on the Atlantic coast, which was controlled by the Bani Gudala. When that tribe revolted against the Almoravids, the salt route from Awlil became more isolated from the hegemony that was developing in the central Sahara under Almoravid protection. It became easier to bring in salt from Teghaza, and it was of excellent quality.

Medieval Arab writers described Teghaza as the most impressive source of salt in the Sahara. Ibn Battuta tells us that the buildings were made of salt.[47] The desert floor in that area was like a quarry of marble. Miners of salt cut thin rectangular slabs about eight inches thick out of the floor of the desert. The traders sold much of their manufactured goods from the north at Teghaza in exchange for this salt, which was very much in demand south of the desert. The merchants exaggerated only slightly when they said that the traders sold salt for an equal weight of gold. The traders were good storytellers, but the truth is that salt was very expensive in the south. And the salt of Teghaza was the best that could be bought. Then there was the cost of transporting it. The caravaners charged as much as 80 percent of the salt's value to transport it to market in Timbuktu.[48] Much, perhaps most, of the gold exchanged for this salt was headed for Sijilmasa.

The cycle in the trade triangle—manufactured goods for salt, salt for gold, and gold for manufactured goods—was continuous. From Sijilmasa, much of the gold was sent to ports all over the Mediterranean world, but much of it, too, was destined for the mint at Sijilmasa, which had been striking gold coins for many generations, for one regime after another. Some of the gold was transported in the form of dust, but most of it was transported as refined gold, melted down and poured into shapes more convenient for transportation: bricks, bars, or blank coins.[49] And huge quantities of gold were shipped—by one estimate, three to four tons a year (at peak) during the time of the Almoravid and Almohad dynasties.[50]

Our own quantification of gold coins struck by North African and Andalusian regimes confirms this estimate.[51] We have already shown how the Fatimids and Umayyads competed for control of the gold routes and that peaks and valleys in their gold production were inversely proportional to each other. But overall averages in the production of gold coinage remained remarkably close. For the first half century of the Fatimid presence in North Africa, an average of 1.18 Fatimid coins per year have survived, compared to 2.12 coins per year during the second half century. Our analysis of sources of gold based on copper impurities in gold ore show that even after the Fatimids moved their base from Ifriqiya to Egypt, they continued to benefit from West African gold through their vassals the Zirids. For their part, Zirid dinars have a survival rate of 2.1 coins per year. Their chief competitors, the Umayyads, score a

Figure 4.6.
Tuareg with
two slabs of salt.

little higher, 2.91 dinars per year, that is, unless we combine the Fatimids and the Zirids. Some scholars argue that the Fatimids and Zirids suffered a steep reduction in their supply of gold when the Bani Hilal invaded North Africa and cut the routes to the west and south. Our radiochemical analysis of Fatimid dinars shows that while they controlled North Africa, 47 percent of their coins were struck from West African gold. After that, only 24 percent were.[52] They still needed, or at least wanted, West African gold. But it had become much harder to get. What changed because of the Bani Hilal was not the availability of gold, but rather control of its flow from West Africa across the Sahara and through North African port cities like Sijilmasa.

The Almoravids took over the gold routes. During the first half of the eleventh century, the Sanhaja confederation, of which the Almoravids were part, controlled the desert between Morocco and the western Sudan. The

year after the Almoravids' conquest of Sijilmasa, they took the city of Awdaghust, the principal commercial entrepôt to the south. In control of both port
cities and the vast ocean of sand in between, the Almoravids were in the best
possible position to dominate the gold trade. Their production of gold coins
attests to it. They got off to a slow start. For thirty years, the Almoravids
struck coins only in Sijilmasa and only in the name of Abu Bakr in absentia;
the extant coins average 3.4 a year. But once Yusuf Ibn Tashfin opened mints
in several other North African cities, the average jumps to 10.0 dinars a year.
And for a period fifteen years, the Almoravids struck coins in ten Andalusian
cities, for which there are an average of 21.1 extant dinars a year compared
with the 2–3 dinars a year that have survived from previous North African and
Andalusian regimes. The Almohads maintained this same level of production.
Their production is more difficult to track in detail, because Almohad dinars
bear no dates or mint names, but we can tabulate an average of 16.2 extant
Almohad dinars per year.[53]

Why did Yusuf Ibn Tashfin strike coins in Abu Bakr's name long after
the latter was gone from Sijilmasa? Only Ibn Idhari records Yusuf's response
to Abu Bakr, who conceded authority to his nephew in Sijilmasa and the
Maghrib: "I will not decree anything without your authority, nor will I, God
willing, hold back anything from you."[54] With those words, Yusuf agreed that
Abu Bakr would be titular head of the Almoravid state. The coins struck in
the Sijilmasa mint bear that out. The *dar al-sikka* (mint) continued to issue the
official coinage of the state in the name of Abu Bakr until the latter's death.
Only then did Yusuf begin to issue coins in his own name as amir, still from
the mint at Sijilmasa rather than from his new capital at Marrakech. Craftsmen cast the die with the inscription in mirror image in a clear, simple, authoritative script. They placed the blank gold discs between the two faces of
the die and struck the upper piece with a mallet: "There is no God but God
and Muhammad is his Prophet—the amir Yusuf Ibn Tashfin!" On the lower
part of the die, they inscribed: "In the name of God this dinar was struck in
Sijilmasa in _____ [date]—*al-imam* Abd Allah, *amir al-mu'minin*." To that
last phrase, "*al-imam* Abd Allah, *amir al-mu'minin*," they sometimes added
al-Abbasi (the Abbasid). By this gesture, the Almoravids continued to recognize, at least in name, the Abbasid caliph in Baghdad.

The mint at Sijilmasa established and maintained the minting policies
for the entire Almoravid Empire throughout its history. Almoravid die engravers in Sijilmasa introduced new techniques that would be used in all the
new mints soon to open.[55] They made maximum use of the *mim* punch even
for letters that are not normally circular. Almoravid coins are symmetric and
have a circular blank stripe separating the field and the margin. The Almora-

Figure 4.7.
Dinar of Yusuf Ibn
Tashfin, reverse
side, showing the
Sijilmasa mint name.

vids introduced a new Quranic phrase on their coins: "And whoever desires other than Islam as a faith, then it will not be expected from him, and he will be in the hereafter amongst the losers" (Quran 3:79). Because this inscription was so long, the die makers linked all the words in the marginal inscription and often used the same letter for two words. The Almoravids were consistent about putting the date and mint name on their coinage, making it easy to compare their mint production in Sijilmasa with that of their other mints over the span of their ninety-year reign.[56] For thirty-eight years, Sijilmasa was the Almoravids' only mint. Then they opened five in the Maghrib and ten in Andalusia. The coins struck in all of these mints were identical to those struck in Sijilmasa except, of course, for the name of the mint. Such a multiplicity of mints is unique in western Islam. Other than Sijilmasa, the only Maghribi mints in operation under the Fatimids, for example, were in Qayrawan—soon to be replaced by one in al-Mansuriya—and al-Mahdiya, and for a very brief run of a year or two, Zawila. In the Maghrib, the Umayyads struck coins only in Sijilmasa.

The first dinar struck in the capital city of Marrakech was produced in 485/1092. The next year, a new mint opened in Aghmat, just eighteen miles south of Marrakech, still the dominant commercial center in the region. In the years to follow, mints were opened in Fez and Tlemcen, and later still in several Andalusian cities. Even with the opening of new mints, the official coinage remained standardized. The coins were weighed against precisely crafted glass weights that bore the stamp of the ruler. The *sikka*, the official insignia of the Almoravids, guaranteed the same fineness of gold that was first established in Sijilmasa.[57]

The value of Almoravid dinars was such that they circulated all around the Mediterranean world, in Muslim and Christian lands alike.[58] We see the term *marabotin* (Almoravid dinars) showing up in texts in Iberia as early as 1084, and in France by the beginning of the twelfth century. The *Liber Censum* (manuscript of 1192) of the Roman Church recorded its revenues from France, Italy, Germany, and England in units of *marabotini*, even though the actual payments may have been in other currencies. Dinars struck by the Almoravids were found in a number of hoards in Europe. The most important one was at the Monastir del Camp in southwestern France. Seventy-five coins were found in 1851, ten of which were Fatimid, the rest Almoravid. Other hoards were found at Vernoux, Saint-Romain, Meslay-le-Vidame, and London. Many Almoravid dinars that went to Europe were then reexported to the East.[59]

Within the Muslim world, Almoravid dinars commanded a favorable rate of exchange. A letter in the Cairo Geniza describes the effort of a merchant in al-Mahdiya (in modern Tunisia) to buy Almoravid dinars. He bought *bakriyya*, dinars struck in the name of Abu Bakr between 1058 and 1087 in the Sijilmasa mint; and *aghmatiyya*, dinars struck in Aghmat beginning in 1088, all at an exchange rate of 2.66:1.[60] The same merchant submitted an account in which he paid 170 al-Mahdiya dinars for 60 Fatimid dinars, 80 al-Mahdiya dinars for 30.92 Almoravid dinars, and 78.92 al-Mahdiya dinars for 30.12 Almoravid dinars. The exchange rate of al-Mahdiya for Fatimid dinars is 2.83:1. The exchange rates of al-Mahdiya for Almoravid dinars are 2.66:1 and 2.58:1 respectively.[61] The Egyptian dinars were slightly more expensive than the Almoravid ones, even though they were on average 3 percent purer in gold. It was the reputation of the "gold of Ghana" that was driving up the value of Almoravid dinars.

Within the Muslim world, Almoravid dinars commanded a favorable rate of exchange. Merchants in Egypt, for example, made a concerted effort to obtain them, some even insisting on being paid in Almoravid dinars.[62] Which was a bit ironic, since the mean fineness of Almoravid dinars was 92.2 percent, more than 3 percent less pure than contemporary Fatimid dinars struck in Egypt. Refining techniques in Sijilmasa were not as sophisticated as those in Egypt, but Almoravids struck coins with "gold from Ghana," gold that was renowned for being the "purest of all the gold in the world." It was the reputation of the source of gold as well as the name of the Almoravid amir that ensured their value. Al-Bakri said that the gold from Awdaghust, the southern port city that fed Sijilmasa, was "better and more pure than that of any other country in the world."[63]

The Impact of West African Gold

If most of the gold that came north across the desert passed through Sijilmasa, can we somehow assess what impact that gold had on the known global economy of the time? What effect did the influx of West African gold have on North Africa and the Mediterranean world? To answer this question, we need to measure fluctuations in the value of the precious metals in different markets—which is difficult to do, since most references to the use of currency, salaries, prices, the cost of living, and so on do not specify the kind of currency used. One would expect the value of gold to vary according to its availability: where gold is plentiful, its purchasing power is less. So we would expect the purchasing power of gold to be low in the western Sudan. And it was, at least according to the few references that we have found. An officer in the court of the king of Mali, for example, received an annual salary of 50,000 *mathaqil* of gold, which seems like a highly inflated amount. One hundred *mathaqil* of copper sold for 66.6 *mathaqil* of gold.[64] Salt, as we have already seen, sold for an enormous quantity of gold.

In North Africa, there was a gradual increase in salaries at all levels of society from the eighth century through the eleventh. During the eighth and ninth centuries, a laborer in Egypt received less than one dinar a month. At the beginning of the tenth century, the same laborer received just about one dinar a month. A skilled laborer received as much as two dinars a month. Because of inflation, though, these workers experienced a decrease in buying power. A worker earning 0.6 dinars in the eighth century could by 923 *artal* (approximately 500 grams) of bread with his earnings, whereas the man earning one dinar in the tenth century could buy only 465 *artal* of bread.[65] Wages continued to rise in the eleventh century: the minimum wage for a common laborer was 1.5–1.67 dinars, a skilled laborer received 2.5 dinars, and a specialized tradesman like a master mason received 3–6 dinars a month.[66] The cost of bread is a good measure of the value of currency. The average cost of wheat in the tenth century was 0.59 dinars for 100 *artal*; it rose to 1.09 dinars in the eleventh century and 1.4 dinars for a short time at the beginning of the twelfth century before dropping back down to 1.09 dinars.[67]

There are indications that Ifriqiya began to feel a pinch on the supply of precious metal after the invasion of the Bani Hilal in the mid-eleventh century. Within a few years of the invasion, dinars were no longer being struck in the mints of Ifriqiya. Merchants deposited currency with bankers in the form of silver dirhams and received credit expressed in gold dinars.[68] Before the invasion, Ifriqiya had been able to pay for wheat from Sicily with large quantities of gold. After the invasion, when the need for imported wheat was even greater, the Sicilians continued to insist on payment in gold—naturally, since the western Sudan via Ifriqiya was the main supplier of gold to Sicily. This placed tremendous pressure on Ifriqiya to purchase gold coins from the new dynasty that was in position to monopolize the gold trade—the Almoravids.

The Almoravids, the Gold Trade, and the Crusades

We are not quite willing to say that the Almoravids caused the First Crusade (1095–1099), but the evidence shows that their control of the gold trade must have been a factor. Once the Umayyad dynasty collapsed, vassals of the Umayyads carved out kingdoms of their own, about three dozen independent city-states in all. The leaders were called *muluk al-tawa'if*, or *taifa* (party) kings, because their loyalty was first and foremost to family or tribe—hence, to a party. There were no fixed boundaries between the city-states, which often changed hands as they battled against one another. They sometimes formed alliances, even with Christian states, sometimes to the point of becoming mere tributaries of Christian kings. Eventually, the more powerful *taifa* states swallowed up the smaller ones. By the time the Almoravids were in Morocco, there were nine or ten powerful states left. An Andalusian poet once likened Andalusia under the Umayyads to a pearl necklace, beautiful, highly cultured, and rich. When the caliphate collapsed, the necklace was broken and the pearls were scattered on the floor, but each was still a pearl.[69] Collectively, the *muluk al-tawa'if* lacked the political cohesion of the former Umayyad caliphate of Cordoba, but individually, each was still rich.

For the *muluk al-tawa'if* combined, there is an average of 2.84 extant dinars per year, slightly less than the Umayyad average of 2.91. One of the ways the *taifa* kings managed to survive was by paying *parias* (tribute) in gold—gold from West Africa that more than likely passed through Sijilmasa—to the stronger Christian kings to the north. One of these kings was Alfonso VI of Castile, who also happened to be the single largest contributor to Cluny Abbey (between Dijon and Lyon). He pledged an annual contribution to Cluny of 2,000 gold dinars, double what his father had contributed.[70] But those payments came to an end when the Almoravids came to Andalusia and defeated Alfonso at the Battle of Zallaqa in 1086.

We have yet to find direct evidence of the Cluniacs indicting the Almoravids for cutting their source of wealth. We do know, however, that the monastery depended on Alfonso's support for its ambitious project of building a new abbey basilica, and that the building progress almost ground to a halt after the Almoravids appeared on the scene.[71] In addition, Cluny Abbey spearheaded the First Crusade.[72] The main thrust of the crusade movement was the Levant, where the enemy was Muslim, but the enemy had to be confronted on every front. Church leaders urged French and Spanish knights to carry the crusade to Andalusia. Pope Gelasius II granted crusade indulgences to all who joined the campaign in Andalusia.[73]

When the Muslim city of Toledo fell to the Christian king Alfonso of Castile, the inhabitants found their new master to be even less tolerant than they had imagined. The prospect of *reconquista* forced the Muslim kings of southern Spain to invite the Almoravids to their shores. The Rock of Gibraltar loomed across the straits much as Sijilmasa must have appeared to the Almoravids some thirty years earlier when its inhabitants made a similar plea. The Almoravids were reluctant to go to Andalusia, but once they got there, they were even more reluctant to leave. It was a wealthy land, its prosperity derived from the introduction of new crops and agricultural technology, which were described by two mid-tenth-century writers, the Muslim Ibn Hawqal and the Christian Recemund. It was a consumer of raw materials and a producer of fine industrial goods. It was the western end of the east-west axis of trans-Mediterranean trade. All in all, it was a considerable prize for a dynasty from the western Sahara.

The Almoravids rescued the *taifa* kings and made Andalusia part of their empire. They soon found themselves in an ideological dilemma. Their war in Andalusia had forced them to raise taxes. The two cornerstones of their ideology, jihad and "no non-Quranic taxes," turned out to be mutually exclusive. Worse still, as they were waging jihad against the Christians in northern Spain, a new threat was emerging on their southern fringes. The Almohads descended on them from the Atlas Mountains, threatening their control of the gold routes to the south and challenging their legitimacy in the Maghrib.[74]

The Almohad Challenge

The founder of the new movement was Ibn Tumart, born in the small village of Igiliz, high in the Anti-Atlas Mountains south of Taroudant.[75] He left home to make the hajj in 1105. Over the next fifteen years, he spent time in several centers of learning, including Cordoba, Alexandria, Bagh-

dad, and, ultimately, Mecca. In each of these places, he studied with some
of the most prominent Malikite theologians. It is likely that he even met the
famous al-Ghazzali, whose books the Almoravids burned in 1109. Central
to Ibn Tumart's teaching was the absolute unity of God, what Muslims call
tawhid, a notion contrary to the much more personal image of God held by
the Malikite theologians who had taught the Almoravids and provided them
with their basis for law. Ibn Tumart openly criticized the Almoravids, calling them *mujassimun*, anthropomorphists. He criticized them for their strict
reliance on books of Malikite law rather than on interpretations of the Quran
and traditions of the Prophet. He taught that an imam should be a person of
impeccable virtue, and that it was his (Ibn Tumart's) duty to promote good
and combat evil, even if that meant rebelling against an imam.

When Ibn Tumart arrived in the Almoravid capital of Marrakech, he went
unnoticed until he began to censure the mores of the people. As he had done
in other cities on his way home from the East, he went around overturning
vats of wine and smashing musical instruments. The final blow came when
Ibn Tumart met the Almoravid amir's sister riding through the streets of
Marrakech. She, like all Lamtuna women from the Sahara, did not veil her
face. Ibn Tumart ordered her to cover herself at once. He slapped the haunch
of her mount, and the animal threw Ali's sister to the ground. Ali Ibn Yusuf
ordered Ibn Tumart to leave town. The latter fled to his ancestral home, Igiliz, where he built a small *ribat* (a convent) and gathered around him a band
of followers. The Atlas Mountain tribes of the Masmuda confederation became his main support.

The Almoravid response to this threat was to build a string of fortresses
along the outer rim of the Atlas ranges from the Atlantic coast to Sijilmasa.
We think that the easternmost fort in this chain was the one atop Jebel Mudawwar, sixteen kilometers (ten miles) due west of Sijilmasa. As described
earlier, this could well be the fortress that sheltered the fugitive Ibn al-Fath
at the time of the Fatimid invasion of Jawhar, fully one century before the
Almoravid conquest. The Almoravids, who were quite good at adopting useful
features from those they conquered, could well have occupied the hundred-
year-old fort at Jebel Mudawwar and even have used it as a prototype for the
forts they built to defend themselves from the Masmuda Berbers, who were
defecting to the Almohad reformers. The new fortresses (Qasba Tadla, Qasba
Dai near Tadla, Tasghimaut south of Marrakech, Tasanult on the Atlantic
coast) were built hurriedly out of rock rubble laid in alternating thick and thin
courses. The Almohad threat was imminent.

In 1144, the Almoravid amir Ali Ibn Yusuf, who had succeeded Yusuf Ibn
Tashfin in 1105, died and was succeeded in turn by his son Tashfin Ibn Ali.

He was an able ruler, but opposition to Almoravids was rapidly rising. The end came quickly. Within a year of becoming amir, Tashfin Ibn Ali lost his life trying unsuccessfully to defend the city of Oran. Fez was the next to fall, followed by several other cities in the Maghrib: Meknes, Ceuta, and Salé. In March 1147, the Almohads appeared before the gates of Marrakech. After a long siege and five inconclusive pitched battles on the plains outside the city walls, a band of Almohad warriors built ladders and succeeded in scaling the walls and opening the city's gates to their comrades. The Almoravids surrendered the city.

By then, the battle cry of the Almohads was being heard all the way to Sijilmasa. The conquest itself is described vividly by Solomon Cohen, a resident of Fustat (in Egypt), in a letter to his father, based on what he heard from Jewish and Muslim refugees from Sijilmasa.[76] At the news of the Almohad conquest of Oran and Tlemcen, where many citizens had been killed, the residents of Sijilmasa rose against the Almoravid governor and expelled him and his garrison from the city. They then sent a delegation of surrender to Abd al-Mu'min, leader of the Almohads. On entering the city, the Almohads tried to convert the Jews to Islam by debate and persuasion. After seven months without success, they resorted to more violent persuasion. A letter from the Cairo Geniza indicates that the leader of the community of Sijilmasa was the first to convert, and he apparently convinced a number of other Sijilmasan Jews to do the same.[77] Those who did not convert either fled or were killed. The chronicles report that over 150 Jews died for clinging to their faith.[78]

Just how Jewish was medieval Sijilmasa? There were stories of anti-Semitism before the Almohad conquest. As elsewhere in the Islamic world, Sijilmasa saw expressions of anti-Jewish sentiment. Al-Bakri reports that the profession of mason, considered a vile trade, was reserved for Jews.[79] That would have been on the eve of the Almoravid era. The anonymous *Kitab al-Istibsar* dates persecution of Jews back to the beginning of the tenth century when the Fatimids attacked the city to rescue their Mahdi, Ubayd Allah. The story goes that it was a Jew who exposed Ubayd Allah to the authorities, which led to his arrest; in retaliation, the Fatimids executed the wealthy Jews of the city, confiscated their property, and allowed only those Jews to remain who would serve as masons or cleaners of cesspools.[80] The *Kitab al-Istibsar*, written during the Almohad era, says that they were confined to the humiliating trades because they had originally settled in the region to get rich, believing that gold could be found there more easily than anywhere else in the Maghrib. The same sentiment was expressed again much later, suggesting that many Jews had become merchants and had accumulated great wealth, and indicating, too, that more often than not Sijilmasa had been tolerant toward its

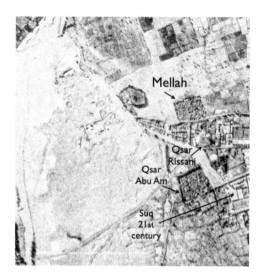

Figure 4.8. Aerial photo showing the location of the Sijilmasa *mellah*. Photo obtained from the Moroccan Division de la Carte; used by permission.

Jewish population. Jewish scholars viewed Sijilmasa as a city of "learned and wise men," a city of scholars, and the only rabbinical city in the South.[81] The *mellah* of Rissani, the "Jewish quarter," which was inhabited by Jews until the early 1970s, is located on the northwestern edge of modern Rissani. We know that the eastern edge of medieval Sijilmasa overlaps the western edge of Rissani, making it impossible to find the precise border. It is possible, then, that the location of the *mellah* did not change as the city shifted in an easterly direction. The current *mellah* could well be the original one.

The Almohads and the Sijilmasa Mosque

The most obvious archaeological evidence for the arrival of the Almohads in Sijilmasa is the orientation of the Grand Mosque. When the Almohads took Marrakech, their ruler, Abd al-Mu'min, at first refused to enter the city. When the *fuqaha* (religious scholars) asked why, he said that it was because "the mosques of your city are not exactly facing the true *qibla*." So the *fuqaha* promised that the city would be "purified by demolishing the mosques because of their faulty orientation, the divergence of the *qibla* and its inclination toward the East."[82] They did in fact demolish the first mosque that they had built in Marrakech, which was pointed 154 degrees east-southeast, and replaced it with a new mosque facing five degrees farther south. Our archaeological research confirms that they did the same thing in Sijilmasa.

We continue to describe the archaeology of the Sijilmasa mosque in reverse order from what we actually did. In the previous chapter, we discussed the lowest occupation level under the mosque, the first level to be occupied, but the last to be found. As we removed the floor of the Filalian mosque, the second floor from the top, approximately 30 centimeters (12 inches) from the surface floor, we uncovered the third of four levels, a plaster floor immediately beneath the Filalian one. But the floor plan for this level revealed a different series of column bases from that of the Alaouite mosque on the surface. Again, there are twenty-four column bases, this time arranged in three rows front to back. They divide the prayer hall into four bays front to back and nine aisles of unequal width side to side. The third and fifth aisles from west to east are wider than the others (see fig. 4.2). Embedded in this floor are two narrow trenches and wooden beams or ties running perpendicular to the narrow trenches, along with traces of wooden rails connecting the beams.

Suspecting that these could have been the remnants of the wooden rails for a movable *minbar*, we examined existing *minbars* in the oasis. They were virtually identical to the feature we excavated in the Sijilmasa mosque. The *minbar* on wheels or rollers is the normal type of *minbar* all over the Maghrib.[83] There is evidence for it as early as the Great Mosque of Sfax (849) and in the Zaytuna Mosque in Tunis (864). The earliest textual reference to a *minbar* on wheels was for one in the Great Mosque of Cordoba under Hakam II (966–976); the *minbar* itself has not survived. The earliest *minbar* on wheels to have survived is the Almoravid *minbar* of the Great Mosque of Algiers, dated 1096. The oldest archaeological evidence for a *minbar* on rails, at least as far as we know, is this one found at Sijilmasa, built by the Almohads shortly after they took over the city.[84]

As we examined the construction at this level, we noticed that the nature

WEST SECTION OF AXIS TRENCH

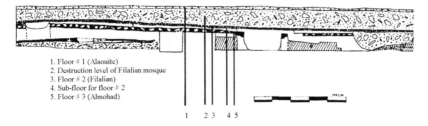

1. Floor # 1 (Alaouite)
2. Destruction level of Filalian mosque
3. Floor # 2 (Filalian)
4. Sub-floor for floor # 2
5. Floor # 3 (Almohad)

Figure 4.9. West section of central axis trench in the mosque.

of the plaster floor changes as we move from the western to the eastern half of the structure, going from a well-constructed white plaster with a very high lime content to a less well-constructed grayish plaster containing less lime. The gravel subfloor is also made of different materials: very coarse gray gravel in the western portion and finer pink gravel in the eastern portion. Finally, the column bases in the western side are smaller than those on the eastern side.

There is only one explanation for all of this. It became clear that we were dealing with an original structure that had become the western part of the prayer hall, and an expansion of that prayer hall to the east. The western part of the building is the Mosque of Ibn Abd Allah, the Grand Mosque at the time of the Almoravids (described above). As we have seen, the Almoravid mosque was almost square, 22.5 meters long by 19.5 meters wide (73.8 feet by 64 feet). The eastern part is an addition built by the Almohads shortly after their conquest of the city in 1147. The Almohads redesigned the mosque by bringing the back wall in, shortening the mosque to 18 meters (59 feet) long, but also by extending the east wall, almost doubling the width of the mosque to 37.5 meters (123 feet). These renovations explain why the third and fifth aisles are wider than the others. The fifth aisle is the center aisle, directly in front of the *mihrab* of the mosque after the expansion by the Almohads. The third aisle was the center aisle of the mosque before the expansion.

That dramatic event, the conquest of Sijilmasa by the Almohads, is the clearest datable event in the archaeological record of Sijilmasa. And that is crucially important. It establishes a central marker on which the chronology of Sijilmasa can hang. There are three convincing pieces of evidence that the expansion of the mosque, so clearly visible in the archaeological record, occurred shortly after the arrival of the Almohads in the middle of the twelfth century. First, we discovered a section of a column and a column capital in the destruction level in the vicinity of the *mihrab*, a slender column with a floral motif on its capital, just like the ones flanking the *mihrab* of the Almohad mosque at Tinmal (in the High Atlas, about 100 kilometers south of Marrakech).

Second, we discovered fragments of camouflaged plaster, carved and painted in red and black, in the same destruction level, another trademark of the Almohads. On the eve of the Almohad conquest of Fez, say the chronicles, the shaykhs of the Qarawiyyin Mosque ordered that the decorations around the *mihrab* be camouflaged to prevent them from being destroyed.[85] Archaeology tells a different story. Henri Terrasse found the camouflaged decorations, but he suggests that the work of plastering the designs was done by the Almohads themselves sometime after 1148 to reflect the ascetic style of the new regime.[86]

The third, and most convincing, clue that the expansion was the work of the Almohads concerns the orientation of the mosque. The original mosque, the Mosque of Ibn Abd Allah, was oriented 163 degrees east-southeast. The orientation of the addition is 166 degrees east-southeast, that is, three degrees farther south. The Almohads were famous for "rectifying" the orientation of Almoravid mosques, even though they established a different wrong orientation. The Almohads' "corrected" orientation was almost sixty-five degrees off the true orientation toward Mecca—so far off that when we first failed to find any trace of a *mihrab* along the wall closest to the correct *qibla*, we questioned whether the structure was a mosque at all. We later learned of the now well-known work of Michael Bonine (1991) on the orientation of mosques in Morocco, as discussed in chapter 3.[87]

We were not alone in being at first misled by the orientation of the mosque. In 1996, an *alim* (religious scholar) from Fez visited the site. As we pointed out the foundation of the *mihrab* and the emplacement for the movable *minbar*, he shook his head in disbelief at the possibility of these structures being what we described them to be. Our only defense was what we could point out on the ground. We could not explain it. Why are so many mosques in Morocco facing so far south? There are several theories and a considerable literature on the subject.[88] In the first two centuries of Islam, Muslims had no truly scientific means of determining the exact *qibla*. They knew roughly the direction of Mecca and the road that pilgrims took to go there. In some cases, they used the direction of that road as the *qibla*. That was not the reason for the incorrect orientation in Sijilmasa. Pilgrims from that city went north to Fez, where they joined larger groups of pilgrims.

Medieval geographers addressed the issue of the *qibla*. They divided the world into zones, anywhere from seven to twelve. The *qibla* for each zone was defined in relation to the rising or setting of a prominent star or star group, or generally as being in a certain direction. The problem with this system is that, according to some schemes, such as that of the ninth-century geographer Ibn Khurradadhbeh, Sijilmasa is in the same zone as Cordoba, but also in the same one as Egypt and Syria. If all of the mosques in the same zone are oriented in the same way, that is, if Sijilmasa's *qibla* were established in the same way as those in Egypt, it would face, as it does, south-southeast.

Yet another explanation goes back to the very beginning of Islam, a time when Mohammed and his companions faced Jerusalem when they prayed. Sixteen and a half months after the *hijra* (migration) to Medina, Mohammed began to face Mecca instead in order to face the ancient religious shrine, the Ka'ba. The Quran places great importance on this change. It says: "The fools among the people will say: 'What hath turned them from the *qibla* to which they were used?' Say: 'to Allah belongs both East and West'" (2:142).

Tradition tells us that Mohammed said, "What is between east and west is a *qibla*," and he himself prayed while facing due south, toward Mecca. Many early Muslims emulated the Prophet and interpreted what he said literally; they used south for the *qibla* wherever they were. Mosques from Andalusia to Central Asia attest to this, including the two slightly different orientations of the Sijilmasa mosque.

Why did the Almohads expand the mosque to almost twice its size? Undoubtedly because of a rapidly expanding population. Urban growth was stellate along the road leading south to Timbuktu. The richest neighborhood that we found in Sijilmasa is located in this area of urban sprawl at the southern end of town, south of the modern tarmac road, now covered and "protected" for the foreseeable future by a brand-new bus station, a lycée, and the local headquarters of the national gendarmerie. The richest house that we found in Sijilmasa is from this period, a house worthy of the growing merchant class living off the gold trade.[89] It had several rooms of adobe walls; it was built on a solid stone foundation; and it was covered with the rich decor of carved stucco, simple geometric patterns, and stylized floral patterns that are an imitation or an elaboration of the simple patterns of the much earlier, prototypical artwork of the Bani Midrar.

The Grand Mosque of Sijilmasa continued to attract distinguished scholars from other important centers of learning during the Almohad period. The "faculty" included Ali Ibn Mohammed Ibn al-Kattan al-Katami al-Fasi, a scholar of hadith and *fiqh* who taught for a while in Marrakech before coming to Sijilmasa. Ashab Ibn Mohammed al-Assari, a Shafiʻi scholar from Baghdad, studied in Murcia, Granada, and Fez before coming to Sijilmasa.[90] Abu Ali Ibn Salem al-Susi studied *fiqh* in Fez before becoming a professor in Sijilmasa in c. 1193. Al-Tadili lists several local students who distinguished themselves in their scholarship, all of them also noted for becoming Sufis.[91] It seems that the Almohads encouraged Sufism as a way to democratize and deepen the Islamic faith.[92]

The Last Medieval Image of Sijilmasa

When Ibn Battuta visited Sijilmasa in 1352, the city was at the height of its glory. It was the richest period in Sijilmasa's history. The gold trade was at its peak. The Merinid sultan Abu'l-Hassan received at least three embassies from the Kingdom of Mali south of the great desert, the first being that of the famous Mansa Musa, whose embassy must have come shortly after 1331. Ibn Khaldun tells us that Mansa Musa died while his ambassadors were in

Morocco. Abu'l-Hassan responded by sending a delegation bearing sump-
tuous gifts for Mansa Musa's successor.[93] Also during this period, Sijilmasa
began to show up on European maps. Genoese merchants resident in Sijilmasa
made the Sahara known for the first time to their nation's cartographers.[94]

But the story of the Merinids in Sijilmasa did not begin on such a high
note. They came to power in Morocco in 1248, but did not effectively control Sijilmasa until 1274. In the dead of winter of that year, Sultan Abu Yusuf Ya'qub led a huge force made up of his own royal army supplemented
by Zanata Berbers and Ma'qil Arabs. They laid siege to the city for eight
full months and finally, in September, took the city by storm. This was the
first time in Sijilmasa's five-hundred-year history that machines of war, cata-
pults, blew holes through its massive adobe walls. Ibn Khaldun reports that
the garrison was put to the sword, the two governors were killed along with
members of the Abd al-Wadid family, and the population that was not killed
was taken into slavery. Sijilmasa was the last city-state in Morocco to oppose
Merinid rule, and it was now soundly defeated.[95]

To emphasize the point, Abu Yusuf Ya'qub struck dinars, the only Merinid
sultan to do so in his own name; other sultans struck coins anonymously.[96]
Our count of extant coins (3.7 dinars a year) shows that the Merinids produced a steady flow of gold coinage, comparable to that of the North African
regimes that struck gold before the outburst of production by the Almoravids
and Almohads. There were two periods when the Merinids' production was
significantly higher than their average: the period following Mansa Musa's
pilgrimage (6.7 coins a year) and the period leading up to the crisis that caused
the Merinids to lose control of Sijilmasa (6.2 coins a year). A puzzling observation is that during the three years that followed the civil war of 1393, the
number of extant dinars reaches its peak of 12 a year.

Sijilmasa and the Merinids

The Merinids had earlier tried to control Sijilmasa. They held it briefly from
1255 to 1258 when a man named al-Qitrani, the Merinid commander of the
garrison, rebelled against the central government. For two years, he transformed Sijilmasa into an independent principality, but he did not have the
strength to stand alone for any length of time. In 1260, remnants of the Almohad dynasty regained control of Sijilmasa. In 1262, the Merinids tried to take
it again, but local residents offered too much resistance; they burned the siege
engines and turned the besiegers away. Finally, in 1263, Sijilmasa fell to the
Bani Abd al-Wad, the rulers of Tlemcen, bitter enemies of the Merinids who

incited opposition to the latter wherever and whenever they could, including in Sijilmasa. The Bani Abd al-Wad ruled Sijilmasa for eleven years before being expelled in 1274.

The chronicles are silent about the history of the Merinids in Sijilmasa between the conquest in 1274 and Abu Ali's coming to power in Sijilmasa in 1315. We have to assume that the Merinids remained firmly in control, or at least that there was no significant opposition to the central regime in Fez.

Unlike the Almoravids and the Almohads, the Merinids did not rely on religious reform to legitimize their authority. They did, however, seek to ally religious orthodoxy with Sufism as a means of propping up state authority. The link between the two was the institution of the madrasa.[97] All over Morocco, the Merinids built madrasas, institutions that supplemented mosques as centers of higher learning. Scholars at madrasas studied the traditional sciences of Islam, Quranic exegesis, hadith, *fiqh*, and Arabic literature. What made them institutionally different from mosques as centers of learning is that they provided residential lodging for out-of-town students. The teaching in the Merinid madrasas reflected the legalistic religiosity of the ulama and must be seen as part of an effort by the Merinids to legitimize their authority by drawing the Malikite ulama into the orbit of the state.[98] Ultimately, it did not work.

Merinid madrasas excel in decorative detail but lack, according to Abdallah Laroui, the grandeur of Almohad art. Visually as well as culturally, their decoration was "borrowed splendor, a last flowering of waning Andalusia."[99] The ultimate failure of the Merinids to promote imperial unity as the Berber dynasties that preceded it had done, that is, their inability to express or to unify society in the Maghrib, led to the immediate and lasting success of the Sufi brotherhoods, which became more autonomous as central authority became less effective.

The Merinids lavished great expense on the building of their madrasas. They are characteristically decorated with intricate details, stylized plants, and arabesques—seemingly infinite interlocking geometric designs carved in stucco and olive wood or laid out in colorful mosaics. There is no hard evidence, either textual or archeological, for the Merinids' having built a madrasa in Sijilmasa. The building adjacent to and attached to the Grand Mosque, still visible today in Sijilmasa, is indeed a madrasa. We know for sure from textual sources that it served as one during the reign of the Alaouite sultan Moulay Ismail.[100] The mosque itself dates to the middle of the fifteenth century, and the madrasa to no later than a century after that.[101] There are two levels of occupation directly beneath that madrasa. The lowest level, where we found extensive construction, including the remnants of a stone wall and a stone pillar, is, we suspect, the earliest mosque built in Sijilmasa, back at the city's

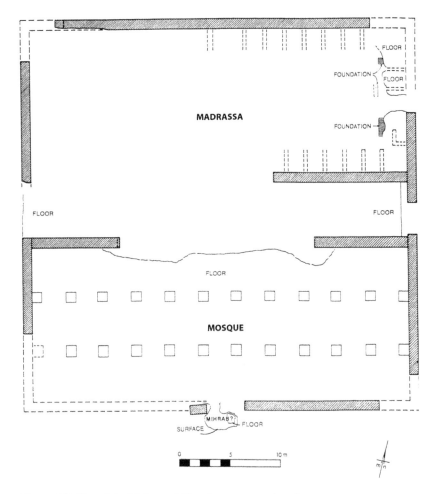

Figure 4.10. Plan of the Filalian and Alaouite mosque and madrasa.

founding. The level between the uppermost and lowest levels is identifiable neither by date nor by function—we did not retrieve enough archaeological evidence to be sure. But it is quite possible that it was a madrasa during the Merinid era. Leo Africanus, writing in 1526, noted the presence of a madrasa in Sijilmasa.[102]

In 1315, the Merinid sultan ruling the empire from his capital in Fez was Abu Sayid Uthman II (1310–1331). Like later Merinid sultans, he had a rebellious son, Abu Ali, who made a bid for power and forced his father to abdicate, but only briefly. Abu Sayid quickly regained his authority. Abu Ali surrendered to his father and offered to turn over everything that he had usurped in return for the governorship of Sijilmasa and its dependencies.[103] The father agreed. The two signed a treaty, and Abu Ali began his rule over Sijilmasa—virtually independent from and at times in opposition to the central Merinid regime. He organized his own administration and his own army and took control of all the *qsur* in the region. From there, he spread his influence over the Draa Valley and into the Sus. To do that, he recruited the service of the Maʿqil Arabs, the last of the Arab nomadic waves to infiltrate the far Maghrib along the Saharan edge. In "alliance with the Zanata Berbers, they constituted a very powerful nomadic mass capable of counteracting the attempts of the settled folk at hegemony."[104] Abu Ali underscored his authority by striking dinars in the Sijilmasa mint. Like most Merinid coins, except those of Abu Yusuf Yaʿqub, they do not bear a date or the name of a ruler, and many bear no mint name. But these dinars of Abu Ali do bear an anti-Merinid slogan devised by the Abd al-Wadid dynasty of Tlemcen when they were on the verge of defeat by the Merinids. The slogan reads *ma aaqraba farija-llah*, "May the relief sent by God be quick," reflecting his own bias against the central Merinid regime in Fez.[105]

When Sultan Abu Sayid died in 1331, his son Abu'l-Hassan, Abu Ali's younger brother, became the new sultan in Fez. Abu'l-Hassan's first thought was to secure control over Sijilmasa. But Abu Ali offered to recognize his brother's suzerainty if he were left in charge in Sijilmasa. Abu'l-Hassan was hesitant. But since he was preoccupied with planning an expedition against the Abd al-Wadids of Tlemcen, he left Abu Ali alone for the time being. It is only when Abu Ali exceeded his jurisdiction, as he was habitually prone to do, and led an expedition into the Draa and on to Marrakech that Abu'l-Hassan decided to take charge. In the fall of 1332, he marched on Sijilmasa. He commissioned an army of workers to build siege machines as well as a temporary town for his own troops beneath the great walls of Sijilmasa. For a full year, he held tight the noose. Finally, on September 30, 1333, after a long and bitter siege, Sijilmasa capitulated to Sultan Abu'l-Hassan.[106] Abu Ali was taken prisoner, led from Sijilmasa on an ass. After spending a few months in prison in Fez, he was executed. Sultan Abu'l-Hassan assumed the responsibility of raising his brother's two sons, each of whom would later briefly appear as the ruler of Sijilmasa. In the meantime, Abu'l-Hassan appointed his own governor in Sijilmasa. The siege of 1332–1333 left such a bitter taste among the Sijilmasans that for a long time they considered the sultan a tyrant. Some say that the assault was so devastating that it took thirty years for the city to recover.

We have already seen that on the eve of Ibn Battuta's journey to Sijilmasa, the Merinid dynasty was on the brink of war between Sultan Abu'l-Hassan and his son Abu Inan. Sijilmasa was caught in the crossfire. When Abu'l-Hassan returned to Morocco from his failed campaign in Tunisia, only to find that his son had usurped the throne in Fez, it was in Sijilmasa that the father took refuge, escorted by those Arab nomads who had remained loyal to him. The people of Sijilmasa, upon hearing that he was coming, went out to greet him, even the young women, proof that they still saw him as their rightful sovereign. The commander of the Sijilmasa garrison, who had been appointed by the usurper son, fled. How quickly fortunes turn. Abu Inan marched against Sijilmasa with a large force, large enough to induce Abu'l-Hassan's supporters to defect. Abu'l-Hassan found himself yet again on the run, and his son chased him all the way to the Atlas Mountains, where Abu Inan finally caught up with his father and forced a final surrender. One has to wonder whether Abu'l-Hassan remembered the words of his own brother, Abu Ali, himself besieged in Sijilmasa some twenty years earlier: "However long the duration, Time does not keep the same face—it fatally takes with it both joy and sadness. Where are the kings who overpowered lions in the forest? They lay shrouded in their tombs, and all traces of what is beautiful have faded away."[107] Abu Inan controlled Sijilmasa from his capital in Fez for the next ten years.

In 1361–1362, Abd al-Halim, with the support of the Ma'qil Arabs, was recognized as suzerain of Sijilmasa. But later in 1362, a quarrel broke out between two tribes of the Ma'qil: the Awlad Hussein, who supported supporting Abd al-Halim, and the Ahlaf, who supported his younger brother Abd al-Mu'min. The latter won the confrontation, and in turn was recognized as suzerain. Both were seen by the Ma'qil Arabs as opponents of the Merinid sultans in Fez. As long as one or the other was in power in Sijilmasa, the Ma'qil could continue collecting tribute in the region. Before the year was out, the central regime in Fez sent an army large enough to induce the Ma'qil Arabs to abandon the sons of Abu Ali and, at least for the moment, recognize the authority of Fez. But that support lasted only until 1365, when a grandson of Abu Ali, Abd al-Rahman, was proclaimed ruler of Sijilmasa by a rebellious vizier in Fez, Mas'ud Ibn Massa. Again, the threat was short-lived. Both Abd al-Rahman and his sponsor, Mas'ud, went to Andalusia to engage in holy war against the Christians. Merinid control of Sijilmasa remained stable until the crisis that precipitated the "fall" in 1393.

Mas'ud later returned to Fez and made one final attempt to overthrow the regime; again the locus of opposition was Sijilmasa. The year was 1387. The governor of Sijilmasa, appointed by the sultan in Fez, was Ali Ibn Ibrahim, a cousin of Mas'ud Ibn Massa. Mas'ud convinced his cousin to support another grandson of Abu Ali, Mohammed Ibn Abd al-Halim, as suzerain of Sijil-

masa. Ali agreed. Mohammed assumed his role in Sijilmasa. Shortly there-
after, following what the chroniclers describe as a falling-out between the
new sultan and the governor Ali Ibn Ibrahim, Abd al-Halim abandoned his
position and sought refuge at the court of the Abd al-Wadids in Tlemcen,
leaving his governor hanging, so to speak, between two sultans, supported
neither by the regime in Fez nor by the descendants of Abu Ali. This left Sijilmasa ripe for what Leo Africanus described a little over one year later as the
last days of Sijilmasa.

At the death of Abu al-Abbas in 1393, the province of Sijilmasa revolted.
The inhabitants killed the governor and demolished the circuit wall. The city
was deserted, and the people withdrew to the many *qsur* in the region. Among
those *qsur*, some maintained their independence and others fell under the
control of the Maʿqil Arabs. Leo Africanus described what he saw in Sijilmasa (elegantly paraphrased by the modern Lebanese-born French author
Amin Maalouf):

> Of its walls, once so high, only a few sections remain, half-ruined, and
> covered with grass and moss. Of its population, there remain only various
> hostile clans, each living with its chief in a fortified village near to the ruins
> of the former Sijilmasa. Their main concern is to make life difficult for the
> clan living in the neighboring village. They seem merciless towards each
> other, going so far as to destroy the water channels, cutting the palm trees
> down to the ground, encouraging the nomadic tribes to lay waste the lands
> and houses of their enemies, so that it seems to me that they deserve their
> fate.[108]

Leo ended up staying in Sijilmasa for several months. What did he see? What
stories did he hear? Were they the same stories that we heard from 1988 to
1998? And what does it all really mean?

CHAPTER 5

Moroccan Rulers at the Desert's Edge: The Filalians

Did Sijilmasa collapse after the civil war of 1393 as Leo Africanus described so explicitly? His narrative of the war is the primary textual reference for this event, but he wrote it well over a century after the fact. His account is supported by a rich body of folklore, much of which we gathered systematically in a series of interviews in the Tafilalt. In our first season of work at Sijilmasa, we began to hear the story of Sultan al-Khal, the Black Sultan, whom today's Filalians still blame for Sijilmasa's ultimate ruin. "Why has Sijilmasa fallen into ruin?" is the question we asked several Tafilalt inhabitants. Five men, a forty-five-year-old mill worker, a seventy-year-old merchant, a sixty-nine-year-old retired soldier, and two other men, ages sixty-five and seventy-three, who described themselves as "unemployed," told of interesting legends. The mill worker said that one of the sultans of Sijilmasa saw a woman with her son drawing water from the river. He wanted to see her face, but she refused. The sultan threatened to cut her son's throat, and she still refused. So when the muezzin issued the call to morning prayer, rather than saying, "Asbaha lillah w'al-hamd" (Good morning and praise be to God), he said, "Allah ikhliha!" (May God make it void!). The merchant told the same story with a slight variant. The sultan, called the Black Sultan, wanted to have a sexual relationship with a woman who came to the river with her children only at night to do her washing. She refused the sultan's demand, so he cut her child in two with his sword and fed it to the dogs. So when the muezzin issued the call to morning prayer. . . . Thus Sijilmasa crumbled. The retired soldier embellished the story a bit, saying that the sultan tossed the child in the air and sliced it in two with his sword as it fell to the ground.

The seventy-three-year-old unemployed man told us that Sijilmasa collapsed because its residents did not thank God for their blessings. Jalil, one of our Moroccan students, reflected on this and concluded that the people of the oasis today, most of them poor, seem to have a disdain for the rich, as they envision the people of medieval Sijilmasa to have been. The mill worker said that the sultan wanted to divert the water from the Timedrine springs, but the people near the springs in turn diverted the water back to themselves. This diversion went back and forth several times until the source eventually dried up. The soldier said that there were once many springs, but the Black Sultan filled them all with copper and wool except the spring at Meski, which still flows, because a woman begged him to spare it. The common theme in all these stories is that Sijilmasa suffered from a lack of water.

The folklore of Sijilmasa's demise points to the Merinid dynasty. The Black Sultan has been identified as Sultan Abu Yusuf Ya'qub, who took the city by storm in 1274 and allegedly destroyed the spring of Timedrine to punish the inhabitants of Sijilmasa.[1] Another candidate is Sultan Abu'l-Hassan, who took the city by storm in 1333 after a painful, yearlong siege that left the city in despair. And the Black Sultan may have been the last governor of Sijilmasa, whose name we do not know but who, according to Leo Africanus, was killed by its inhabitants in 1393.

For the first three seasons of MAPS's work, we too were convinced of Sijilmasa's late-medieval collapse, when the central city all but disappeared and the Filalians scattered to the four corners of the oasis, just as Leo Africanus described. From the beginning, we referred to the period following the civil war, up until the Alaouite restoration of the citadel, as the Filalian period, a time of salutary neglect when, we assumed, the Tafilalt was under some form of local rule.

But our archaeological work on the site, by our fourth season, began to tell a different story. At least the central city, "downtown" Sijilmasa, survived and, indeed, was restored to some level of magnificence. The clearest evidence of this is in the Grand Mosque itself. The last restoration was done during the reign of Sultan Sidi Mohammed Ibn Abdallah in the late eighteenth century. But there had been an earlier, much more substantial remodeling of the Mosque of Ibn Abd Allah at some point after the Almohad expansion in the mid-twelfth century of the Almoravid mosque. This restoration consisted of new walls and a new roof and ceiling supported by square brick columns on very large square footings. When did this restoration occur? In the thirty centimeters (twelve inches) of debris beneath the floor of the mosque as it was restored by Sidi Mohammed Ibn Abdallah, we found several fragments of wood, presumably from the roof that had been removed and replaced. Dates established by carbon-14 analysis for the three samples are remarkably consistent: 1435, 1445, and 1460, with a margin of error from 1400 to 1525. This means that the mosque that Sidi Mohammed Ibn Abdallah restored, the floor plan and extant walls of the surface mosque, and the adjoining madrasa just to the north of the mosque were all established during the century that followed the "destruction" of Sijilmasa as a result of the civil war of 1393. That revolt marked the end of the Merinid dynasty in Sijilmasa. But it certainly did not mark the end of urban development in the central city.

How did later historians get it wrong? It is not so much a question of their getting it wrong as of being virtually silent about Sijilmasa from the fifteenth century on. As Sijilmasa's importance as an urban commercial center and as a seat of political power declined, late medieval and early modern Arab chroniclers lost interest in it. Perhaps our most significant revision of the standard history of Sijilmasa is to point out that it not only survived the civil war of 1393, but also thrived for at least another half millennium. The archaeological proof is in the Grand Mosque.[2]

The mosque-madrasa complex, as visible on the surface today, measures 39 meters (128 feet) east to west and 33 meters (108 feet) north to south. This is larger still than the mosque after it was expanded by the Almohads. The quality of construction of these walls is superior to that of the other mud walls standing on the site. They are made of rosy-pink mud containing stone aggregate and lime, a mixture that dried into an extremely durable form of concrete. The walls are uniformly 1 meter thick and nearly 6 meters (20 feet) high. Putlog holes are consistently a half meter apart, establishing courses 1 meter high. The madrasa is in the northern half of the structure, and the prayer hall of the mosque is to its south. The roof and ceiling of the prayer hall were supported by twenty-four columns arranged in two rows, front to back, dividing the prayer hall into three bays and eleven aisles of equal width. The *mihrab* (prayer niche) was naturally aligned with the central aisle. Judging by the large number of green glazed roof tiles found in the excavation, a peaked roof of green tiles covered each of the three bays, and a fourth peaked roof covered a corridor between the mosque and madrasa. At least twelve two-story cells for students were laid out around the central courtyard of the madrasa, the courtyard itself being open to the sky. A door at each end of the corridor gave access to the madrasa and to the mosque. The quality of construction, the uniformity of the walls and of each successive course, and the quality and durability of the building material in the mosque-madrasa complex are much superior to anything else we have seen in the archaeological record of Sijilmasa.

The Wattasids

As Sijilmasa moved into the fifteenth century, following the civil war, it continued to enjoy salutary neglect by the Merinid regime, which was increasingly plagued by two problems: dissension among the royal family and incursions into northern Morocco by the Portuguese. A stabilizing factor that allowed the Merinids to survive was the presence of the Wattasids, a related family that had been established in the Rif Mountains since the last days of the Almohad dynasty and whose members had held important posts under the Merinids intermittently during the fourteenth century. When the Merinid sultan Abu Said died in 1420, the Wattasid Abu Zakariya rose to power as regent-vizier for the sultan's one-year-old son, Abd al-Haqq. And so the Wattasids sustained the Merinid dynasty and kept the Portuguese at bay. But when Abd al-Haqq came of age, he sought to rid himself of the Wattasids. In 1458 he dismissed his Wattasid vizier, and the Portuguese took the city of Tangier. The Idrisid *shurfa* (Arabic plural of "sharif"; religious and tribal leaders) in northern Morocco became increasingly disenchanted with the Merinids. They revolted and took Fez in 1465, effectively marking the end of Merinid rule. Seven years later, in 1472, the Wattasids under the leadership of Mohammed al-Shaykh defeated the *shurfa*, occupied Fez, and claimed sovereignty over all of Morocco.

The Wattasids ruled Fez until 1549 and maintained varying degrees of authority in other parts of Morocco, but they were never able to grow to the stature of national rulers. To come to power, they had surrendered the coastal city Asilah to the Portuguese in exchange for support against the *shurfa*. In the years to come, they allowed Portuguese penetration into Morocco to reach its peak. Tribes in Morocco saw the Wattasids as continuing Merinid rule and as incapable of protecting the country from foreign incursions.

Can we assume that Sijilmasa was at least theoretically under the authority of the Wattasids following the fall of the Merinids? The texts are for the most part silent about Wattasid involvement, except for four references. In 1524, they sent aid to a local Filalian chief. In 1526, they dispatched an expedition of reprisal against the local authorities. In 1536, they concluded a treaty with a local ruler. Also in 1536, they invaded with a force of three thousand lancers, sacked the city, and "took much booty."[3]

Beyond these few instances of the central government's involvement in the affairs of Sijilmasa, it is likely that Sijilmasa was controlled by local shaykhs and that a dynamic of local politics began to play out among the *qsur* of the oasis and the central city of Sijilmasa, with its newly restored mosque and madrasa. Leo Africanus says that there were as many as 350 *qsur* in the Tafilalt when he visited there in the early sixteenth century.[4] Each was governed by a local lord who commanded the political allegiance of the inhabitants. The largest and most secure of them, according to Leo, was Tabouassamt, located about five kilometers (three miles) south of Rissani and the ruins of Sijilmasa, but on the opposite (west) bank of the Ziz. Members of the MAPS team visited Tabouassamt many times. The oldest structure in the *qsar* today is the mosque, which dates back to around 1400. The heavy polygonal pillars in the prayer hall support arches with elaborate stucco designs. Likewise, the *mihrab* is laced with carved stucco whose motifs and inscriptions are reminiscent of Merinid decorative motifs from the late fourteenth and early fifteenth centuries.[5] During Leo Africanus's time, this *qsar* was heavily populated with foreign merchants as well as Jewish artisans and merchants. During Leo's six-month stay in the Tafilalt, he lived in the *qsar* of al-Ma'mun.[6] It, too, was quite populous, home especially to many Jewish and "Moorish" merchants. A comment by Leo that caught MAPS's attention is that rulers in these *qsur* struck coins on their own authority, both gold and silver. To our knowledge, none of these coins has survived. On the other hand, the Saadian dynasty, soon after it asserted some degree of authority over the Tafilalt in 1537, reopened the mint of Sijilmasa, inscribing on some of their coins the mint name "Tafilalt" rather than "Sijilmasa," suggesting that the Saadians point of reference was the oasis as a whole rather the city at its center.[7]

The Saadians

The Saadian dynasty was one of the richest in Moroccan history. It sought to dominate the salt industry in the Sahara and the gold trade with West Africa, and sought as well to trade with Europe, as far north as England.

The Saadians were originally from the Hijaz (in western Saudi Arabia); they migrated to the Maghrib in the thirteenth century and settled in the village of Tagmadart in the Draa Valley, not far to the west of Sijilmasa. The ascent to power of the Saadian *shurfa* began when the religious and tribal leaders of the Sus sought their protection against the Europeans. The head of the Saadian house, Mohammed al-Sa'adi al-Qa'im bi Amri Allah, established his headquarters in Afughal in the Sus, at the *zawiya* (sanctuary) of al-Jazuli, the Sufi teacher who formed a brotherhood that became devoted to the ideal of resisting foreign influence, especially that of the Portuguese.[8] Mohammed al-Sa'adi not only identified with the Jazuli movement, but also claimed the status of sharif.

Shurfa were, or at least successfully claimed to be, direct descendants of the Prophet Mohammed. Most *shurfa* in Morocco claim descent from the Prophet either through the line of Moulay Idris, founder of the Idrisid dynasty in the eighth century, or through the line of Moulay Ali Sharif, founder of the current ruling Alaouite dynasty. There are many *shurfa* in Morocco today, the largest concentration being in the Tafilalt, the homeland of the Alaouites. Some have official endorsement as *shurfa* from the Ministry of Religious Affairs. Others have genealogies that establish their connection. Most do not exhibit any behavior suggesting that they are endowed with sharifian *baraka* (special blessings or powers that come from God).

Some people of religious distinction are known as *murabitin* ("saints"; singular, *murabit*).[9] At least eight *murabitin* lineages in the Tafilalt today trace their origins back to saints of the sixteenth, fifteenth, fourteenth centuries, some as far back as late Almohad times, when local scholars who became Sufis during the last years of the Almohad Empire achieved *murabitin* status. There was at least one such scholar during the last days of the Almohads, Sayyid Abd Allah al-Daqqaq, whose tomb is still revered in the Tafilalt today. The *qsar* in which his tomb is located, to the immediate west of the ruins of Sijilmasa, is the village in which most of our workers live. What distinguished these *murabitin* was their great *baraka*, a channel through which God's blessings could be transmitted to others. "Without them [*murabitin*] the sky would not send rain, the earth would not cause its plants to grow and calamities would pour upon the inhabitants," claimed Abu Jafar Kittani, the founder of one of the major Sufi brotherhoods.[10]

All over the Maghrib it was believed that this *baraka* attaches to the lineage of the saint and resides in a holy place, the *zawiya*. The head of the *zawiya*, the shaykh, was usually a living saint in his own right who embodied that *baraka*. Each holy man attracted loyal followers to form a religious brotherhood, a *tariqa*. By default, the shaykhs assumed more and more of the functions that an effective government would normally have performed. They were agents of political mediation. They arbitrated disputes among the local population. They provided education for the children. In short, they were the center of community life. The people rewarded the *zawaya* (plural of "*zawiya*") with gifts (*ziyara*) for their public service.

When the concepts of "sharif" and "*murabit*" merged in one person, he could be propelled to national prominence and leadership. That is exactly what happened in the case of Mohammed al-Sa'adi. Whether or not he was truly *shurfa*, he made good the claim. He rose to power as a ruler in the Sus in 1509–1510, and his influence grew from there and was passed on to his descendants. Following his death, conflict arose between his two sons. Al-Arraj, the older one, became sharif in Haha, to the north of the Sus, from where he went on to conquer Marrakech. His younger brother, Mohammed al-Shaykh, remained in the Sus. In spite of the competition between the two, the Saadians took control of all of Morocco. The Saadian *shurfa* defeated the Wattasids in 1536 and forced them to recognize the authority of the Saadians everywhere south of Tadla. The Saadians established their authority in the Tafilalt in the next year. They laid siege to Sijilmasa and bombarded it with artillery they had taken from Fez. They granted the local Filalian ruler some lands for his subsistence and left a garrison of their own to ensure his ability and willingness to uphold Saadian interests.

For the rest of the sixteenth century, the Saadians remained more or less in control of the Tafilalt. For the Saadian ruler, its rich resources and relative isolation made the oasis an ideal place to isolate potential opposition from within the family. But who was the establishment and who the opposition? War broke out between the two Saadian brothers in 1542. Sijilmasa was caught in a seesaw battle between them. The Wattasids took advantage of the conflict and very briefly regained control of the Tafilalt. But almost immediately, the younger of the two brothers, Mohammed al-Shaykh, prevailed in the war with his brother, ousted the Wattasids from the Tafilalt, and sent his defeated older brother, al-Arraj, there. Al-Arraj enjoyed his "sovereignty" in Sijilmasa from 1543 to 1550. Mohammed al-Shaykh then took it back, lost it again to al-Arraj in 1554, took it back the same year, and held it until his death in 1557.

Mohammed al-Shaykh was the first Saadian to strike gold coins in the Sijilmasa mint. It was a good way to assert his sovereignty over the Tafilalt. In fact, Saadian coinage helps chronicle the political relationship between the Saadian central authority and Sijilmasa. Mohammed al-Shaykh used the mint name "Tafilalt" instead of "Sijilmasa," as did Abd Allah al-Ghalib (1561–1573). Are these the coins that Leo Africanus says were minted in the *qsur* outside Sijilmasa? The mint name "Sijilmasa" returned to the coinage under Abd al-Malik al-Mu'tasim (1575–1578) and survived to the end of the dynasty. In fact, these were the last gold coins struck at the Sijilmasa mint, a testimony to the importance of Sijilmasa in the Saadians' goal to reestablish direct control over the gold trade with West Africa.[11]

Most extant Saadian dinars from the Sijilmasa mint bear the name of Ahmad al-Mansur. He was known as al-Dhahabi, the "Golden Sultan." He conducted an expansionist campaign south of the Sahara and succeeded in conquering Gao in 1591 and Timbuktu in 1594. In that year, he received his first tribute of thirty mules laden with gold. Ahmad al-Mansur here achieved what earlier Saadians had tried to do. Both Al-Arraj and Mohammed al-Shaykh had tried but failed to control the salt mines in Teghaza. Not since the time of the Almoravids had a ruler in Morocco exercised so much control over the gold routes to the western Sudan as did Ahmad al-Mansur. That control lasted twenty-five years or so; the sultan appointed governors to Timbuktu as late as 1618. But during that short period of time, control of trade provided an enormous source of wealth to the Saadian state.

The chroniclers describe the reign of Ahmad al-Mansur as one of the richest times in Moroccan history. Wealth poured in from his monopoly over the gold trade with West Africa and came from within the empire as well. Ahmad al-Mansur developed the sugar-refining industry, primarily in the region west of Marrakech, where the ruins of a large sugar refinery can still be seen along the dry riverbed three kilometers east of the small town of Chichaoua. The Saadians granted a monopoly for sugar export to the English and to the French, who paid dearly for it. Finally, Ahmad al-Mansur levied canonical taxes at a rate higher than earlier sultans had, provoking intense complaints from his subjects.[12]

The wealth was most prominently displayed in the Badiʿ Palace in Marrakech, the capital of the Saadian Empire. Although in ruins today, the Badiʿ Palace is still impressive for its massive walls and huge Andalusian *riyad* (enclosed garden) with four rectangular sunken gardens, one in each corner, separated by paved walkways. In the past, the air would have been filled with the scent of sweet-smelling flowers. One description of the palace reads:

> Walls and ceilings incrusted with gold from Timbuktu. . . . Its vast halls were filled with fountains, and in looking glass ceilings far overhead the fish appeared to swim, reflected from the cool waters of marble basins. There was a domed hall where golden stars set on a blue ground gave the appearance of the heavens themselves. . . . Long ponds between the alleys ended in grottoes and arbors. . . . [There were] gaily decorated boats to entertain [the sultan] and his guests in the cooler hours of the evening.[13]

In another practice reminiscent of the Almoravid era, Ahmad al-Mansur summoned annually the leading ulama to the Badiʿ Palace. It was probably at such a gathering that the decision was made to launch an expedition to conquer the land of gold.

It stands to reason that routes west of the main one from Sijilmasa to Timbuktu would come to be heavily traveled. Caravans left the capital of Marrakech, went southwest to the coastal city of Massa, and continued south to Timbuktu. Others followed in the wake of the Saadian armies that left from the Draa Valley, bent on conquest. Some argue that the Draa Valley became the main caravan head for the gold trade with the Sudan, replacing Sijilmasa in that role.[14] Leo Africanus is a key source for this idea. He describes the route from the Draa to Timbuktu; he also describes the market of Teg-daoust in the Draa as being the preeminent market in the south of Morocco, important enough to hold two markets a week: a major market for gold and the main regional market for slaves.[15] But Leo traveled those roads before the Saadians came to power.

Ahmad al-Mansur's reign was the autumn of the gold trade. His conquest of the Sudan was a last-ditch effort to directly control the gold trade at its source and, at least for a time, to reverse what was a downward trend in the trans-Saharan trade in general and the gold trade to Sijilmasa in particular. It is clear, especially from the dinars struck at the Sijilmasa mint, that gold flowed steadily to Sijilmasa to supply the mint. The political focus of the Saadians was undoubtedly on Marrakech and the Draa Valley, but Sijilmasa was an indispensable part of their overall economic plan.

Like the Wattasids and the Merinids before them, the Saadians were content to place Sijilmasa in the hands of a peripheral member of the royal family, sometimes even a dissident member, or in the hands of a loyal Filalian governor. For limited periods, Sijilmasa achieved some degree of autonomy. From time to time though, like the Merinids and Wattasids, the Saadians were compelled to make a show of force, to reassert their control over the Tafilalt. Such control came to an end in 1603.

Toward the end of the century, in 1595, Ahmad al-Mansur granted the Tafilalt to his son, al-Shaykh, along with a force of one thousand lancers. In October 1602, to isolate his insubordinate son al-Ma'mun, Ahmad al-Mansur offered him the government of Sijilmasa and the Draa, as well as all the revenues of the two provinces to sustain him—yet another example of a rebellious member of the royal family in comfortable exile.

Ahmad al-Mansur's sons were quick to grab whatever they could of their father's empire. Sijilmasa was caught in the middle of this struggle. His son Moulay Zaidan was proclaimed sultan in Fez immediately upon Ahmad al-Mansur's death, but he was quickly put to flight by his brothers. He fled to Sijilmasa, only to find that the Filalian *qa'id* (local governor) was ruling in the name of one of his brothers. But the previous *qa'id*, who had been loyal to al-Mansur and was still in the Tafilalt, rallied to Zaidan's support with twelve hundred cavalrymen. The new *qa'id* fled, along with the troops from the garrison. Zaidan gained control of Sijilmasa but left fifteen days later to wage war in the Sus. Over the next two years, Zaidan won the Sus, defeated his brother in Marrakech, and became the recognized ruler in the whole of southwestern Morocco. But he lost control of Sijilmasa in 1607 to his brother al-Ma'mun.

Marabouts

This breakdown in central authority in Morocco gave rise, by default, to maraboutic leaders. People in the Tafilalt, like people everywhere in Morocco, found themselves having to give their allegiance to a powerful local shaykh. One of the first to take up the call was Ahmad Abu Mahalli. Born in the Tafilalt in 1560, Abu Mahalli studied religion with his father. When he was thirteen years old, he left to study for five years in Fez. Then, in 1579, he joined the *zawiya* of the Sufi shaykh Sidi Mohammed Ibn Mubarak al-Zaeri, just south of Rabat. Around 1593, the shaykh decided to send Abu Mahalli back to his home in the Tafilalt. When it came time to bid farewell, so the story goes, the shaykh offered his graduating student his staff, his burnoose, and his shoes. He placed a bonnet on his head as an insignia of his religious mission.[16] And thus Abu Mahalli went home. Within a year, he left Sijilmasa to perform the hajj. Returning home in 1594–1595, Abu Mahalli chose not to settle in Sijilmasa, but rather retreated with his whole family to the Oued Saoura, about one hundred kilometers (sixty-two miles) to the southeast. Why did he abandon his home in the Tafilalt? This was during the reign of Sultan Ahmad al-Mansur. It could be that Abu Mahalli was emerging as the most powerful authority in the Tafilalt and therefore was becoming a locus of opposition to the central authority of the sultan.

At this same time, Ahmad al-Mansur was striving to neutralize the authority of the shaykh of the *zawiya* of Zouddharha in the Western High Atlas as well as the shaykh of the *zawiya* of Tazeroualt in the Western Anti-Atlas.[17] It could be that Abu Mahalli was afraid that he would be the next holy man to fall. For the next fifteen years or so, remote southeastern Morocco offered him a safe haven where he could consolidate his power. He was seen as one learned in the law, an imminent jurist, a reformer, a saint possessing great *baraka*. People came from near and far to seek his blessing and to offer gifts.

There was a tradition that foretold of a native of Sijilmasa who would be sent to bring peace, to revive the law, and to rescue the country from the bad government of the Saadians. This marabout would find a drum in the *zawiya* of Sijilmasa. When he beat on the drum, the people would come forth and proclaim him king.[18] Abu Mahalli fulfilled this prophecy.

The ceding of Larache (a harbor town southwest of Tangier) to the Spanish in November 1610 was the impetus for Abu Mahalli's revolt. Toward the end of that year, he marched toward Sijilmasa, where the *qa'id* al-Hajj al-Mir recognized the authority of Moulay Zaidan. The story goes that Abu Mahalli had only one tent, three or four loyal followers, two horses, two camels, and one mule. But en route, some 180 horsemen and 200 foot soldiers joined him.

When they arrived at Sijilmasa, they faced an army of about 4,000—the odds, ten to one, were not in their favor. Still, Abu Mahalli preached to them, perhaps reminding his followers of the promise in the Quran (8:65-66) that God would intervene on behalf of those Muslims who fought against adversity, even against ten-to-one odds. Abu Mahalli's *baraka* inspired his troops to carry the day. He immediately set about reforming abuses and reestablishing the rule of Islamic law—a story that much resembles the Almoravid victory in Sijilmasa a half millennium earlier.

From the fall of 1611 to the spring of 1612, Abu Mahalli conquered the Draa Valley. By controlling both trailheads for routes crossing the Sahara, he effectively cut off a major source of income of the Saadian rulers. On May 20, 1612, Abu Mahalli defeated the forces of Moulay Zaidan at Marrakech. Zaidan sought refuge in Safi in the *zawiya* of yet another maraboutic figure, Sidi Yahya of Zouddhara. Abu Mahalli occupied the royal palace and for a year and a half was the dominant religious and political figure in Morocco. On November 30, 1613, he was killed by Sidi Yahya, the rival marabout who had sheltered the defeated Saadian ruler. Sidi Yahya himself took up residence in the royal palace in Marrakech, but almost immediately relinquished it to the Saadian sultan, who promised reform.

So the struggle between the central regime of the Saadians and maraboutic shaykhs for control of Sijilmasa continued. It appears that Moulay Zaidan reasserted his authority over Sijilmasa at the death of Abu Mahalli, since the *qa'id* there ruled in the Saadians' name. The next time that Sijilmasa appears in the chronicles is in 1623. The son of Abu Mahalli led a campaign to take the city. Moulay Zaidan sent one of his sons to intercept him. The sultan's *qa'id* feigned support for Ibn Abu Mahalli, but then betrayed him. The son of a local Filalian saint who dared to oppose the central regime was beheaded. Sijilmasa remained, at least from a distance, under the control of the Saadian dynasty. But Moulay Zaidan's days were numbered; other powerful maraboutic saints were poised to fill the void. Sidi Ali, the great-grandson of a great Sufi saint and founder of a *zawiya* in Tazaroualt in the Anti-Atlas, and Sidi Mohammed Ibn Abu Bakr, the son of a saint and the founder of the *zawiya* of Dila in the western Middle Atlas Mountains, faced off against each other as they strove first to overthrow the last of the Saadians and then to control the rest of Morocco. For good reason, these marabouts saw the control of Sijilmasa as the key to both objectives. The competition between them resulted in polarized allegiances among the people of the Tafilalt.

In 1626, Sidi Ali conducted a campaign into the valleys of the Draa and the Ziz, seizing control of both trailheads of the trans-Saharan gold trade with the Sudan. This not only cut off a major source of the Saadians' income but also gave him a source of goods from West Africa, which he could then trade with Europeans who came calling at the port of Agadir, also under his control. Sidi Ali took up residence in Sijilmasa and regularly sent caravans to the Sudan carrying European goods that were exchanged for gold and ivory.[19] His actions brought about the fall of the Saadians and ushered in a new dynasty—indeed, a new era in the history of the Tafilalt and of Morocco itself.

The Cityscape of Filalian Sijilmasa

Before we move on, let us pause for a moment to walk the streets of Filalian Sijilmasa with Leo Africanus as one of our guides and the archaeological record as the other. The western wall along the Oued Ziz was still standing during the Filalian period and was still the western border of the city. We know that the Filalians dumped their garbage over the western city wall. Debris from the exterior of the tower that we excavated in 1992, on the river side of the wall, was replete with material primarily from the fifteenth and sixteenth centuries. During the 1992 season, a MAPS crew spent a considerable amount of time excavating a series of units near the dry riverbed of the Ziz in the northwest corner of the site. The first feature to come to light, in the uppermost (most recent) level of occupation, was a tower along the western wall of the city. As it turned out, this was the northwest corner tower, which had a wall turning to the east toward the citadel. Inside the wall was a series of structures whose distribution of pottery told us that we were in a residential quarter from the eighteenth or nineteenth century. At a lower (earlier) level, though, the tower had features reminiscent of the housing for a noria, a waterwheel that would have lifted water from the river and dumped it into a canal carrying it into the city. Among the ceramics collected at this level were a large number of sherds from clay noria pots, pots that would have been lashed to the wheel itself and served as vessels to lift the water. Leo Africanus said that he saw such a waterwheel when he was in Sijilmasa.[20]

In color, composition, and form, pottery from the Filalian period is virtually identical to Sijilmasan pottery except for a few chemical components in the clay, indicating that it came from a source closer to the Oued Ziz. The forms are primarily small utilitarian ware. Lahcen Taouchikht believes that the same potters or their descendants moved from their place of production near the Oued Gheris and established workshops among the ruins of medieval Sijilmasa.[21] That said, we did not find a single pottery kiln in Sijilmasa. We did find a number of kiln wasters and separators at various levels of occupa-

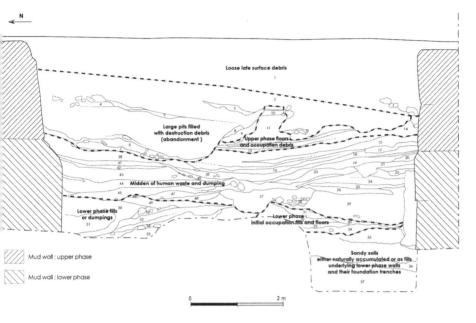

Figure 5.1. East section of trench 6.

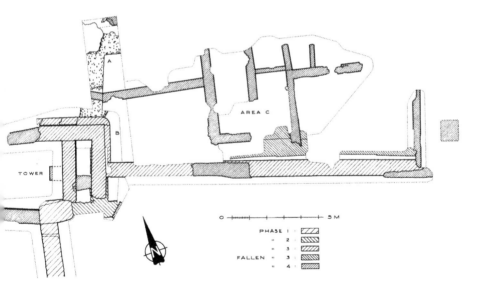

Figure 5.2. Plan of trench 8, noria housing and adjacent walls.

Figure 5.3. Housing for a noria.

tion, from one to four meters deep, in the southwestern corner of the site. But that alone is not conclusive evidence of pottery production in that location.

During the six weeks or so that we worked on these excavation units, we had daily interaction with passersby, residents of the Qsar Moulay Abd al-Daqqaq on the west side of the Sijilmasa ruins who were riding their donkeys across the ruins of the medieval city on their way to modern Rissani. The donkey path was in effect a road, the same road that must have passed directly past the corner tower and northern wall that neither we nor twentieth-century Filalians knew existed before our excavations began. It could well have been the road that passed along the irrigation canal of a period before that, namely, during the Filalian period. It could well have been the road along which Leo Africanus entered Sijilmasa. If it was, did he see the noria in a state of ruin? Had it already gone out of use? He does say that intravillage wars destroyed irrigation canals that carried water from the river to the fields. He even observes that it would take large sums of money to restore them to their original function.[22]

Fifty meters (164 feet) due west of the Grand Mosque, MAPS excavated what remains of a series of public latrines and, possibly, baths, both of which were used during at least two successive periods. Our evidence shows that they were definitely not the baths described by al-Bakri, which were built by the city's founder, al-Yasʿa. And if we are to believe al-Bakri's description, these later ones were certainly better built.[23] The last phase, especially of the baths, is clearly of the Filalian period. At a level of occupation directly below the Alaouite level, stone canalization connects what appears to be a hypocaust (hot-water heater) to a pair of basins. Those basins, in turn, empty into a cistern below the basins. One of the basins was covered by a baked-brick pavement, suggesting that it was used during two phases of occupation. A latest

Figure 5.4.
Noria pot.

Figure 5.5. Basins west of the mosque.

possible date was established for the construction of the basins, based on car-
bon-14 analysis of material inside one of the basins, but under the pavement
that covered the basin. That date is 1585, with a range of 1430–1670. That is
also the earliest possible date for the pavement covering the basin, proving
that the bath was in use during the Filalian period. This is not a surprise, since
this time was shortly after the major renovation of the mosque-madrasa complex, which established the current floor plan for the surface mosque. New
mosque, new baths with hot running water. The complex is clearly an im-

Figure 5.6. Basin beneath a basin.

Figure 5.7. Medieval "refrigerator."

provement over what al-Bakri described in the middle of the eleventh century as baths that were "poorly built."

Immediately to the west of the bath complex is a series of stone-lined cesspits. They are surrounded by an underground drainage field of coarse river gravel. At least one of the cesspits seems to have been constructed and used in three separate phases, only the first of which was stone lined. Charcoal from that level was dated by carbon-14 analysis to 1290, with a range of 1175–1420. So the oldest phase of this cesspit is from the Almohad or Merinid period. It was in continuous use for two more phases of occupation, including the Filalian.

To our surprise, we found that the residential quarters of the city did not fall into decay in the immediate aftermath of the civil war of 1391, contrary to what one would guess from reading Leo's description of the mass migration of people from the city to the surrounding *qsur*. We found architectural and ceramic remains from the Filalian period in several excavation units in the residential area west of the Grand Mosque, in the residential quarter in the northwest quadrant of the city, in the southwest quarter, and along the western wall. In the excavation units in the southwest quadrant there is an abundance of common utility and cooking wares, several hearths or cooking pits, and what now have been interpreted as food storage pits. These storage pits are bell-shaped sand pits approximately 75 centimeters (2.5 feet) in diameter and 100 centimeters (3.3 feet) deep, sunk into the floor of the houses. Some pits were lined with straw, and one was lined with mud or plaster. Each house had a number of these storage pits and at least one pit in which a large storage jar, a medieval "refrigerator," was placed. Our senior laborer, Bel-ʿAid Ben Barrak, amid the rhythmic songs he sang and the wonderful folk tales he told of Sijilmasa past, convinced us that his own grandfather had used such a storage facility to keep food and liquids cool—keeping butter from melting, for instance, even in the heat of summer.

We know that this part of town remained essentially residential. A residential area is characterized by having a relatively low percentage of low-replacement items. One rarely had to replace a "refrigerator." One or two "refrigerators" per excavation unit indicates a residential area. Had we found an area with, say, thirty-five "refrigerators," we would have been in a place that either made or sold "refrigerators." We found no such evidence in the southern part of the cityscape.

The city that Leo Africanus described was not the city of imperial Sijilmasa at its peak. Nor was it the city at the end of the Merinid period, during the civil war in 1393. What probably disturbed Leo, the destruction that he described in the early sixteenth century, might well have been the crumbling walls separating the *gamaman* rather than the walls around the city proper, and perhaps the abandonment of some of the outlying villas to the north and south of the central city. That process continued well on into the Alaouite period, when central Sijilmasa was reduced to about half its size and came to be called *madinat al-ʿamra*.

CHAPTER 6

Out of Sijilmasa: The Alaouites

The current Alaouite king of Morocco traces his roots back to the Tafilalt oasis. His ancestors came to the Tafilalt with the great influx of Arab tribes in the middle of the thirteenth century. They readily became and remained highly respected as *shurfa*. Adding even more to their prestige, two maternal ancestors, so the story goes, were descendants of the Almoravids, who had conquered Sijilmasa back in the eleventh century.[1] By the seventeenth century, their many offspring inhabited fifteen or so *qsur* in the Tafilalt. But they remained in the political background until the Tafilalt became the focus of competition between the two maraboutic powers of Tazaroualt and Dila (described at the end of chapter 5). The rivalry between those brotherhoods polarized the loyalties of the tribal communities within the Tafilalt. The Alaouites supported Sidi Ali, the shaykh of Tazaroualt.

The residents of Sijilmasa, the city itself, were loyal to the Alaouites. Because of the relationship between the Alaouites and Tazaroualt, Sijilmasans supported the same brotherhood. On the other (west) side of the river, the Bani Zubir, residents of Tabouassamt, were longtime rivals of the Alaouites. Naturally, they supported Dila.

The maraboutic shaykh of Dila, Sidi Mohammed Ibn Abu Bakr, decided to march on Sijilmasa in 1630, a year after Sidi Ali withdrew from the city. The saint from Dila was turned back, however, by Moulay Ali Sharif, a local Alaouite sharif who had supported the shaykh of Tazaroualt and who, in turn, had been supported by that marabout. In any event, the people of Sijilmasa proclaimed their local Alaouite hero, Moulay Ali Sharif, to be their uncontested leader.[2] With him came a new national dynasty—indeed, a whole new era in Moroccan history.

In 1632, two years after Dila's failed attempt to conquer Sijilmasa, the armies of both *zawaya* converged in the Tafilalt on the outskirts of Tabouassamt. The saint of Dila immediately saw that his adversary had much stronger weapons, having obtained firearms from trading with Europeans. Dila petitioned for peace, and Tazaroualt complied in order to "avoid spilling the blood of Muslims."[3] The residents of Tabouassamt reluctantly swore allegiance to the shaykh of Tazaroualt, hoping to drive a wedge between the latter and his ally Moulay Ali Sharif. They did. In retaliation, Moulay Ali Sharif's son attacked Tabouassamt in 1634. At the head of two hundred cavalry, he stormed the *qsar*, massacred the soldiers of the garrison in their sleep, and seized the treasures within.

Sidi Ali was furious. He instructed his representative in the Tafilalt, Abu Bakr, to capture Moulay Ali Sharif in any way he could. Abu Bakr invited the Alaouite to his *zawiya*, about ten kilometers northwest of Sijilmasa. This, too, was on the west bank of the Ziz, where, apparently, the power base for the Alaouites was still nonexistent. When the Alaouite arrived, he was taken into custody and shipped off to Tazaroualt, where he lived for the next five years under house arrest.

Sidi Ali had focused most of his attention on securing the western portion of his realm and on establishing trade with Europe. His administrators in Sijilmasa, no longer under the watchful eye of Tazaroualt, raised taxes on "everything" and managed to alienate the population of the Tafilalt. Sidi Mohammed of Dila, for his part, waged war against the Saadian sultan and against the maraboutic ruler of Salé, al-Ayyachi. This allowed Moulay Ali Sharif's son, Mohammed Ibn al-Sharif (the one who attacked Tabouassamt), the opportunity to assert himself in Sijilmasa. His father still in exile, Mohammed Ibn al-Sharif was accepted by the people on the left bank of the Ziz as their undisputed leader, even though Sijilmasa was still nominally under the control of Sidi Ali. From this base, Ibn al-Sharif conducted raids up the valley of the Moulouya as far as Taza, following the same path, it might be noted, taken by the Almoravid Yusuf Ibn Tashfin almost six hundred years earlier. The booty that he amassed in his campaigns allowed him to finance a growing army and to pay the ransom that set his father free from Tazaroualt. He went on to take Oujda, then Tlemcen. In the spring of 1645, the dey of Algiers sent an envoy to Ibn al-Sharif in Sijilmasa, and the two concluded a treaty fixing the border between their territories. The Alaouite signed a similar treaty with Sidi Mohammed of Dila, establishing the summit of the High Atlas Mountains as the border between their respective domains. Ibn al-Sharif had become a regional hero and established the Alaouites of the Tafilalt as a major player in the overall Maghribi balance of power.

In 1650, Mohammed Ibn al-Sharif was at the peak of his power. The people of Fez, in revolt against their governor, who was allied to Dila, appealed to him. He came in June of that year, imprisoned the Dilaite governor, was proclaimed king of Fez in July, and was promptly congratulated by the Saadian sultan in Marrakech. But he was king for only a month. The Dilaites once again forced him to withdraw to Sijilmasa.

The year 1659 was fateful for Sijilmasa and all of Morocco. The last Saadian sultan, Moulay Ahmad al-Abbas, was killed in Marrakech by Arabs of the Shabana tribe. Sidi Ali, the marabout of Tazaroualt, died that same year. His political power, already weakened, was dissipated among his numerous descendants. Moulay Ali Sharif, patriarch of the Alaouite dynasty, died in Sijilmasa. As long as he was alive, his oldest son's power and popularity were uncontested. But after his death, conflict broke out between Mohammed Ibn al-Sharif and his younger brother Moulay al-Rashid. The day after his father's death, al-Rashid fled Sijilmasa to amass a following loyal to himself, in defiance of his older brother. The fugitive went first to Dila, where he stayed, unrecognized, for perhaps as long as a year. He then went to the lower Moulouya valley, where, in 1664–1665, he settled among the Bani Iznassin, whose shaykh respected the descendants of the Prophet. He revealed his identity, and with the support of the local shaykh, he received the loyalty of the surrounding tribes.

In that same year, the armies of the two brothers faced each other on the left bank of the lower Moulouya River. Mohammed Ibn al-Sharif's 5,000 cavalry and 9,000 infantry squared off against Moulay al-Rashid's 2,600 cavalry and 8,000 infantry. Ibn al-Sharif was killed near the outset of the battle, and his troops threw their loyalty to Moulay al-Rashid, who went on to take Taza in the fall of 1664. Moulay al-Rashid next turned his attention to the conquest of Sijilmasa.

Mohammed Ibn al-Sharif's son was in Sijilmasa, poised to offer resistance to the advance of Moulay al-Rashid. Al-Rashid mounted a siege to the city that lasted nine months. Finally, in the summer of 1665, al-Rashid prevailed. After restoring the ramparts of the city, he placed one of his brothers, al-Harran, in charge and then consolidated his authority over the rest of Morocco. While the siege of Sijilmasa was still going on, al-Rashid had gained control of the Rif Mountains, crucial not only for protecting his rearguard in the upcoming campaign against Fez, but also for ensuring his access to the northern coast and contact with Europeans.

In June 1668, Moulay al-Rashid defeated the *zawiya* of Dila. In July he took Marrakech. In the spring and summer of 1670, he neutralized the last of his major rivals, the shaykh of Tazaroualt. The *zawiya* there continued to play a political role throughout the eighteenth and nineteenth centuries, and a strictly religious role in the twentieth. Sidi Ali left eighteen to twenty sons.

After his death, conflict and division among them prevented the *zawiya* from mounting much of a political threat to the Alaouites.

Moulay al-Rashid died in April 1672. He was succeeded by his son Moulay Ismail, whose reign lasted until 1727. In the first half of that reign, though, he had to take drastic steps to consolidate his authority over the whole of Morocco. In the center of the country, the sultan was faced with opposition from the powerful bloc of Sanhaja Berbers. In the north, major urban areas such as Tetuan and Fez sought regional autonomy. In the south, members of his own extended family posed a threat, especially his brothers Moulay al-Harran, Moulay Hisham, and Moulay Ahmad. The main threat from his siblings involved their attempts to control the trade routes to West Africa, which threatened to cut off his supply of gold and slaves. In 1680, Moulay Ismail's nephew Ibn Mahraz succeeded in taking Taroudant and sought to take the salt mines of Teghaza. To counteract this decentralization of power, the sultan solicited the support of those *zawaya* that he could win over and tried to eliminate those he could not. He built a string of *qasbas* (fortified castles) throughout the country and manned them with an increasingly large professional army that at first was a traditional army, that is, one based on tribal contingents. But he wanted an army that was not dependent on individual tribes or tribal confederations. The solution was an army of black slaves from the Bambara kingdom of the Sudan, new converts to Islam. They were called *abid al-Bukhari* (slaves of al-Bukhari) because they swore an oath of loyalty to the sultan upon the book of hadith compiled by al-Bukhari. These troops developed an esprit de corps as strong as or stronger than any tribal solidarity (*asabiya*).

Military reform followed tax reform. Moulay Ismail restored the taxes of *makus*, that is, taxes on market purchases. These were non-Quranic taxes, and as had happened so many times before, they were strongly criticized by the ulama. They criticized the non-Quranic taxes and the harsh means by which they were collected.

By the end of the seventeenth century, Moulay Ismail was in control of virtually the whole country. He divided the provinces of the Maghrib among his older sons, thereby hoping to strengthen the ties between the provinces and the capital in Meknes. To rule over Sijilmasa and the Tafilalt, he sent his son al-Ma'mun al-Kabir. Moulay Ismail built a new *qasba* outside Sijilmasa and stationed his son there with a garrison of five hundred black cavalrymen.[4] The *qasba* in Sijilmasa itself had suffered considerable damage during the Alaouites' rise to power, particularly during the nine-month siege of the citadel in 1664–1665 against Moulay al-Rashid and a second, more recent siege during the revolt of Moulay Ismail's brother Moulay al-Harran.

Moulay Ismail's Restoration of the Sijilmasa Citadel

When Moulay Ismail rose to power, the citadel of Sijilmasa was essentially the one that had been built on the elevated plateau north of the Grand Mosque. An exclusive interview describes exactly what Moulay Ismail's restoration of that citadel consisted of. Although the exact date of the restoration is not known, it must have been done in the mid to late 1670s. A French lieutenant colonel named Henri Dastugue spoke with Sidi Suleiman Ibn Abd al-Rahman, the grandson of Sultan Moulay Suleiman, who described the restoration of the citadel in some detail.[5] He stressed that Moulay Ismail restored only the northern part of Sijilmasa, which had come to be known as *madinat al-'amra*, the "inhabited city," and not the southern part of the city, which Sidi Suleiman said was destroyed by a Merinid sultan whose name he could not remember, but who is identified by Ibn Khaldun. Here Sidi Suleiman is perpetuating the notion that Sijilmasa collapsed after the civil war of 1393. What Moulay Ismail restored were the walls of the citadel and the roofs of the buildings within the walls. The roofs would have been made of wood and supported by wooden beams, much more vulnerable to fire in a siege than the thick, solid adobe walls, which apparently survived. The walls of the citadel that we see today in Sijilmasa, formidable-looking walls, especially as seen when approaching the city from the north, were part of Moulay Ismail's restored citadel. The southwestern section of the citadel wall, mapped as a "subsurface wall," was completely covered by a long, narrow, and very high sand dune. During a brief visit to the site in October 2011, we saw part of that section of wall that had recently been exposed by "mining" the sand for construction purposes. The wall and corner tower that we saw then for the first time can be described as *massive*. We observed Filalian pottery (late fifteenth to early seventeenth century) embedded in the building material of the wall, indicating that the wall dated to either the late Filalian or early Alaouite period. More than likely, it was in the same place as an earlier wall of the Almoravid-Almohad-Merinid period.

The Alaouite restoration was much larger than the Almoravid citadel of the medieval period, which it encompassed. It was not immediately clear to MAPS excavators whether the citadel included only the northeastern portion, where there are traces of the walls above the surface, or whether it also included the entire northern half of the city extending to the river. Pottery provides the best answer. There is a distinctive type of pottery called Bhayr because of its place of production in the Qsar Bhayr al-Ansar, now in ruins, on the west bank of the Oued Ziz on the southwest corner of medieval Sijilmasa. Bhayr pottery dates from the eighteenth and nineteenth centuries. The

Figure 6.1. Bhayr pottery.

paste is similar to that of Filalian pottery of the fifteenth through seventeenth centuries, and the forms consist of small domestic items such as bowls, plates, jugs, bottles, lamps, and cups. Bhayr pottery, though, is much thicker and heavier than Filalian and is often covered with a monochrome glaze of green, yellow, or brown. The presence of large quantities of Bhayr pottery in our surface collection of 1988, along with the excavation of a residence in the northwest quadrant of the site in 1992, indicates that the whole northern sector was occupied during the Alaouite period. Major subsurface walls in the northwestern sector, projected by remote sensing in 1996, seem to align nicely with the surface walls in the northeastern sector to form the outline of the restored citadel of Moulay Ismail, which covered an area of approximately 500 meters (1,640 feet) east to west by 400 meters (1,312 feet) north to south. When people talked of the *madinat al-'amra*, this whole enclosed area, 49.4 acres, is what they must have meant.

So what exactly was the *madinat al-'amra*? A residential quarter to be sure, as suggested by the name given to the quarter during this later period as well as by our excavations in the northwest zone. Clearing a surface layer of mostly windblown sand exposed the tops of an entire complex of walls consisting of what we first thought to be a tower, but then identified as a possible housing for a noria, and to the east of that, a whole series of rooms. This complex is at the very northwest corner of the city. The western perimeter wall extends from the "western tower" (described in chapter 5) to this complex. We dug nine small trenches to find where the wall went from here, and discovered that it zigzagged northeastward toward the visible surface walls of the citadel. This complex of rooms is then considered to be outside the perimeter wall of the city. It appears to have been constructed in four phases, as indicated in the plan (figure 5.2). Ninety percent of all the diagnostic pottery in this excavation unit came from the most recent phase of occupation. Thirty-three percent of the diagnostic pottery was Bhayr pottery. There was no diagnostic pottery from the pre-Filalian period. Our best judgment at present, then, is that these near subsurface walls date from the Bhayr period, that is, the eighteenth or nineteenth century. There is not enough diagnostic pottery from the lower phases to suggest the period. But those phases probably date from the same period as the lower phase of the "western" tower, that is, pre-Filalian.

A short distance south of this northwest corner of the city, within the city wall, we excavated a well-defined central room of a house. As we traced the faces of the room on its west, north, and east sides, it became apparent that they bore a thin lime plaster. The uppermost level of occupation yielded two coins, beads, a piece of flat glass, a small copper strip, a firm piece of sawn wood, and a good number of broken glazed tiles in green, white, blue, yellow, and black, including cement fragments bearing their impressions. Near the center of the room, a mud brick partition divided the east-west width of the

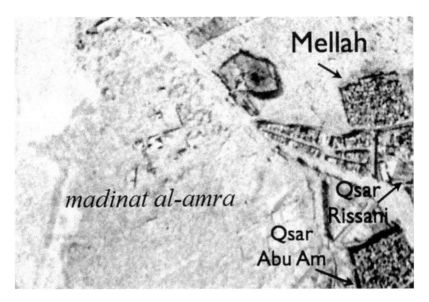

Figure 6.2. Aerial photo showing the *madinat al-ʿamra*, the *mellah*, Qsar Rissani, and Qsar Abu Am.

room in half. The partition was built directly on the floor, using plano-convex mud brick, which had already been found in an inner, later wall in the complex of rooms outside the city wall. Only one and a half courses were found in situ, unplastered and perhaps unmortared, and with laid headers on one side and stretchers on the other. The headers lay stacked one on the other rather than flat, and may have continued up originally in classic Sumerian fashion in a herringbone pattern. A pair of beaded rings was found lying close to the south wall. One ring is broken into two parts; each is a triple string of glass beads on a copper wire. About 60 percent of the diagnostic pottery from this excavation unit is Bhayr pottery. The remainder, except for a few pieces of Filalian pottery, is crude ware. The coins that were retrieved at the upper floor levels are eighteenth- and nineteenth-century Alaouite coins. The three floor levels near the surface are definitely recent, that is, eighteenth and nineteenth century. All this suggests a fairly sophisticated residence. The floor levels beneath the layer of midden could date from the Filalian period. There is at least one level of occupation below that, still to be excavated.

The *madinat al-ʿamra* was, first and foremost, at least at the beginning of the reign of Moulay Ismail, the seat of government for the Tafilalt and the official residence of the *makhzan* (literally, "storehouse," but here meaning "central government"). The *dar al-imara* remained within this *qasba*. At the time of the revolt of his brother Ibn Mahraz, the sultan appointed as *qaʾid* of the Tafilalt and the Draa a man named Musa al-Manugi. The *qaʾid*'s specific commission was to monitor relations with the tribes of the Sahara and to oversee the *diwan al-jund* (ministry of the army) for Timbuktu.[6] According to Sidi Suleiman, Moulay Ismail appointed an *amir al-bilad* (a commander in charge of imperial troops), who, like the troops in the nearby *qasba* at Tizimi under the command of the sultan's own son, was to "keep the region secure." Sidi Suleiman stressed that Moulay Ismail did not restore the mosque and madrasa, which had not sustained any damage during either siege.[7] Within the walls of the citadel, then, were the Grand Mosque, complete with its theological school; the *dar al-imara*; a small garrison of troops; a gunpowder storehouse; and a small number of residences to support this political and religious infrastructure. Judging from our excavations outside the perimeter wall, a service population attached itself to the city just outside the citadel.

A Seventeenth-Century Pilgrimage

Sijilmasa remained a central place for pilgrims to gather and prepare to make the hajj. Some Alaouite *shurfa* became famous for organizing caravans for such pilgrims. We have the travelogue of a pilgrim from Teghaza who traveled with such a pilgrimage guide in 1685.[8] His name was Ahmad Ibn Moham-med Ibn Daʿud al-Gazuli al-Tamuli al-Hashtuki. The caravan left Teghaza on April 3, 1685. It had not been gone long when it was overtaken by a messenger bearing a letter to be delivered to a sharif at Sijilmasa. Its contents and sender remain a secret. Another defaulted payment of tribute, perhaps, by the *qaʾid* of Teghaza to the *makhzan*? As part of Moulay Ismail's effort to centralize administration, he placed the family of Uqba Ali al-Teghazi in command of the *qasba* of Teghaza, giving it jurisdiction over the rich salt mines of that re-gion of the Sahara. Al-Teghazi was responsible for an annual tribute of 52,000 *mithqals* in gold. We have it on record that in 1692, Abd al-Malik al-Teghazi could not make the payment; he had only 22,000. He was instructed by the sultan to borrow the rest from merchants in the Tafilalt.[9]

This caravan traveled under the guidance of Sharif Moulay Ibn Hashim Ibn Umar, whose father was even more famous as a pilgrimage guide. Ahmad the pilgrim chose this guide and felt safe with him because of his great *baraka* as well as that of his ancestors, going all the way back to the Prophet. These *shurfa* had a reputation for protecting the weak and for protecting pilgrims from marauders who preyed on travelers in the desert. The respect that such *baraka* commanded provided an additional layer of security to all who came under the protection of such a guide. When Ahmad Mohammed's caravan passed through the region of Tabelbelt, Moulay Ibn Hashim recognized the sheep of the Bani Mani immediately, and more importantly, the shepherds recognized him as well. In fact, they informed the sharif that a rebel tribe of the Ait Atta had recently attacked a group of travelers from Qsar Man-la-Yahaf in the southern Tafilalt. The guide was not surprised. He had earlier seen footprints in the desert sand that he recognized as those of the suspected marauders.

The pilgrim Ahmad likely knew all about the nature of relationships among the segmented nomadic tribes, but here he could get a sense of how those played out in the Tafilalt. The two largest tribal groups competing in this area were the Bani Mani and the Ait Atta, both of whom were tent dwellers who depended primarily on raising camels, sheep, and goats for a living. They supplemented their income by gaining control of certain palm groves in the oases, by engaging in the caravan trade, by selling protection to merchants passing through their territory or to sedentary residents of the oases, or by staging raids to obtain booty. The Bani Mani were Arabs. They inhabited the area east of the Tafilalt, and in the course of the seventeenth century, they ex-panded their domain toward the Oued Guir and the Oued Zousfana. Intent on protecting the pasturelands there, the Bani Mani took a defensive posture toward outsiders. Not so the Ait Atta. These Berber nomads, starting from the Jebel Saghro region west of the Tafilalt, expanded in every direction, including into the Ziz Valley. The Bani Mani joined the Ait Yfalman, a tribal defense alliance against the Ait Atta. Their rivalry became a dominant theme in the history of Sijilmasa through at least the early twentieth century.[10]

Ahmad's journey from Teghaza to Sijilmasa took eighteen days. He arrived on April 21, 1685. He described the oasis at the peak of its glory. The rivers were overflowing with water. The crops were tall and green and swayed with the wind. The date palms showed promise of an abundant fall crop. No wonder, then, that he described the Tafilalt as one of the most beautiful places in the whole world to live, the place chosen by God as the home of the descendants of the Prophet.[11] As in the days of old in Sijilmasa, the caravan did not go into the city itself, but set up camp in al-Ghurfa, on the southeastern edge of the oasis. This settlement served the same function in the seventeenth century that Suq Ben Akla, to the west of Sijilmasa, had served in the medieval period: the staging area for large caravans crossing the Sahara to West Africa. It was capacious and well provisioned enough to receive a large influx of itinerant people and beasts of burden, the latter numbering in the hundreds or thousands. Ahmad referred to al-Ghurfa as a district within Sijilmasa, obviously referring to Sijilmasa in this case as the entire region. Locally, people referred to al-Ghurfa as a tribe.

Ahmad was overwhelmed by the hospitality. Several *shurfa* whom he thanked by name invited him to stay at their homes or at least to share a meal. Likewise, several *fuqaha* (lawyers), ulama, and *murabitin*, all of them prominent men in the various *qsur* of the Tafilalt, invited him as well. How familiar this sounds to those of us who worked in the Tafilalt between 1988 and 1998.

The Grand Mosque of Sijilmasa, within the restored citadel of Moulay Ismail, continued to be a center for religious and intellectual debate, as it had been from the beginning of its existence. Ahmad Mohammed had the chance to interact with famous shaykhs from other parts of Morocco who came to Sijilmasa to teach, consult, and sometimes debate with the *fuqaha* and other ulama. He was curious to learn which ones supported the *makhzan*, that is, the central government, and which ones did not. Among those who had invited Ahmad to stay at his home was Shaykh al-Tagmuti Abd al-Malik, the most famous *faqih*, according to Ahmad, in the whole of the Tafilalt and an ardent supporter of the *makhzan*.[12] Ahmad inquired about two other shaykhs who had recently visited Sijilmasa and who had engaged in debates with al-Tagmuti. Similar debates that won support for the *makhzan* were happening all over Morocco. Moulay Ismail won the support of some of the *zawaya* and tried to suppress others, all in his effort to control the tribes of the country.

Opposition from more and more *zawaya* was on the rise; ultimately, it was fear of the army that held most of them in check.

In the end, Ahmad profusely thanked the many shaykhs who had extended him hospitality. He decided to stay with the family of the guide of his caravan. His travelogue is unclear about where they lived, but it was not in al-Ghurfa. It could have been Qsar al-Ahannus, the *qsar* that was the home of the Alaouites when they first arrived in the Tafilalt, the *qsar* that shelters the tombs of their ancestors.[13] After staying in Sijilmasa for eight days, Ahmad returned to al-Ghurfa to rejoin the caravan. He spent one night in al-Ghurfa before leaving for Mecca.

What did Ahmad do during those eight days? He visited notables of the oasis in several of the *qsur* surrounding Sijilmasa. And he shopped in the *suq* for provisions for the long journey that lay ahead of him. Ahmad insisted that the suq of Sijilmasa, by unanimous agreement of the merchants and travelers that he knew, was the best in the whole region for obtaining the supplies needed for the long journey to Arabia. He advised getting only enough food to allow the beasts of burden to get to Figuig, 150 miles to the northeast. The market was also the place to shop for specialty items for which Sijilmasa had become famous—dates, certainly. When Ahmad Mohammed was there, Tafilalt dates were being shipped to Europe, a highly sought product in the luxury food markets of London.[14] Even today, mail-order catalogues for gourmet foods sometimes advertise "Tafilalt dates." They are still perhaps the best dates in the world.

There is a Tafilalt specialty called *sawic*, which is made of wheat, ground dates, sugar, butter, and pepper. It is highly nutritious, easy to carry, and lasts a long time. It is the perfect staple for a long journey. Ahmad bought some when he was in Sijilmasa and recommended it to his readers. (Our Rissani friends taught us to make this specialty during the 1992 season.) Ahmad advised shopping for small mirrors, knives, nutcrackers, combs, cloth, and gunpowder, all items that could be traded for profit along the way. And, of course, gold. Gold dust bought in Sijilmasa, so Ahmad observed, could be sold for a high price in Tripoli and an even higher one in Cairo. Minted gold was worth even more.

It is clear from Ahmad Mohammed's pilgrimage guide that by the time of Moulay Ismail, the term "Sijilmasa" was often used interchangeably with the term "Tafilalt," referring to the whole region or to the whole oasis. But it is also clear that the term was also still used to describe the city itself. According to tradition, sometime between 1672 and 1689, Moulay Ismail built the *qsar* of Rissani on the southeastern corner of Sijilmasa (the northwestern corner of modern Rissani), immediately south of what was and is the Jewish quarter.

He built it in order to move the seat of government there.[15] The process of the famed medieval city becoming legend was well in progress.

From Moulay Ismail to Sidi Mohammed Ibn Abdallah

When Moulay Ismail died in 1727, competition among his sons launched Morocco into three decades of instability. The Tafilalt fared no better. Funds to support the madrasas ceased to arrive. The schools were closed, and the students and professors moved from Sijilmasa to the surrounding *qsur*, although some people remained in the *madinat al-ʿamra*.

In Morocco as a whole, it was assumed that the army, and more specifically the *abid al-Bukhari*, would play a large role in choosing the sultan's successor. And, indeed, it did for a while, at great expense to the royal treasury. At first the army supported the designated heir, Moulay Ahmad al-Dhahibi, but then replaced him with his brother Abd al-Malik. It then returned Moulay Ahmad to power because Abd al-Malik had "granted no dirhams to the soldiers."[16] But the power of the *abid* began to decline with the accession of Moulay Abd Allah in 1735. His reign was interrupted more than once by competition from several contenders supported either by the *abid* or by tribal contingents. In fact, he was deposed five times. The chronicles say that Moulay Abd Allah gave the *abid* free rein to "devastate the countryside [around Fez], to demolish buildings, to cut trees, to destroy crops."[17] It got to the point that people were most afraid of the forces of the *makhzan*, forces supposedly responsible for maintaining law and order. Tribal forces, on the other hand, began to push into less inhospitable regions. In the south, the Ait Atta continued its drive into the Draa Valley and the Tafilalt. It fell to Sultan Sidi Mohammed Ibn Abdallah (1757–1790), a grandson of Moulay Ismail, to check these moves through a series of reforms (ideological, administrative, tax, economic, urban), all of which affected the Tafilalt as well as the kingdom as a whole.

Sidi Mohammed Ibn Abdallah based his power as ruler on his role as the sole religious leader of his subjects. As the repository of spiritual power, he opposed every attempt to revive the power of the marabouts. He launched a jihad against those foreign powers that held port cities in Morocco. His administration would look like the one that governed Morocco in the time of the Merinids. In the major cities, the *qaʾids* that he appointed had considerable power. He appointed elites who had the loyalty of local populations to the position of *qaʾid* and to high posts such as *hajib* (gatekeeper), *katib* (secretary), *qadi* (judge), and *muhtasib* (marketplace supervisor). He was determined to avoid becoming dependent, as his grandfather had been, on the military. He raised an army from tax-exempt communities settled on state lands. A main function of the army had been to collect taxes, which were seen as oppressive. Sidi Mohammed tried to remedy that by assessing taxes on foreign trade. Customs duties were set at a flat but enforceable rate of 2 percent. And the sultan did everything he could to encourage foreign relations and commerce with other countries. He negotiated trade agreements and friendship treaties with Denmark (1757), the United Kingdom (1760), Sweden (1763), Venice (1765), and the United States (1777). In fact, Morocco became the first nation in the world to recognize the independence of the infant country in America.

Sidi Mohammed Ibn Abdallah was a builder. He built the new city and the port of Essaouira. The principal architect of the new city and port was a Frenchman, Théodore Cornut, an architect famous for his design of fortifications. The result, a city with straight streets, monumental gates, and European-style bastions, was unlike any other city in North Africa. Consuls of the leading foreign powers took up residence there. Europeans called it Mogador. The economic life of the new city was placed in the hands of Jewish merchants. To attract European merchants, the sultan lowered import duties there. He intended the city to be the primary port for the Atlantic trade. Moroccan exports as well as exports from Morocco's trade with West Africa would make their way to Europe through Essaouira. One or two enormous caravans a year, each comprising several thousand camels, as well as several smaller caravans made their way from the Sahara to Essaouira every year. In this way, the sultan's new urban creation was linked to Sijilmasa, his ancestral home in the Tafilalt.

More Restoration in Sijilmasa

In 1783–1784, Sultan Sidi Mohammed Ibn Abdallah paid a visit to his ancestral home. He gave special attention to Sijilmasa, where he focused on urban renewal. Henri Dastugue's interview with Sultan Moulay Suleiman's nephew, Sidi Suleiman Ibn Abd al-Rahman, is once again a crucial source that informed our archaeological findings.[18] The sultan ordered the reopening of the madrasa attached to the mosque, and decided to maintain by state support some five hundred students. The sultan also commissioned a major reconstruction—the last—of the Grand Mosque and madrasa. Primarily, the renovation consisted of replacing the roof of the mosque, a much bigger task than it might sound. It involved replacing the wooden roof supported by wood beams, replacing the glazed tiles on the top side of the roof, and redoing the carved stucco work of the interior frieze and the capitals of the columns.

Debris from what was torn out—wood, tiles, and plaster—accumulated in a destruction level approximately thirty centimeters thick and lying above the existing floor, which had been built in the mid-fifteenth century. A new floor was installed above this destruction level. Within these thirty centimeters of debris between the two floors were samples of wood that had supported the old roof. Analysis of them produced carbon-14 dates ranging from 1430 to 1460, giving us a construction date of the mid-fifteenth century for the earlier mosque. We now have three specific points of reference for the chronological development of the Grand Mosque of Sijilmasa: the expansion of the mosque soon after the Almohads conquered the city from the Almoravids in 1147, the major remodeling in the mid-fifteenth century, and a remodeling by Sidi Mohammed Ibn Abdallah in the late eighteenth century.

The Tafilalt also saw new construction outside the city of Sijilmasa. One way to keep his sons from threatening the stability of the state was to keep them content with their lives in the Tafilalt. They lived on the outskirts of Sijilmasa in *qsur*, strung along the *route touristique* to the south of modern Rissani. These impressive fortresses have massive square towers, the upper third of which are beautifully decorated with a complexity of designs, chevrons, crosses, and herringbone patterns, all carved into the adobe walls.

Administration of the Tafilalt under Moulay Rashid

Following the death of Sidi Mohammed Ibn Abdallah in April 1790, Sijilmasa as a city entered its final stage of decline. The last administrative function to move from the city was the gunpowder storehouse built during the time of Moulay Ismail. It was transferred to Qsar Rissani. Again, the students left the madrasa adjacent to the Grand Mosque and took up residence in the various *zawaya* in the oasis. The weekly market moved east to the open space outside of Qsar Abu Am, where it has been ever since.

Opposition to the central regime was concentrated in the Tafilalt. For the first half of the nineteenth century, there were several changes of power in the central government. More often than not, there were corresponding changes in the governorship of the Tafilalt. At least one failed revolt, that of Moulay Abd al-Salim against his father, originated in the Tafilalt.

In 1859, the new sultan, Sidi Mohammed Ibn Abd al-Rahman, appointed his son, Moulay Rashid, governor of the Tafilalt and other pre-Saharan oases. For the rest of the nineteenth century, the Tafilalt experienced relatively stable government. Moulay Rashid was not just the governor of the Tafilalt, but also a *khalifa'l-sultan*, that is, a special representative of his father, one of three in

the kingdom; the other two were in Fez and Marrakech. As *khalifa*, Moulay
Rashid governed in his father's name and in his absence. He oversaw the work
of local officials and judges appointed by the central government, presided at
Friday prayer in the Grand Mosque, and exerted a kind of moral authority.[19]
The *khalifa* was a *sharif*, after all, endowed with the *baraka* of the Alaouite
dynasty. He lived in Qsar Rissani and was supported by a small detachment,
usually just a few dozen, of royal troops. The *khalifa* was to mediate feuds
among the *qsur* in the oasis, as well as among the tribes in and around the
Tafilalt. And he was to keep an eye on the potentially rebellious *shurfa* who
had been banished to the Tafilalt.[20]

In an effort to administer the region more efficiently, Moulay Rashid divided the Tafilalt into six districts or clusters of *qsur*: Sifa, in the northwest
part of the Tafilalt; Bani Mohammed, directly south of Sifa; Tanejiout, in the
Southeast, where the Alaouite Qsar al-Fida was among the *qsur*; Seffalat, in
the Southwest, which included the important Qsar Tabouassamt; al-Ghurfa,
also in the Southeast, where caravans from the Sahara first stopped upon their
arrival in the Tafilalt; and Oued Ifli, the very heart of the Tafilalt. In this last
district, we find Qsar Rissani, the administrative center; Qsar Abu Am, the
economic center; and at least three other *qsur* directly controlled by the central government—Abbar, Oulad Abd al-Halim, and al-Ma'mun (the same
qsar where Leo Africanus stayed), where the shrine of Moulay Ali Sharif,
the great ancestor of the Alaouite dynasty, is located. These same six districts
divide the Tafilalt today, each one overseen by a shaykh. They are the basis
for the distribution of government grants, projects such as the installation of
public wells, and the like.

Each individual *qsar* in the Tafilalt was a political and economic unit. Each
qsar had its own assembly, the *jama'a*, the supreme executive and judicial body
of the village, which deliberated on all matters of concern to the inhabitants.
The *qsar* elected its *shaykh al-jama'a* to serve as spokesman for the assembly.
From time to time, representatives of all the *qsur* in a district would meet to
address an issue that affected them all, such as resistance to a common foe.
This provided the district with some sense of political identity that went beyond the *qsur* and bound them together. In one of the districts, the Bani Hammad, the people were united also by tribal kinship, so they, like other tribes,
elected a *shaykh al-qabilah*.

One of the most important functions of the *khalifa* was to ensure law and
order in the marketplace. To do that, he appointed a *qa'id al-suq*, a director
of marketplace supervision, who in medieval Sijilmasa was called the *muhtasib*. Moulay Rashid usually appointed to this position an Alaouite *sharif*
whose association with the *baraka* of the Alaouite lineage might transcend

divisions among the merchants of the several *qsur* and among the tribes that came to trade. In Sijilmasa, the *qa'id al-suq* had at his disposal some 50–100 royal troops, who were garrisoned in Qsar Rissani, just a stone's throw north of the market.

Trade in the Tafilalt in the Nineteenth Century

Abu Am is a large *qsar* located on the southeastern edge of medieval Sijilmasa, less than a quarter of a mile south of Qsar Rissani. During the nineteenth century, it became the economic heart of the Tafilalt. As Ross Dunn describes it: "Barely a mile southeast of the crumbling walls (of Sijilmasa) the market of Abu Am arose to take its place. Abu Am inherited from its predecessor a dissipating trans-Saharan trade, but it served nonetheless as the commercial nerve center of southeastern Morocco."[21] (Abu Am is in fact less than a mile from Sijilmasa.) At that time, the weekly market days were Sunday, Tuesday, and Thursday. And so it is today. The large open space in front of the *qsar* is where beasts of burden were tethered, replaced later in the twentieth century by the many buses coming daily to Rissani. Just to the south of that were small domed earthen structures that Walter B. Harris likened to beehives, where sellers offered their wares. Other vendors displayed their goods in small tents.[22] That was the market of Abu Am. Today it is in exactly the same place, and it is known as the Rissani market, described in at least one guidebook as "more for locals than tourists, though it often turns up a good selection of local Berber jewelry."[23]

During the first half of the nineteenth century, Abu Am competed for the trans-Saharan trade with the oasis of Figuig, located about 150 miles to the east. But once the French gained control of Algeria and began to enforce the abolition of the slave trade throughout their empire, slaves that would formerly have been sent to Figuig began to be channeled through the market at Abu Am. Jean-Louis Miège gives us the numbers. Slaves coming into Morocco from West Africa reached their peak from 1840 to 1855: 3,500–4,000 annually. Then trade declined significantly. From 1875 to 1885, Miège estimates that 500–1,000 slaves arrived annually at Tinduf. For the slave market in Abu Am, he estimates the number to be 200–300 annually from 1800 to 1900.[24] Most of the slaves were sent to Fez, Marrakech, or some other market in Morocco. There was little need for slaves in the Tafilalt except among a few men of wealth who wanted females as concubines or domestic servants.[25]

In addition to slaves, Filali leather and dates were the most important products to leave the market of Abu Am for other parts of Morocco. Fez and

Marrakech had large tanning industries of their own, but the Tafilalt had become famous for the quality of its leather, which was exported to be crafted by leather workers in other parts of Morocco. Caravans of as many as one hundred animals left for Fez carrying nothing but Filali leather.[26] The Tafilalt was even more famous for the quality of its many varieties of dates, harvested every year from late August through October, when the annual date festival continues to be celebrated.

Most of the merchants in the market of Abu Am were Filalis, including many wealthy *shurfa* families and many Filali Jews. The Bani Hammad, who lived in the southeastern district of the Tafilalt of the same name, dominated the trade going south by organizing caravans to Timbuktu. Some even took up residence in Timbuktu as commercial agents for Moroccan merchants. They were successful largely because of their alliance with the Ait Khabbash, the tribe of the Ait Atta confederation that dominated the region from the Tafilalt to Touat to the southeast. The nomadic Ait Khabbash supplied the caravaners with camels and drivers as well as armed escorts across potentially hostile territory. Other than Filalis, merchants from Fez were the most numerous in Abu Am. Fasi commercial houses maintained agents and warehouses in Abu Am. Ross Dunn describes one particularly successful Fasi, Ibn Idris, who resided in Abu Am and used the profits of his trade (in European or Moroccan currency) to perform informal banking services.[27]

By the late nineteenth century, the Tafilalt began to suffer from an imbalance in trade. An ever-increasing number of European goods began to show up in the marketplace. The main imports from Europe were sugar, coffee, spices, and various manufactures, including modern firearms.[28] Many of these goods came into Morocco at Tangier and were carried to the Tafilalt via Fez, but an even larger quantity came into Essaouira and arrived via Marrakech.

Sultan Moulay Hassan and the Tafilalt

The nineteenth century witnessed the true collapse of the city of Sijilmasa. By the end of the century, Sijilmasa as a city was but a nostalgic memory for the residents of the Tafilalt as well as for the central regime, although the spot continued to command a great deal of reverence. Each year on the great feasts of the Aid al-kabir and the Aid al-saghir, a community of pious Filalis gathered to pray in the ruins of the old mosque. In 1893, Sultan Moulay al-Hassan I paid his respect to Sijilmasa of old and prayed in the half-ruined Grand Mosque. He came to the Tafilalt officially to visit the tomb of his ancestor and the founder of the dynasty, Moulay Ali Sharif. He was accompanied by some of the highest officials of the *makhzan*: the grand vizier, the chamberlain, the foreign minister, the minister of the army, the commander of the artillery, the *qa'id* of the *mechouar* (the area of the palace where the king makes public appearances), and a French physician who was his highness's personal physician. This was clearly intended to show his royal presence, the authority of the *makhzan* over the Tafilalt, especially in view of the intensity of tribal warfare in the region at the time. It was in this year that the sultan built yet another fortress at Tigmart and stationed another corps of *makhzan* troops at the disposal of his brother the *khalifa*, Moulay Rashid.

The expedition left in June 1893 and arrived in the Tafilalt in November. His entourage established a sprawling camp in the center of the Iglis district, probably among the ruins of the city of legend. Walter B. Harris, an English traveler who was visiting the Tafilalt at this same time and who joined the expedition once he arrived, numbered the king's expedition at forty thousand. He described the city thus: "Immense blocks of *tabia* lie scattered in every direction for some five miles along the east bank of the Wadi Ziz. . . . Several *ksor* of more or less modern construction exist among the ruins."[29] Apparently, he saw Sijilmasa much as we did on our first visit, in 1986. He says that a minaret was still standing when he was there in 1893. Our archaeological research showed no evidence of there ever having been a minaret at the Sijilmasa mosque. Very near the mosque are the remains of a large square tower, part of the circuit wall of *madinat al-'amra* as refortified by Moulay Ismail. Could it be this tower that Harris mistook for a minaret?

The expedition, arriving from the north, probably did not pass through the Bab Fez, now known as Bab al-Rih, since it was then a freestanding gate without the attached curtain walls. As the caravan traveled the two kilometers from the Bab Fez to the citadel of Moulay Ismail, the travelers would have passed not the splendid villas of the late-medieval period, but rather a few isolated, simple dwellings belonging to local farmers, like that of our senior laborer Bel-'Aid Ben Barrak, who lives just south of the Bab al-Rih. The walls of the citadel would still have been rather imposing when they came into sight, as they are today. How much of that wall was still standing when Moulay Hassan arrived is hard to say. Only the northern side and part of the eastern wall are visible above the surface today. The southernmost part of the western wall has been buried by windblown sand, but a portion of it has recently been exposed, as mentioned above, by miners of sand. Within the walls, amidst the rolling mounds of sand covering fallen structures, were a number of wall fragments, rather crudely built. Today, the freestanding, mostly broken walls within the citadel contain sherds of Bhayr pottery as part of the aggregate. That means that these crude walls were rather recent at the time of Moulay

Hassan's visit, yet were in a poor state of repair, probably the makeshift homes of a transient population. The irony is that at the time of the last royal worship in the Sijilmasa mosque, the site was no longer an urban space, but was as it had been on the eve of the founding of the city in the mid–eighth century.

The sultan had traveled, at great expense, to the Tafilalt to pray at the tomb of his great ancestor and at the Grand Mosque of Sijilmasa, but he also had other motives for the visit.[30] The *makhzan* was once again losing control of this traditionally vital part of the realm. The sultan stayed in the Tafilalt for three weeks. He distributed gifts to the leading *shurfa* and granted them special subsidies, all in the hope of minimizing opposition from dissident members of the royal family. He tried to mediate disputes between the rival tribal groups, especially between the Berber-speaking Dawi Mani, who were affiliated with the Ait Yfalman, and the Arabic-speaking Ait Khabbash of the Ait Atta. These tribes, each in its own way, competed to control the economic life of the oasis. The Dawi Mani controlled most of the area east of the Oued Ziz. They were herders for the most part, but had succeeded in controlling most of the date palms of the region. The Ait Khabbash, on the other hand, were caravaners who controlled the trade routes going south from the Tafilalt across the Sahara to Timbuktu, as well as the route going north to Fez. The tribes were in direct competition with each other to control the economic life of the Tafilalt. Often enough, the competition broke out into outright feuds. Walter B. Harris described the warfare between the Arabs and the Berbers as "unceasing": "At the time of my stay in the Sultan's camp a skirmish took place between the two [tribal confederations] in the very presence of Moulay el Hassen, several on both sides being killed, altogether some fifteen it is said. The sultan promptly imprisoned the ringleaders of each party; but the prisoners' fellow-tribesmen brought such force to bear that he was obliged to release them in the course of a few days."[31] The sultan saw this competition as playing right into the hands of the French, who had begun to make inroads into southeastern Morocco from their land base in Algeria. This threat of foreign invaders was probably another reason for the sultan's presence.

The sultan failed to mediate between the rivals, and the Dawi Mani began to align themselves with the French as trading partners, further driving a wedge between the tribal factions. The Ait Khabbash, with the help of local *shurfa* in the Tafilalt and the *khalifa* himself, tried to impose an embargo on the Dawi Mani, depriving them of Filali dates and Filali leather, both highly in demand in other markets. But it did not work. In the year when Sultan Hassan made his "pilgrimage" to the Tafilalt, the French entered Timbuktu far to the south. They were then in a position to dominate the trans-Saharan trade, making it a virtual satellite of the Franco-Algerian trade network.

The French Advance into the Tafilalt

The French had begun to penetrate farther and farther into neighboring Algeria as early as the 1830s. The Treaty of Lalla Maghnia in 1845 established the border between Algeria and Morocco, but only as far south as Taniat al-Sassi, some seventy miles inland from the Mediterranean coast. South of that, the border was vague at best, meaning that certain *qsur* could be seen as either Moroccan or Algerian. The French felt that they had free rein to pursue raiders into what was considered Moroccan territory. The presence of the French prompted opposition from the local tribes. An uprising under the leadership of Abu Amama, a resident of Figuig, together with the assassination of the head of the Arab Bureau in Géryville (El Bayadh in modern Algeria) in 1881, provided the French with an excuse to move into the southern Oranie and to establish a fort in Ain Sefra. The railroad was a useful means of extending French influence. By the spring of 1903, the railroad had reached Beni Ounif. The French constructed a market there that immediately began to attract trade from nearby Figuig. They built a road to Figuig and even invited European tourists to visit the oasis while on holiday in the desert. Figuig thus preceded Oujda and Casablanca as a territorial beachhead in France's drive to take Morocco.[32] Because of the railroad and cheaper cost of importing European goods into Algerian ports, the Algerian routes regained the dominance they had enjoyed in the first half of the nineteenth century. By 1905, the French had pushed the railroad even closer to the Tafilalt, as far as Colomb-Béchar, just about seventy-five miles away.

When Sultan Moulay Hassan died, his eldest son, Moulay Abd al-Aziz, succeeded him. In 1904, he contracted a loan of 62.5 million francs from a consortium of French banks. In 1906, France signed an *entente cordiale* with Great Britain, recognizing Morocco as a French sphere of influence and Egypt as a British sphere of influence. Another *haraka* (uprising) was the response from the Tafilalt. The leaders of this one were Moulay Mohammed, a son of the *khalifa*; Moulay Abu, the *khalifa*'s adjunct; and Sidi al-Bukhari, a sharif of the Ghorfa district. The *haraka* failed. Why? Because, according to Ross Dunn, not a single *shurfa* leader "was a reputed saint." This meant that the "Filali *shurfa* community was extremely divisive, and the entire population of the oasis was split on the question of trade with the French."[33]

French forces occupied Oujda in March 1907 and landed in Casablanca in July. This precipitated a move to depose Sultan Abd al-Aziz in favor of his brother Abd al-Hafid, who was willing to call for a jihad against the French. Abd al-Hafid's base of power was in Marrakech, where the ulama had proclaimed him sultan. Both he and his brother knew how vital was the support of the Tafilalt; both vied for the support of their *shurfa* relatives there. Abd al-Hafid chose a son of the Tafilalt *khalifa* to command his forces in the Chaouia region. Abd al-Aziz, for his part, tried to sustain the *khalifa*'s support by continuing his monthly salary through the financial services of a wealthy Fasi merchant.

The sword of resistance was taken up by Moulay Lahsin, an Idrissi *shurfa* from Figuig, an ideological heir of Si Mohammed al-Arbi al-Darqawi, and the founder of his own *zawiya* at Douiret Sbaa. He organized a *haraka* against the French stationed at Colomb-Béchar. The French crushed the resistance forces with superior firepower at the Battle of Boudenib in May 1908.

By 1912, French interest and investment in Morocco had reached critical mass. Having achieved virtual economic control over the country, France pressured Sultan Moulay Abd al-Hafid into signing the Treaty of Fez, which established the French protectorate over Morocco. But like every regime that had come before it, France would learn that to secure its control over Morocco, it would have to extend its own *makhzan* to include the Tafilalt. It was still, after all, the trailhead for routes going to Timbuktu and to French colonies south of the Sahara. Moreover, it was the ancestral home of the ruling dynasty, which it still left in nominal control of the country for a while. A significant number of *shurfa* lived there, as did several *murabitin*, leaders of Sufi brotherhoods. And it remained an area where intertribal conflict threatened French dominance of the southeastern corner of Morocco. These tribes could be potential allies if properly courted, or agents of opposition if left unchecked.

Following the establishment of the protectorate, the Tafilalt continued to offer resistance to the French. The French established a post in the Tafilalt in 1916, but resistance was so fierce that they abandoned it in 1918 in favor of a larger and more defensible one in Erfoud. A new weekly market was established in Erfoud, some say to deliberately shift the economic center of the oasis north of Rissani, the Sijilmasa of old. Our excavation team, living in Rissani, became acutely aware of this shift in economic focus and the subsequent development of Erfoud, at the expense of Rissani, as we compared the number of items (drafting supplies, foreign newspapers and magazines, imported cheese) and services (photo processing, blueprint copying, etc.) available to us in Erfoud but not in Rissani. We can blame it, at least initially, on the French.

From 1918 until 1932, the heart of the Tafilalt remained free from French control. For most of that time, it was controlled by the resistance leader Bil Qasim N'gadi and a following of tribesmen, mostly Ait Atta. Those tribesmen remained a thorn in the side of the French until they were finally defeated in a great battle in their High Atlas stronghold, the Jebel Saghro. The Ait Khab-

Figure 6.3. Center for Alaouite Studies and Research (Centre d'Études et de Recherches Alaouites; CERA), Qsar Rissani.

bash, whose domain was the eastern Tafilalt and beyond, were the last of the Ait Atta, indeed the last Moroccans, to surrender to the French.

The French protectorate was the last of a long series of regimes that struggled to control the Tafilalt and to consider control over the Tafilalt as essential to their strategy to remain in power in the *makhzan*. From the Almoravids to the French, whoever governed the *makhzan* either maintained a local Tafilalt regime sympathetic to themselves or sent rulers of their own to govern directly. The French officer placed in command was Captain Henri de Bournazel, who set up his command post in Qsar Rissani, which had been the local seat of government since the latter part of the reign of Moulay Ismail. Bournazel's administration set about repairing many of the dams along the Oueds Ziz and Gheris, thereby increasing agricultural production. The road from Meknes to Rissani was vastly improved, which allowed the beginning of regular bus service from Meknes to Rissani (through Midelt), essentially the same route that Ibn Battuta traveled some six hundred years earlier, but requiring only one long day of travel rather than weeks. The new administration moved the marketplace from the front of Qsar Abu Am to the south of that open space and enclosed it with a wall. The abandoned open space served as a parking lot for buses coming from Meknes and Fez, at least until the new bus station, built over the southern edge of medieval Sijilmasa, opened in 2002. Qsar Rissani, incidentally, is still an important arm of the *makhzan*. It is now the home of the Ministry of Cultural Affairs and houses the Center for Alaouite Studies and Research (Centre d'Études et de Recherches Alaouites), a library, a museum, and a research institution dedicated to the current Moroccan dynasty, which was born in Sijilmasa.

CHAPTER 7

Using Models of the Islamic City as Guides

The relationship between an evolving, theoretical model of the Islamic city and the reality of Sijilmasa as seen on the ground through our interdisciplinary approach produced a dynamic that has become central to our study. An important starting point in the evolution of our theoretical model is the work of Dale Eickelman, who outlines four discernible patterns of spatial order in precolonial Middle Eastern cities: the presence of the central power, often represented by a fortified quarter, a *qasba* (citadel), and marked by a conspicuous externality or otherness in relation to the urban population; a complex of economic activity, the *suq*, where commercial and craft activities tend to be separated from places of residence; the religious institutions, the mosques and maraboutic shrines; and the residential quarters or neighborhoods within which residents claim multiple personal ties.[1] A second guidepost are the three themes introduced by Amira K. Bennison and Alison L. Gascoigne: "urban transformations occasioned by the rise of Islam and their conceptualisation by Muslims" (legends of early Islamic idealism played a big role here); "the impact of Muslim regimes on urban development"; and "the ways in which religion may have affected the functioning of public amenities."[2] What follows is a recapitulation from the preceding chapters of those aspects of Sijilmasa's urban fabric that confirm or reflect some aspect of one or another of the Islamic city models that we have encountered. Our first run at a model is divided into four quadrants representing the political institutions (*dar al-imara*), religious institutions (mosque-madrasa), economic institutions (markets and industry), and residential quarters.

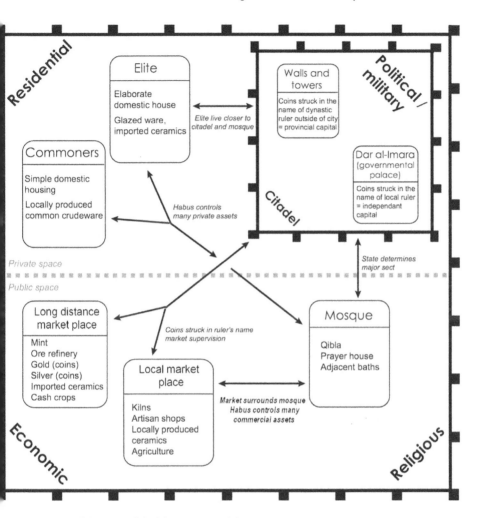

Figure 7.1. Schematic of the Islamic city model.

Dar al-imara

We begin with the political-military sector of the city, the *dar al-imara* (literally, "the house of government"), which might also include the citadel or reside within it. In figure 7.1, we have placed a dark line around this quadrant to indicate that it is typically within the city walls, but that the citadel, the seat of government, the prince's palace, and the military barracks, often placed on a height, are all clearly marked off from the rest of the city. They are sometimes enclosed within fortifications of their own inside the city, providing protection against the local populace as well as against forces from without.[3]

MAPS places the earliest *dar al-imara* of Sijilmasa on the same high plateau in the center of the site as the earliest settlement. More than likely, it was the elite residence that we excavated directly beneath the three levels of mosque on this elevated plateau. Later, Sijilmasa's seat of government moved to within the walls of a citadel. This move conforms to the urban model described by Frej Stambouli and Abdelkader Zghal for precolonial North African cities. In the case of Sijilmasa, we cannot be sure when the seat of government was moved from its original location to the high ground to the north and was enclosed in its own curtain walls. Both the Fatimid rulers in the midtenth century and the Almoravids beginning in the middle of the eleventh century were unquestionably viewed as "foreign" rulers by the resident population of Sijilmasa. We are inclined to say that it was the Almoravid dynasty that moved the *dar al-imara*. Remember, in the year when they took Sijilmasa, the local population rebelled and killed the Almoravid rulers in the mosque, which brought about a second conquest of the city the following year. Such events would certainly create a sense of "conspicuous externality or otherness in relation to the urban population," as Stambouli and Zghal put it, and stir the Almoravids to rule from behind the walls of the *qasba*.[4] Paul Wheatley echoes this idea: "As religion and government began to assert substantial degrees of autonomy in their operational spheres, there developed a tendency for caliphal residences and government *diwans* to be incorporated in elaborately conceived extramural palatine complexes, sometimes well removed from main population foci." In the case of Sijilmasa under the Almoravids, the *dar al-imara* and citadel remained within the circuit wall of the city, but was walled off from the rest of the city itself.

The seat of government was institutionally connected with the religious quadrant. It determined, at least officially, the *madhab* (school of law and denomination) that would be followed in the city. Sufriya Kharijism was the *madhab* of the Midrarids, and thus the *madhab* of Sijilmasa until the arrival of the Fatimids in the tenth century, who introduced Shi'ite Islam. It changed to Malikite Sunni Islam under the Maghrawa and Almoravids in the eleventh century, and so it has remained ever since.

In the early years of Sijilmasa, Sufriya Kharijism helped shape the early layout of the central town. Followers of that sect firmly believed that all citizens were equal before the law, so much so that they insisted that the ruler should be elected from a community of equals. Hence, the ruler lived in the midst of the community next to the mosque, which was at the heart of the city. Legend played an important role in the conceptualization of what the first city in Sijilmasa would be. It may not be more than legend, but the first leader in Sijilmasa was Isa Ibn Mazid al-Aswad, "the Black."[5]

The founding fathers of Sijilmasa not only were egalitarians, but in their Kharijite worldview also insisted on each person's responsibility for his or her actions. The only fragment of a monumental inscription that we found in Sijilmasa, a fragment of wall plaster with the words *"wus'aha . . . kasabat . . . 'alayha"* (Quran 2:286: "On no soul doth God place a burden greater than it can bear. It gets every good that it earns, and it suffers every ill that it earns"), attests to their belief that faith alone was not sufficient for salvation. It affirms that individuals are responsible for their own actions.

When the Fatimids took control of Sijilmasa, the *madhab* changed. The Fatimids brought Isma'ili Shi'ism to Sijilmasa. But we found no archaeological evidence that Shi'ism affected the religious life of the city or had any impact on the urban landscape. On the other hand, when the Bani Khazrun asserted their independence from the Fatimids, they converted to the Malikite *madhab* of Sunni Islam and forever changed the sect of Islam that would be the basis of law in the city. Malikism has been the law of the land in Sijilmasa and the Tafilalt to the present day.

Religious Institutions

The noted author Titus Burckhardt once used the metaphor that the mosque is the heart of the Islamic city. The Arabic word for mosque is *masjid*, from the root *s-j-d*, "to bow down" or "to worship." The mosque is a place to worship. A *masjid jami'* is a great mosque or central mosque, where Muslims come together to pray on Friday. The root word for *jami'* is *j-m-'*, which means "to come together" or "to meet." The mosque was also a gathering place. Finally, it was a place for teaching and learning, a function that became institutionalized in the madrasa, from the root *d-r-s* ("to study" or "to learn"), associated with the mosque. The most distinguishing architectural feature of a mosque is its *mihrab*, the niche that indicates the direction to face when praying. Most mosques have a *minbar*, the chair from which the imam delivers the Friday sermon. Many mosques have a minaret from which the muezzin sings out the call to prayer. But the minaret is not an indispensable element. A small mosque near where MAPS members lived in Rissani does not have a minaret. The muezzin simply stood in the street in front of the mosque to call the people to prayer. Finally, somewhere close to the mosque or as part of the structure is a place for people to do ritual ablutions before praying.

The Grand Mosque of Sijilmasa is the most obvious remnant of the religious institutions in Sijilmasa's physical landscape, and MAPS has documented five phases of its existence. The earliest mosque is not in the same place as is the next. We might not have found it without referring to Nezar al-Sayyad's model of early Islamic garrison towns. That model places the *dar al-imara* on the *qibla* side of the Grand Mosque. Paul Wheatley confirms al-Sayyad's observation about the positioning of the *dar al-imara* on the *qibla* side of the mosque and adds that it was "perhaps to suffuse administrative decisions with the power of prayer flowing down from the *qiblah* to Makkah (Mecca)."[6] Knowing that the *qibla* of the Sijilmasa Mosque, like that of most early mosques in Morocco, faces almost due south, and assuming that the lowest level within the surface walls of the mosque is the *dar al-imara*, and assuming further that al-Sayyad's model holds true for Sijilmasa, then the earliest mosque should be on the north side of the *dar al-imara*. And there it was. All that is left of it are a couple of circular column bases. Everything else of the first mosque was eradicated for the construction of new buildings, including the madrasa.

The madrasa became an important institution in Morocco under the Merinids. In Sijilmasa, we know that the mosque had its adjacent madrasa from the time of the Alaouite sultan Moulay Ismail, and we have the archaeological evidence to prove it. It is the uppermost level of construction over the site of the first mosque. It is possible that the Sijilmasa madrasa goes back as far as the Merinids, but we cannot conclusively prove that. On the west side of the mosque-madrasa complex in Sijilmasa are the public ablutions area and the public latrines.

The issue of mosque orientation is one obvious way that the ruling regimes affected the physical landscape of the city. First, we might never have found the *mihrab* of the Sijilmasa Mosque had we not learned that most early mosques in Morocco and the rest of North Africa are consistently 63–65 degrees off the true orientation.[7] Most consistent of all of the Moroccan ruling dynasties were the Almohads, who changed the orientation of at least two mosques, the Kutubiya Mosque in Marrakech and the Sijilmasa mosque. It was a visible symbol of their reformist ideology, of their determination to correct the errors of the Almoravid regime. Our archaeobotanical evidence confirms that reformist ideology. The almost complete absence of grapes from deposits dating from the mid-tenth to the mid-twelfth centuries supports the textual evidence that both of these puritan reformist regimes enforced a strict prohibition against alcohol, demonstrating another link between political and religious institutions.

To recap all of the levels of occupation within the surface mosque: it is here more than anywhere else on the site that the stratigraphic levels can most easily be discerned, producing in essence a series of time-lapse photographs spanning the history of Sijilmasa. At the earliest level, dated with some precision by carbon-14 analysis to the first century of Sijilmasa's urban existence, is the elite residence that we tentatively identified in chapter 3 as the *dar al-imara*. At the center of the structure is a garden covering approximately 36 square meters (387.5 square feet). To the west of it is a sunken central court stepping up to rooms on the eastern and western side. Quite possibly there were rooms to the north and south as well, but traces of them have not survived. To the east of the garden are four smaller rooms, approximately 10 square meters (108 square feet) each. To the north of the garden is a kitchen area, evidenced by several fire pits and a trash pit that was filled with cooking utensils and food refuse. This was beyond a doubt an elite residence, highly decorated with geometric designs painted in black on a white background and carved in stucco, designs that we have to describe as prototypical Bani Midrar art, not seen by modern eyes until now. It was a residence befitting the Midrarid Kharijite rulers of Sijilmasa, who, to reflect their Kharijite belief in salvation by works, painted a Quranic inscription on the wall of the residence.

By the time the Almoravids arrived in Sijilmasa in the middle of the eleventh century, this structure was no longer the *dar al-imara*; it was not a residence at all. The Almoravids moved their seat of government behind walls within the city, high on the plateau to the north of the mosque area. The elite residence was torn down and a mosque was built in its place, quite possibly the Mosque of Ibn Abd Allah, as we suggested in chapter 4. It was modest in size, almost square in shape, 22.5 meters north to south and 19.5 meters east to west. The prayer hall was divided into five bays and five aisles, the center aisle being wider than the others, as is typical of most mosques. At the south end of this central aisle, we saw only slight traces of the *mihrab*. What we did not see were any traces of an emplacement for a *minbar*. This does not necessarily mean that there was no *minbar*, only that no traces remain. If there was no *minbar*, it would not have been a Friday mosque and, thus, not the Mosque of Ibn Abd Allah—hence, the reason for some uncertainty in our identification.

In the second half of the twelfth century, the Almohads decided that the mosque was too small. They almost doubled the size of the prayer hall, to 18 meters north to south, a little shorter than the Almoravid mosque, but 37.5 meters east to west, again with the central aisle wider than the others. The reformist Almohads also decided that the mosque was incorrectly oriented. As we pointed out earlier, they were right about that, but changed the orientation to one that was further from the correct one than the original. But tradition is a powerful force. The Almohad orientation survived two later restorations of the Sijilmasa Grand Mosque. From the archaeological evidence, we can also picture an aesthetically more modest mosque. We have evidence that the Almohads camouflaged the carved stucco with a coat of plaster, just as they did in the Qarawiyyin Mosque in Fez.

In the mid-fifteenth century, fully a half century after the alleged destruction of Sijilmasa under the late Merinid rulers in 1393, the Sijilmasa mosque saw its most substantial restoration: new walls, new pillars, a new roof, and a completely new floor plan. It was slightly larger than the Almohad mosque, but the interior space was divided quite differently, having only three bays on the north-south axis, but eleven bays on the east-west axis. Most likely, the madrasa was added to the immediate north at this time. This major restoration compels us to reject the notion, put forward by Leo Africanus, that Sijilmasa collapsed as a city at the end of the fourteenth century. The local rulers reasserted themselves with this architectural statement that Sijilmasa was alive and well.

More than three centuries passed. When Sultan Sidi Mohammed Ibn Abdallah restored the mosque in the 1770s, as we describe in chapter 6, he maintained the walls, pillars, and floor plan of the Filalians. But he replaced the ceiling, the roof, and the splendid green tiles on each of the peaked bays, giving the mosque a brand-new appearance.

In this one enclosed area are distinguishable archaeological traces of each of these phases of occupation—a complete series of time-lapse photographs of the successive periods of Moroccan history.

Economic Institutions

Early in the twentieth-century formation of the Islamic city model, in 1955, Gustave von Grunebaum, working from an observation made by Ibn Battuta, wrote that markets "do exhibit everywhere in Islamic lands the same general structure."

> For one thing, the producers or retailers of the same kind of goods will always occupy adjacent stalls; in fact, each trade is likely to have one of the market lanes completely to itself. More important still, the order in which the several trades follow one another in the layout of the market is apt to be substantially the same wherever we go in Muslim territory. Near the mosque was a religious center we will find the suppliers of the sanctuary, the suq of the candle merchants, the dealers in incense and other perfumes. Near the mosque as an intellectual center we will find also the suq of the booksellers,

the suq of the bookbinders and, as its neighbor, the suq of the leather merchants and the makers of slippers, all of whom are in one way or another
concerned with leather goods. Adjoining this group of markets we enter
the halls of the dealers in textiles, the *qaisariya*, the only section of the suqs
which is regularly roofed and which can be locked and where, therefore, precious materials other than fabrics will also be stored and exchanged.[8]

This view of the market in the Islamic city is often seen as stereotypical.[9] Yet
we do see cities, especially in North Africa (Fez, Sefrou, Tunis) that follow
this model. The question is, is it Islamic? Much of it could be attributed to
common sense: trades that service activities in the mosque tend to be located
near the mosque, bookbinders near the booksellers, slipper makers who work
in leather near the bookbinders, and so on. Or did the arrangement, as Ibn
Abdun, an early twelfth-century writer of *hisba* (manuals for marketplace
supervision), suggests, make each particular trade easier to regulate?[10]

The institutional connection between the *dar al-imara* and the economic
institution was the *muhtasib*, the director of marketplace supervision, whose
functions we described in chapter 4. The *muhtasib* also regulated the location
of cemeteries (on the edge of town) as well as proper behavior for visiting
cemeteries. In Sijilmasa, the medieval cemeteries were located just outside of
the inhabited urban landscape. The main cemetery was between the southwestern edge of the city and the east bank of the Oued Ziz. Suq Ben Akla's
cemetery was on the northeastern side of the city's edge.

As far as "foul" trades are concerned, pottery production certainly fell into
that category, because of the soot coming out of the kilns. At first, it was
suggested that the earliest pottery production in Sijilmasa was located along
the banks of the Oued Gheris and then moved to the southern part of Sijilmasa itself in the fourteenth or fifteenth century, after that part of the city
fell into decline. Finally, in the seventeenth and eighteenth centuries, pottery
was produced in Bhayr al-Ansar, on the west bank of the Ziz, southwest of
Sijilmasa.[11] Those scenarios were based on the discovery of kiln trivets (tri-
pods used to separate stacked plates or bowls inside the kiln) and on laboratory analyses that identified sources of clay for ceramics along the Gheris and
the Ziz. But the location of raw material is not evidence of production. Raw
materials can easily be transported a few kilometers to a place of production.
Archaeological research during the 1993, 1994, and 1996 seasons specifically
looked for physical evidence of pottery kilns in and around the limits of medieval Sijilmasa, but produced no such evidence except for the seventeenth- and
eighteenth-century kilns at Bhayr al-Ansar. The most likely scenario, then,

is that Bhayr al-Ansar was the primary location for pottery production from the medieval period on — outside the city itself, on the west bank of the Oued Ziz.[12]

A common practice in many North African cities and towns is to have market days once, twice, or even three times a week. Sellers and buyers come from near and far. Typically, sellers set up temporary stalls in a given area and then dismantle them at the end of the day. This is what MAPS observed every Tuesday, Thursday, and Sunday in Rissani from 1988 through 1998. It is still the case today.

The enclosed market square located about 60 meters (196 feet) southwest of the Sijilmasa mosque would have been this kind of market, conforming to the von Grunebaum model. What is unique about the case of Sijilmasa is Suq Ben Akla, the staging area for the large caravans that connected Sijilmasa with markets south of the Sahara. It is one feature that we generally do not find in other Islamic cities. Not that it is unusual for a secondary market to be near the edge of a city or even just outside a city. That arrangement was and remains fairly common. But for the secondary market to be larger than the one that served the city itself, to be far from the central city, and to have a permanent resident population is not common at all. Picture Suq Ben Akla as the center of an economic network. Imports came there from four directions. From *bilad al-Sudan* came gold, of course, plus slaves, ivory, ebony, salt, ostrich feathers, and *lamt* hides. From the Sus and Awlil to the west and southwest came brass, alum, ambergris, and salt. Merchants from the Maghrib and points beyond brought all sorts of manufactured goods: textiles, leather, ceramics, metalwork, glassware, and books. Merchants, craftsmen, and farmers from Sijilmasa brought goods to Suq Ben Akla: ceramics, leather, metalwork, dates, wine (except during periods of prohibition), and coins.

Only some of these imports would have made the short trip to the Sijilmasa market for consumption by Sijilmasa's residents. Most of the gold was destined for the Sijilmasa mint. Some of the slaves would have served as domestic servants of the urban rich. Some of the manufactured luxury goods would have appealed to the same group. Alum and ambergris would have supplied Sijilmasa's industries. But most of the manufactured luxury goods imported from the north were exported south and west to the *bilad al-sudan* and to the Sus and Awlil. Products shipped north from Suq Ben Akla included gold coins from the Sijilmasa mint, Sijilmasa's own industrial products (ceramics, textiles, leather goods, metalwork), and Sijilmasa's cash crops (dates and sugar).

After the monetary reforms of the Umayyad caliph Abd al-Malik (d. 705), the minting of coinage was the exclusive prerogative of the state through-

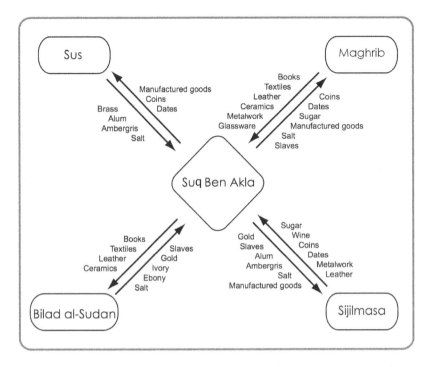

Figure 7.2. Schematic showing Suq Ben Akla as the hub of a vast economic network.

out the *dar al-Islam*. The presence of gold coinage struck in mint cities all over the Maghrib testifies to the role that governments played in commerce, both local and long-distance, and to the extent that they benefited from the gold trade. The founders of Sijilmasa viewed the town and its environs as an independent city-state. At least one Midrarid ruler, Mohammed Ibn al-Fath, asserted his independence from the Fatimids by striking dinars in his own name beginning in 943.

It was in the best interest of the central regime to control and protect the trade routes that connected the empire to the trade centers beyond its jurisdiction, as well as those routes that connected various cities within the empire. The Fatimids and the Umayyads competed intensely with each other to control Sijilmasa and the routes that connected it with the Sudan. The Fatimids' mint output was directly proportional to their success at controlling Sijilmasa. For a time, the Sijilmasa mint struck as much as one-fourth of their official gold coinage. When the Almoravids took control of the city, they struck coins only in Sijilmasa for thirty-five years, but then struck coins in six centers in the Maghrib and eight in Andalusia, representing at least five geographic links between the Mediterranean and West Africa, namely, Marrakech/Aghmat, Fez, Tlemcen, Andalusia, and Sijilmasa. These centers were not only the major commercial centers of the empire, but also administrative capitals for the five provinces of the state.[13] Sijilmasa's mint continued to be a governmental institution of paramount importance to the city's economic life for many regimes to come. The innovative research of Choukri Heddouchi, who elucidated six distinct phases in the development of die-engraving technology, has shown that the Sijilmasa mint not only conformed to the standards of other North African mints, but also took the lead in setting minting policies for them.[14]

Yet another link between political and economic institutions was taxation. In the middle of the tenth century, when the Fatimids controlled Sijilmasa, the Fatimid governor levied numerous taxes: duties on caravans going to the Sudan; the religious tax (*zakat*); the land tax (*khasraj*); the customary duties imposed on the buying and selling of camels, sheep, and cattle; and customs on all merchandise going to or coming from Ifriqiya, Fez, Spain, the Sus, and Aghmat. For the next twenty years, Sijilmasa produced half the tax revenues of the Fatimid state.[15] Taxation remained a critical matter when the Bani Maghrawa, initially as clients of the Umayyads and then as independent rulers of Sijilmasa, imposed non-Quranic taxes. Excessive taxation was one of the grievances that led the population of Sijilmasa to appeal to the Almoravids to liberate them from the oppressive practices of the Bani Maghrawa. As we saw in chapter 4, the Almoravids came to Sijilmasa on a reformist platform of prohibition and "no non-Quranic taxes."[16]

Residential Quarters

The Islamic city model suggests that most Islamic cities were divided into quarters. According to al-Sayyad: "Housing was mainly made up of inward oriented core residential quarters, each allocated to a particular group of residents and each is served by a single dead-end street."[17] Those who look first at social forces shaping cities rather than the form itself also see quarters as one of the main principles of order, "with the households of each quarter claiming multiple personal ties and common interests based on varying combinations of kinship, common origin, ethnicity, patronage and clientship, participation in factional alliances, and spatial propinquity itself."[18] In Morocco, that quality of life is called *qaraba*, "closeness."[19] Stambouli and Zghal call it "links of neighborliness."[20]

People who were close in that way would visit each other on feast days; assist or participate in births, circumcisions, weddings, and funerals; and share in certain collective responsibilities for the well-being of the quarter. Women who would not venture unveiled to the central market would nonetheless feel at ease moving about unveiled within the quarter. Numerous hadith stress this special relationship with one's neighbors. One hadith reported by Ibn Umar Ibn al-Khattab, the second caliph, states: "Allah's Apostle said, Gabriel kept on reminding me about treating the neighbors in a kind and polite manner, so much so that I thought that he would order (me) to make them (my) heirs." Aisha, wife of the Prophet, narrates: "I said, 'O Allah's Apostle! I have two neighbors! To whom shall I send my gifts?' He said, 'To the one whose gate is nearer to you.'" And Abu Rafi, another well-known narrator of hadith, says, "The Prophet said, 'The neighbor has more right to be taken care of by his neighbor (than anyone else).'"[21]

The archaeological record supports the physical presence of quarters. We have identified a residential quarter in the northwestern section of central Sijilmasa, a very large residential quarter in the southwestern quadrant, and an elite residential quarter in the area due west of the Grand Mosque. That residences close to the Grand Mosque tended to be elite residences seems to conform to the model.[22]

Janet Abu-Lughod suggests three elements that facilitate the division of a city into quarters—three ways, she says, in which Islamic cities are Islamic. First are features of city planning that reflect or facilitate distinctions between classes that are juridically distinct in Islam, for example, residential segregation of the *dhimmi*, that is Jews and Christians, who were "people of the Book."[23] It seems that people of the same religion or religious orientation tended to live in the same neighborhood. Since the mosque and school were the center of community life, people often wanted to live within easy walking distance of them. The same was true for Christians and Jews living in Islamic cities. In his study of the Geniza documents, S. D. Goitein saw evidence of religious groups tending to live together in neighborhoods. But it seems to have been a matter of preference rather than law. There was hardly a neighborhood that he looked at, whether in Egypt, Iraq, or North Africa, that was exclusively Jewish.[24] It is true that the Almoravid amir Ali Ibn Yusuf issued a decree forbidding Jews from residing in Marrakech. The Jewish merchants who did business in Marrakech lived in Aghmat and, at least theoretically, had to leave the city by nightfall, before the city gates were closed.

The first *mellah*, Jewish quarter, to emerge in Morocco was in Fez during the late Merinid period. It was located near Fez al-Jadid, the new administrative district built by the Merinids. Sijilmasa, too, had a *mellah* late in its history, as does the city of Rissani today. The latter was inhabited by Jews until the last of them moved away in the late 1960s and early 1970s. Historical texts do not tell us when it was established, but it is quite possible that it was in the late Merinid period. The Merinids are well known for having established a *mellah* in most of their major cities. It could also have been built when the Alaouites restored the *madinat al-ʿamra* in the late seventeenth century, for example, when Moulay Ismail built Qsar Rissani and moved his *dar al-imara* there. The Rissani *mellah* is located immediately to the north of Qsar Rissani, both of which are located on the eastern edge of the ruins of medieval Sijilmasa, a logical direction for urban expansion, since the town was bordered on the west by the river. It could well be that the *mellah* of late medieval Sijilmasa is in fact the one in early-modern Rissani, located in the newest part of medieval Sijilmasa and the oldest part of Rissani.

The second feature that might make Islamic cities Islamic, according to Abu-Lughod, are elements that facilitate gender segregation, which would coincide somewhat with elements that distinguish between private space and public space.[25] The layout of Sijilmasa, as we envision it in the composite GIS map, certainly separates public space from private space. The residential quarters in the northwestern and southwestern parts of town appear to have been enclosed by walls within the city walls. The market area, too, was enclosed. What evidence we have of house plans confirms that entranceways into Sijilmasan houses, like those all over Morocco and the rest of the Muslim world, required a ninety-degree turn to enter the courtyard or the house itself. One cannot see into a house's living space from the entrance on the street. The entrance to a small house excavated in the southwestern part of town, near the modern water tower, required a ninety-degree turn to enter.

The third element that shaped the traditional Islamic city was neglect. By failing to concern itself with matters of day-to-day maintenance, especially in the area of private space, the government relegated those tasks, by default, to other functional units, such as the neighborhood. In other words, since public functionaries like marketplace supervisors were concerned with public spaces, private spaces acquired a large measure of autonomy within the city.[26] As noted in chapter 4, Ibn Abdun's manual for marketplace supervision makes each household responsible for the upkeep of the street outside its door. That practice survived as a custom in the *qsur* of southern Morocco at least through the late eighteenth century, a custom handed down from generation to generation by word of mouth.

Abdulaziz Touri and Mohammed Hammam have found a nine-line text that documents this practice. It says that the council (*jamaʿa*) of the Qsar Tiriqiwt on the Dades River decrees that each individual is responsible for the maintenance of the wall in front of his house, specifically "against water

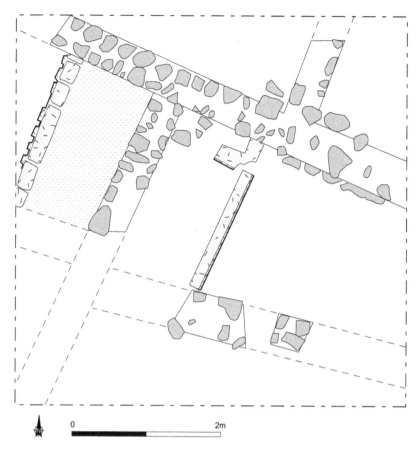

0   2m

Figure 7.3. Plan of trench 55: portion of an elite residence, now under the Rissani bus station.

damage and other destructive factors."[27] Water damage occurred primarily from flooding, a fairly regular occurrence along the banks of the rivers on the edge of the Sahara—so common, in fact, that medieval chroniclers did not record it, except for Ibn Abi Zar, who describes one such flood in Sijilmasa: "A torrential downpour, like one never seen before, came all of a sudden to fill the river Sijilmasa, to the great surprise of the inhabitants who had not seen a single drop of water all that year."[28] In October 1994, MAPS witnessed a flood that might well have exceeded the one described by Ibn Abi Zar. It rained for five consecutive days in early October. The waters of the Oued Ziz swelled and overflowed their banks. The bridge that crosses the river was more than a meter and a half underwater. Schoolchildren in Rissani were let out of school because the school building is located across the river from the town. Residents cleaned up mud for several days. Presumably, Sijilmasa city residents were responsible for repairing any flood damage to the city walls that passed in front of their houses.

The availability of free water, it can be argued, was considered an Islamic right. The Quran states: "We (God) have distributed the water amongst them, in order that they may celebrate our praises." (25:50). Many hadith reinforce this idea. In her chapter "The Water Supply of Tinnis," Alison L. Gascoigne defines three legal statuses of water: freeflowing water, which is essentially ownerless; water that is the subject of a usufruct, that is, obtainable by holders according to certain specified criteria; and water that is the property of a possessor, that is, placed in a canal, irrigation channel, or container.[29] We have seen that water management was an important feature of life in Sijilmasa from the beginning of its existence. The city's earliest rulers undertook the construction of water-delivery systems.[30] Oral interviews conducted by our geographers confirm that over time, an elaborate tradition developed to apportion the water supply among the oasis's inhabitants. In recent times, with the construction of the Hassan ad-Dakhil dam at Errachidia, the traditional water-distribution schedules were threatened and people were extremely anxious about what they called "government water." Today, much of that anxiety has subsided; people have become adjusted to "government water."

All along the way, bearing in mind the characteristics of the Islamic city model, that is, those distinctively Islamic characteristics shared by other Islamic cities, has been a useful guide. Let us briefly review some of those highlights. Dale Eickelman's description of four discernible patterns of spatial order in precolonial Middle Eastern cities has helped us delineate those same patterns in Sijilmasa: the citadel on the northern edge of the site; the mosque-madrasa complex in the center; an elite residence immediately to the west of the mosque, a residential quarter farther to the northwest, and a very large residential quarter in the southwestern part of the site; a small enclosed market area near the town center and a very large market and caravan staging area (Suq Ben Akla) outside town to the west. We see physical evidence of the Islamic practice of locating cemeteries on the edge of cities—on the southwestern edge of Sijilmasa and on the northern edge of Suq Ben Akla. In this way, cemeteries turn out to be helpful in determining city limits. The ceramics kilns of Bhayr al-Ansar testify to the Islamic practice of pushing the "foul" trades to the outskirts of town. The physical relationship between what we think has survived of the earliest mosque of Sijilmasa and what we think is the earliest *dar al-imara* conforms to what we see in other cities built as Islamic cities in the Middle East (Kufa and Basra), which was the key to

our finding the few vestiges of that original mosque. The erroneous orientation of the Sijilmasa mosque, which was consistent with the orientation of
most early mosques in Morocco, confirmed for us the identity of the mosque.
The precedent of the change in orientation by the Almohads in the Kutubiya
mosque that we see replicated in Sijilmasa was invaluable for understanding
the stratigraphy in the mosque itself and then in the rest of the site.

MAPS has learned much about Sijilmasa's past, from its founding to its
role in the medieval empires of the Almoravid and Almohad periods. We
have revised earlier conclusions on the demise of the caravan capital city in
the age of Merinid political dissolution and its recrudescence in the Filalian
and Alaouite periods. While all the trenches we have dug at Sijilmasa have
provided rich information about the ancient city, some have proved more in-
formative than others: an industrial site, likely the ore washery for one of the
most productive mints in western Islam; an elite residence decorated with
prototypical art of the Bani Midrar and a stunning pre-Almoravid (dated to
1025–1050) vase; the likely housing for a noria (waterwheel) along the bank of
the Oued Ziz; fragments of the western wall—the western limit of the cityscape; pottery from the Middle Niger and glass from Egypt; an enigmatic
emplacement west of the mosque that may have been a place for public ablutions and a public latrine; and above all, the mosque in the central site, whose
history and presence in the landscape of the site is the one known place and
function extending from the Sijilmasa past to the Moroccan present.

As we engaged the ghosts of Sijilmasa past, we saw how their Sijilmasa
changed from the pre-Islamic seasonal settlement to the first Midrarid city,
from the much larger but relatively austere city of the Almoravids and Almohads to the more lavish city of the Merinids, from the salutary neglect of
the Wattasids and Saadians to the renewal and eastward movement under
the current ruling dynasty, the Alaouites. From Sijilmasa past to Sijilmasa
present, Sijilmasa is process rather than product, ever changing. To know
Sijilmasa is to know them all.

CHAPTER 8

An Altered Present; An Uncertain Future

A week together in the Tafilalt in October 2011 allowed us, Ron Messier and James Miller, to see a great deal of change. We visited Rissani, renewing old friendships and spending several days at the site and at the Centre d'Études et de Recherches Alaouites (CERA). That visit was prompted by the fact that the storage shed at the center had lost its roof in rains several years before, and much of the carefully marked ceramic collection of the project's six seasons had been covered—rather fortunately, as it turned out—by the caved-in roof. We needed to excavate the materials, sort them out, and rebag them. Our trip to Rissani had been prompted also by the presence of our new friend Chloé Capel, a colleague and PhD student from the Sorbonne who, through a long line of archaeological connections, had found Sijilmasa and our work there and then used them as a basis for her own studies—and had consequently become part of the long chain of scholarly connections that the Sijilmasa project has grown into over the years.

We worked together at the center for several days, doing archaeology of the archaeology, digging out the now-tattered plastic bags from 1992, 1993, 1994, and a few from 1988. The objects of the 1996 and 1998 seasons had been reported as missing, but as it turned out, we found them in the storeroom that had been assigned to us during those last two seasons. No one had seen them since we had left in 1998, when we locked the door and turned the key over to the director of CERA. No one had opened it since. In fact, the key had been lost with the change of administration at the center. We had to remove the hinges of the door to regain access to our storeroom.

The most important objects had not been put in storage. In 1999, we boxed them up and brought them to the United States for a special exhibition in three U.S. cities. When they returned home to CERA, they were displayed in the center's museum. To see them again was like greeting old friends: the carved stucco from the various levels of occupation of the mosque, the large jar "refrigerator" from the southern residential area, the wood veneer painted in prototypical Bani Midrar style, the Quranic inscription that echoed the theological orientation of the Kharijite founders of the city. Notably missing was the beautiful vase with the *al-baraka* inscription retrieved from the very first trench we dug, which is now in the National Museum of Archaeology in Rabat. We also did not see the gold filigree ring that we retrieved from one of the elite residences west of the mosque, ironically, the only gold that we excavated in the City of Gold; it too was on loan to another museum.

Much of the gold from Sijilmasa's heyday had been struck into coins that were now dispersed in collections around the world. For example, we borrowed some dinars for our traveling exhibition from the American Numismatic Society in New York. This in itself is a clear reminder of the role that Sijilmasa played in distributing the gold of West Africa to other parts of the Islamic world in Andalusia and in the Mashriq (eastern Islamic world), and even beyond to the Christian kingdoms in northern Spain in the form of tribute (*parias*) and then on to other parts of Europe. This interesting sidebar led us to think that the gold of Sijilmasa might have contributed to Europe's seemingly insatiable taste for gold and to such global events as the Crusades.

When we worked at the dig, each year we kept a list of the obvious things that we thought would make our task, which seemed daunting at times, a little easier. We called it our "letter to the king." Of course we never sent it, but it was a way of laying out our frustrations and making light of them. But some matters were of high importance to us, and they never got done. Nor have they since. At the top of the list is protection of the site.

Whether it comes down to trained personnel or money or both, it remains a mere idea—an idea that may have been sold down the river by virtue of the fact that the site was afforded a modicum of protection after our 1988 season: a masonry wall along the north side of the tarmac road leading into Rissani. That was seen as a sufficient solution. The Ministry of Culture, with the help of the administration of CERA and MAPS, in 1994 drew up a petition to identify the entire Sijilmasa site as a national historic site. MAPS provided detailed data indicating that medieval Sijilmasa extended as far south as Qsar Qusaibah. The goal of getting Sijilmasa designated a national historic site has yet to be achieved, caught in bureaucratic limbo, having bounced around desks in the Ministry of Culture, Ministry of the Interior, and Ministry of Agriculture in Rabat for more than a decade. The issue illustrates the difficulty of classifying a site in Morocco, even one of such overwhelming importance as

Sijilmasa. Part of the problem may well be that Sijilmasa is different; it is an archaeological site, mostly still underground. Unlike Volubilis, it has no obvious monumental structures on its surface other than the mosque.

As we have seen, erecting a wall along the modern road created the sense among local officials that the road was the limit of the medieval city site, and they have allowed the area south of the road to become urbanized. In early May 1998, the MAPS team discovered a different world of intense activity at the site of the ancient caravan city. All along the southern sector, south of the tarmac road, men and machines were moving earth, striking deep blows into the ancient urban fabric, over a site several hundred meters long in every direction. Foundation trenches three meters deep had been laid, lattice-like, into and through the fiber of medieval Sijilmasa, iron rebar had been laid down, and concrete was pouring in. Dozens of laborers were working extra hours to get their task done in a tableau of dust, payloaders, and dump trucks. As current construction science came to the Tafilalt in a gust of modernization emblematic of Casablanca or the building of dams elsewhere in Morocco, Sijilmasa died a new death under the echoing sounds of screeching wheels and determined foremen. Nothing much, in the context of modern Morocco: a bus station was being built. The die had been cast, the decision made: Rissani needed to take its bus station out of the central part of the town and put it alongside the road at the entrance to the city—a provincial bus station in a country that rides and needs the bus. *Ma kain mushkil,* "no problem," one might say; every Moroccan town needs a new and better bus station, and Rissani had none, only parking for buses in town and in front of the old *qsar* of Abu Am, which is the heart of Rissani. The irony of the "improvement" is that once the bus station opened, Rissani's residents objected to having to go to the edge of town to take the bus and to being dropped off so far from the city's center. Now, the buses make a loop through the center of town, where the journey used to end; then they return to park at the bus station.

But there was a problem, of course: this bus station was being built within the archaeological ruins of Sijilmasa, which was apparent with every scoop of a backhoe shovel and every loading of a dump truck. Not only had the plan for identifying the site as a national historic monument gone nowhere, big powers and deep pockets were at work. Proponents of the bus station cried, "But the Americans have only dug on the north side of the road [which was true], and everyone knows that Sijilmasa was only on the north side of the road!" Things came to a head in our first days at the site, and within a week the team had secured the right to open two salvage trenches at the bus station site within the labyrinth of foundation trenches. Those foundation trenches were three meters deep, we quickly learned, because the underlying ground

Figure 8.1. Construction of the new Rissani bus station south of the tarmac road, 1998.

was unstable because of the mass of Sijilmasa-era strata. The construction workers had to reach pre-Sijilmasa virgin earth, and so did we—quickly! Day after day we hauled luxuryware and elaborately carved stucco back to the lab at CERA. But then it all came to an end. On the last day of our excavating season, as we stepped out of the trench, drawings in hand, the construction company foreman asked, "*Fini?*" Yes, *fini*. The cement was poured and the superstructure of the bus station grew in the same site. Today, the same area has seen continuous growth, and a new housing development has emerged on the back side of Qsar Abu Am on the way into Rissani—all archaeological ground, all Sijilmasa.

On our October 2011 sojourn in Rissani, walks around the site, the Sijilmasa core, made us nostalgic for our work of the 1980s and 1990s. In large part, the trenches we dug then are much as we left them—filled in by us; worn by sand, wind, and rain. The town slaughterhouse, long our bane because of its stink, had been abandoned and replaced by a new one a bit farther south along the river. The Jewish cemetery, now completely walled off and protected within the Sijilmasa site, a place visited each year by the Jews who once inhabited the *mellah*, provided another touchstone to the south—although the size of it, spatially separated and set in relief by its wall, was at first a bit jarring to our vision of things as they had been.

The very central part of the site looked much as we remembered it, the area of the surface mosque and madrasa. Within the remains of the walls, we recognized the polygonal depression indicating where we had dug, allowing us to reconstruct the phases of occupation: the original elite residence (*dar al-imara*); the new mosque of Ibn Abd Allah, just to the south of the original mosque (contemporary with the Almoravids, late eleventh to mid-twelfth century); the expansion of the latter by the Almohads; the restoration by the Filalians in the mid-fifteenth century; and the renovation by Sidi Mohammed Ibn Abdallah in the late eighteenth century. Within the madrasa, we recalled seeing the two circular stone column bases, now reburied, of the first Sijilmasa mosque, which we excavated in the 1998 season.

Approaching the western edge of the site, I (Jim) turned to Ron and exclaimed, "I don't know where I am now." I had the sensation of falling, of being suddenly out of a place I knew well and in a different, altered space. "There's something missing here," I (Ron) noted, equally disoriented. Then we realized where we were. We gazed at the space before us, thinking it was where our wonderful colleague Nancy Benco had excavated her trench in 1993, a hole that proved largely bereft of information, right down to a hard surface. No information in this sense meant the absence of structures down through about 1.5 meters of sand and windblown sediment that, since urban abandonment, had sailed over the western wall of Sijilmasa and filled in the large open market space. The fact that there were no structures and very little pottery or other cultural debris in this trench allowed us to conclude that it was the site of the Sijilmasa market in Almoravid-Almohad and perhaps Merinid times (as opposed to our emerging picture of the transregional market outside the city and across the Oued Gheris at Suq Ben Akla). And what was left was a large, deep mass, largely of sand, that had filled in an area of some 500 square meters (5,380 square feet) sloping up to the top of the western wall, much like snow that had reached the top of a snow fence—such is the nature of sand in the desert.

We suddenly knew what had happened, and it was striking, even thunderstriking: the mining of the site for building material, particularly sand. We plunged forward and down in amazement to find ourselves on the surface of the medieval market. Payloaders and bulldozers had done what archaeologists could not do, namely, remove truckload after truckload of building material— sand infill on the Sijilmasa site—and carry it away. And therein lies a curious story, one that focuses on the nature of the Sijilmasa site, the problems of archaeological method, and the dreams and vexations of those who work in such places. What was left astonished us: nothing! Nothing, that is, except the interior surface of the old city wall itself, protected from the equipment by its strong construction, enclosing an empty Sijilmasa nearly a thousand years

Figure 8.2. Alaouite wall exposed by mining for building material.

later. An easy source of supplies, an unguarded site—perhaps not even a site in the eyes of those who took the sand away. Such is the nature of the site today.

Trash, a reflection of the ever-growing economy of Morocco, is ever-more a problem—not so much domestic garbage as random dumps of refuse from building sites, material dropped off in the middle of the night when no one is watching. Domestic refuse, which has grown commensurately with the rise in the standard of living, is collected and dumped elsewhere. Walking the site of Suq Ben Akla, five kilometers to the west of central Sijilmasa, we saw where the trash goes. Sometime between 1999 and 2011, the site had received Rissani's domestic trash, which was sifted by the harsh weather of the pre-Sahara. Dumping there has ceased, but most of what we knew as pristine ground just a dozen years ago—where the surface itself revealed many elements offering clues to the likelihood of the area's past use—is gone. Archaeology could still reveal what lies underneath, but the surface is a cluttered and despoiled mess.

Equally disturbing was our visit to Round Mountain, Jebel Mudawwar, 15 kilometers (9.3 miles) west of Rissani. The stone fortress on this site, such a fresh and startling discovery for us in the early 1990s, has undergone a series of negative transformations. The negative changes were brought about by the sheer thoughtlessness of modern tourism. In the late 1990s, Hollywood found Round Mountain while scouting locations for the filming of *The Mummy*

(1999). The film crew believed they had found a dormant volcano (they hadn't; Jebel Mudawwar is a round mesa) where the set for "Hamunaptra," the film's mythical ancient Egyptian city of the dead, could be located. When the film was finished, Round Mountain was left littered with styrene building material just inside the Almoravid wall encircling the fort, at the bottom of the appropriately fantastic site, and a new breach in the Almoravid wall had been made at the base of the mountain to facilitate production inside the wall. A year later, it was rewarding to see that the plastic had been picked up and the mountain's environmental integrity restored.

But the passage into Round Mountain had been enlarged, allowing vehicles to enter, and therein lay trouble for the future. Today, a dirt track carved out of Round Mountain leads directly up its interior slope. A travel agency in Erfoud removed the ruins of a medieval encampment to provide for a parking turnaround at the "bivouac" (overnight camp) it has built on the northern rim of the mountain. Most detrimentally, however, is the regular wave of tourists on motorbikes who ride up the mountain's base and attempt to roar up the sandy slopes just inside the wall—coming down is, apparently, a thrill. The constant parade of bikers, sometimes fifty to sixty a day, is having a steady depredatory effect on the mountain's environment.

But there is good news. We know much more about Round Mountain. There have been many new discoveries, and the history of the place is being revealed by our young French colleague Chloé Capel. She has determined that ceramics retrieved so far date almost exclusively to the twelfth century, meaning that what remains of the medieval occupation dates to the second half of the Almoravid period. Jebel Mudawwar may well have been the stone fortress to which Ibn al-Fath retreated when the Fatimids laid siege to Sijilmasa in the mid-tenth century, but it was taken over and refortified by the Almoravids. She has managed to discern and draw the plans of several complete houses within the compound, making it possible to say much more about house plans during that era than is possible from the central Sijilmasa site.

There is more. In 2010, we began to hear murmurs of a new project to excavate Sijilmasa. A French team wanted to dig. The Americans hadn't written anything; their results had not been published; Sijilmasa is too important to be left unexcavated. While the accusations about our not publishing were not true—see the bibliography—the French team sought to redo Sijilmasa in their own way. They presented a large, comprehensive plan to the Moroccan authorities and a year later received authorization to dig at the site. In 2011, just before our visit, they had organized an exploratory survey and dug a small trench outside the western wall where we had observed the mining of sand. More puzzlingly, a year later, I (Ron) made a one-day visit to the site and saw that the French team had spent a few weeks reexcavating a series of trenches, trenches 25, 26, 32, and 42, which covered portions of the bath west of the Grand Mosque.

Suffice it to say, the French team is right—Sijilmasa is too important to be left alone. It needs protection, more than ever, and that may be on its way. A recent visit with the *directeur du patrimoine* revealed that the Ministry of Culture has placed renewed importance on classifying at least the center of the central site, the area around the mosque-madrasa complex, as a national historic site. We are prepared to submit our plan to create an interpretation center in exactly that part of the site. There are a number of possibilities, ranging from a complete reconstruction of the mosque-madrasa in its final occupation phase to a more modest and less costly reconstruction of the floor and pillars, a re-creation of the floor plan of that structure.

Those few days in October 2011 were crowded with numerous trips back and forth to the Rissani market for supplies, seeing old friends, and getting a grip on ten years of change in the region. Fall is the season when dates are harvested, and the 2011 harvest was much better than average. A useful coincidence for us, since we were able to replace the torn plastic bags that stored our ceramics with cardboard boxes used to package dates, boxes available in a variety of sizes and limitless quantities. The market was buzzing with activity. People were happy and had a sense of at least a slight surge of prosperity. In this setting once again, it was not such a stretch to let our minds wander back to a time when just a kilometer or so away was the most vibrant international market on the northwestern edge of the Sahara. Merchants came from far and wide back then. Some guidebooks to Morocco tout the Rissani market today as the last authentic Berber market in the country. That might be right. It attracts tourists, but it is not a market for tourists. It is, although on a smaller scale than in its medieval past, the most important regional market for today's Filalians.

What we learned from our fieldwork during the last decades of the twentieth century, overlaid on our reading of the medieval texts, was validated by our October 2011 visit to the Tafilalt. The Sijilmasa we have described here is a complex, polymorphic place. Its location alone presents a paradox: it was strategically located to be distant and separate from other places and yet be part of trade networks connecting many places. But we are not the first to make this observation. Walter B. Harris lived long enough, and lived long enough in Morocco as the *Times* correspondent in Tangier, to make his own assessment of change, in *The Morocco That Was* (1928). The book's title in its French translation, *Le Maroc Disparu* (1929), is perhaps more evocative of a society being transformed and refashioned by the rapid onslaught of French

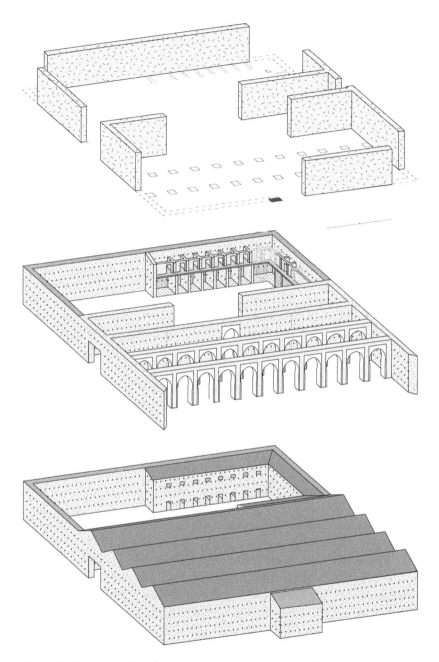

Figure 8.3. Architectural rendition of the restored mosque in its final phase of occupation.

(and Spanish) colonialism in the form of the protectorate that ruled over it from 1912 to 1956. While those changes affected all of Morocco, cumulative change was slow to come to the country's desert regions. In Harris's day, the age of Sultan Moulay Hassan, Sijilmasa was a memory, its urban functions as a center of world trade reduced to the local. The Tafilalt, enshrined as the city of Sijilmasa, with its broad sphere of influence in medieval times, had become a mere center for the regional production of dates and henna, its trade almost entirely redirected to the north, the Moroccan domain of the western Maghrib. There were caravans—Harris encountered them frequently—but they were not carrying the wealth of Africa north anymore. Boundaries had been drawn; French Algeria had been formed; Morocco loomed as a curious and endangered independent state of which the outside world knew little. The outside world was, however, knocking on Morocco's door, and the Morocco that Harris knew had little time left. But what is significant in his portrait of the Tafilalt, including his description of the Sijilmasa site, is that he left a record of elements that we were able to piece together in the 1980s and 1990s. These things had been prominent just a few generations ago, and many essential features of them remained in the landscape and in the memories of those still alive. Today, those elements have become far more distant, fragmentary, and lost forever as the twenty-first century continues the inexorable path of change—a progressive and accumulating decline of the Tafilalt environment, we now realize, that has been going on since the 1970s.

At Sijilmasa, we probed a place that was pivotal to Morocco's role in the world for over a thousand years. It was a place that gave rise to legends of gold. But more than that, it was, and is, a real place. Today, Sijilmasa can play a role anew. It is the same as the purpose of our work in archaeology, history, and geography at the site and in the Tafilalt, which is to bring the world's attention to the power of the "last civilized place."

Moroccan Dynastic Rulers Governing Sijilmasa

The date after a ruler's name is the year he came to power (Gregorian calendar).

Bani Midrar, 758–963[1]

Abu al-Qasim Samgu Ibn Wasul al-Miknasi, 758
Abu al-Yas'a al-Wazir, 784
Abu Muntasir al-Yas'a Ibn al-Qasim, 790
Midrar Ibn al-Yas'a
Ibn al-Qasim, 823/4
Ibn Baqia, 867
Mohammed Ibn Maymun Ibn Baqia, 877
Al-Yas'a al-Munasir, 877

Fatimid Interlude with Midrarid governors, 909–963

Maymun (al-Baqia) Ibn Midrar, 909
Ahmed Ibn Maymun, 913
Al-Mu'tizz Ibn Mohammed Ibn Saru Ibn Maymun Ibn Midrar, 921
Mohammed al-Mu'tizz, 933
Mohammed Ibn al-Fath Ibn Maymun (al-Baqia) Ibn Midrar, 943; rebelled against the Fatimids, ruled independently
Mohammed Ibn al-Mu'tizz, 958
Abu Mohammed Abdallah Ibn Mohammed Ibn al-Mu'tizz Ibn Saru Ibn Maymun Ibn Midrar, 963

Bani Maghrawa, 976/7–l055/6

Khazrun Ibn Falfal al-Maghrawi, 976/7, as a client of the Umayyads of Cordoba

Bani Khazrun, independent after the fall of the Umayyads in 1031

Mas'ud Ibn Wanudin, last Maghrawa ruler of Sijilmasa, killed by the Almoravids in 1055/6

Almoravids, l055/6–ll46/7

Yahya Ibn Umar, 1055/6

Abu Bakr Ibn Umar, 1056

Yusuf Ibn Tashfin, 1071

Ali Ibn Yusuf, 1106

Tashfin Ibn Ali, 1142

Ishaq Ibn Ali, 1146

Almohads, ll30–l242/3

Abd al-Mu'min, 1148 (Almohad control of Sijilmasa begins)

Abu Ya'qub Yusuf, 1163

Abu Yusuf Ya'qub al-Mansur, 1184

Mohammed al-Nasr, 1199

Abu Ya'qub Yussuf al-Mustansir, 1214

Abd al-Wahid, 1223

Abdallah al-Adil, 1224

Yahya al-Mutasim, 1227

Idris Abu Ula al-Ma'mun, 1229

Abd al-Wahid al-Rashid, 1232

Ali al-Said Abu al-Hassan, 1242 (loses control of Sijilmasa in 1242/3)

Merinids, l2l6–l47l

Abu Yahya Ibn Abd al-Haqq, 1255/6 (takes control of Sijilmasa)

Abu Yusuf Ya'qub al-Mansur, 1258

Abu Ya'qub Nasr al-Din Allah, 1286

Abu Thabit, 1307

Abu al-Rabia Suleiman, 1308

Abu Sayid Uthman, 1310

Abu al-Hassan Ibn Uthman, 1331

Abu Inan Faris, 1348

Mohammed al-Sayid, 1358

Abu Salim Ibrahim, 1359

Abu Umar Tashfin, 1360

Abu Zayyan Mohammed, 1362

Abu al-Fariz Abd al-Aziz, 1366

Abu al-Abbas al-Ahmed, 1372

Musa Ibn Faris, 1384

Al-Muntasir, 1385

Mohammed al-Wathiq, 1386

Abu al-Abbas, 1387 (Merinids lose control of Sijilmasa at Abu al-Abbas's death in 1393)

Wattasids, 1472–1549

Sijilmasa enjoyed a period of salutary neglect by the Wattasids, and thus local government developed in separate *qsur* in the Tafilalt oasis. The Wattasids conducted four expeditions in an attempt to exercise some control: in 1524, in 1526, and twice in 1536.

Saadians, 1510–1659

Ahmed al-Araj, 1518 (takes control of Sijilmasa in 1537)

Mohammed al-Shaykh, 1544 (control of Sijilmasa alternates between the two brothers, Ahmed and Mohammed, between 1544 and 1557)

Abdallah al-Ghalib, 1557

Abu Abdallah Mohammed, 1575

Abd al-Malik al-Mu'tasim, 1576

Ahmed al-Mansur, 1578

Succession War, 1603–1627

Marrakech capital	Fez capital
Abu Faris Abdallah, 1603	Mohammed al-Shaykh al-Ma'mun, 1603
Zidan al-Nasir, 1608	Abdallah, 1613
	Abd al-Malik, 1623

Reunified Rule, 1627–1659

Abu Marwan Abd al-Malik, 1628

Al-Walid Ibn Zidan, 1631

Mohammed al-Shaykh al-Asghar, 1636

Ahmed al-Abbas, 1655

Alaouites, 1631–present

Alaouites arrived in the Tafilalt from the Hijaz at the end of the thirteenth century, when Hassan al-Dakhil came to the Tafilalt to serve as imam. The spelling of Alaouite rulers' names is given as usually found in Morocco today, for example, "Muhammed" is usually spelled "Mohammed."

Moulay Ali Cherif (Moulay Ali Sharif), 1631

Mohammed Ibn Sharif, 1636

Moulay al-Rashid, 1664

Moulay Ismail, 1672

Abu al-Abbas Ahmed, 1727 (first time)

Abd al-Malik, 1728

Abu al-Abbas Ahmed, 1728 (second time)

Abdallah, 1729 (first time)

Ali, 1734

Abdallah, 1736 (second time)

Mohammed II, 1736

Al-Mustadi, 1738 (first time)

Abdallah, 1740 (third time)

Zin al-Abidin, 1741

Abdallah, 1741 (fourth time)

Al-Mustadi, 1742 (second time)

Abdallah, 1743 (fifth time)

Al-Mustadi, 1747 (third time)

Abdallah, 1748 (sixth time)

Sidi Mohammed Ibn Abdallah (Mohammed III), 1757

Yazid, 1790

Suleiman, 1792

Abd al-Rahman, 1822

Mohammed IV, 1859

Hassan I, 1873

Abd al-Aziz, 1894
Abd al-Hafid, 1908
Yussef, 1912
Mohammed V, 1927 (first time)
Mohammed Ibn Aarafa, 1953
Mohammed V, 1956 (second time)
Hassan II, 1961
Mohammed VI, 1999

Ceramics Typology

This ceramics typology evolved through a number of stages of development. Initially, Lahcen Taouchikht divided the ceramics into four categories that were predominantly time-sensitive:[1]

1. Sijilmasa pottery: eleventh through fourteenth centuries; characterized by mostly cream-colored pastes and typical forms (bowls, plates, jugs, bottles, lamps, and cups); very thin and of very fine texture.
2. Filalian pottery: fifteenth through seventeenth centuries; similar to the first group, that is, cream-colored paste and small utilitarian forms; generally thicker than Sijilmasa pottery.
3. Bhayr pottery: eighteenth and nineteenth centuries; so called because of its place of production, Qsar Bhayr al-Ansar; forms the same as those in the first two categories; thicker and heavier than the first two categories; often covered with a monochrome glaze of green, yellow, or brown.
4. Crude pottery: from prehistory through the three historic periods above; derives from prehistoric Berber pottery identified at a site approximately six kilometers east of Sijilmasa in the mountainous massif Rich Dar al-Bida; characterized by a crude texture with inclusions of small black stones; ranges in thickness from ten to twenty-four millimeters; large utilitarian wares (jars, basins, cooking vessels, braziers); often with a red or white slip.

In 1993, Nancy Benco developed a new typology in conjunction with stratigraphic information that is consistent with a typology developed at two other Islamic sites in Morocco (Qsar es-Seghir and al-Basra).[2] Her approach distinguishes types according to form, decoration, and wares. A database of 15,400 diagnostic sherds was organized according to the following typology.

Vessel forms are organized first into general functional categories, for example, cooking vessels, jars, bowls, plates, lamps, lids, bases, handles, spouts, and strainers. Cooking vessels are made of coarse paste and have evidence of sooting on surfaces. Jars are closed, or restricted, forms, that is, those with rim diameters that are the same size as or smaller than the vessel's neck or body. Large heavy forms are those with thick vessel walls (c. 10 cm) or large rim diameters (less than 25 cm); they may be open or closed forms.

Within each functional category is a variety of forms. These forms are defined by the shape and size of the rim, neck, body, base, or handle. In some cases, vessel forms are also defined by paste composition and surface treatment if these appear to be commonly associated with the form.

Forms 10–19: Cooking Vessels (*marmites*)

10. Cooking vessel with a round lip, curved inward; no neck; body with rounded shape. Small horizontal or vertical handle sometimes present below the rim. Sooting sometimes on the lower part of the vessel. Coarse ware.

11. Cooking vessel with a round lip, curved inward; no neck; inverted pear-shaped body. Sooting sometimes on the lower part of the vessel. Coarse ware.

12. . . .[3]

13. Cooking vessel with a round lip; short vertical neck; round shoulder and round body; small vertical handle sometimes below the rim. Usually coarse ware.

14. Shallow cooking vessel, c. 7 cm high, with a round or slightly flattened slip; slightly rounded body turned inward toward the base. Impressed appliqué strip sometimes below the rim. Coarse ware.

15. Deep cooking vessel with a flattened rim; slightly out-turned body. Possible sooting on the lower part of the vessel. Coarse ware.

16. Shallow or deep cooking vessel—cannot tell.

17. Shallow cooking vessel with a flat rim; short vertical neck; shoulder extends outward. Soot sometimes present.

18. Cooking vessel with a round lip and vertical neck; impressed strips below rim.

19. Cooking vessel with a round lip flaring outward and an outward-curving body. Handle or impressed strip sometimes below rim.

20–29: Large Heavy Forms (may include basins, jars, etc.)

20. Heavy vessel (basin?) with a thick beveled lip, beveled toward exterior; neck sloping inward. Very coarse.

21. Heavy jar with a beveled lip, beveled toward exterior; sometimes grooved below lip on exterior surface. Neck nearly vertical, but turning outward slightly. Body curving outward. Very coarse.

22. Heavy jar with a triangular lip and inward-sloping neck. Very coarse.

23. Jar with a flat lip, grooved band rim, vertical neck; impressed or incised strip sometimes below rim. Coarse to very coarse.

24. Jar with a triangular lip, thick groove below lip, relatively high vertical neck. Coarse to very coarse ware.

25. Heavy open form with a round lip; impressed strip(s) sometimes below rim. Sooting possible.

26. Heavy jar with an out-flared rim; neck nearly vertical.

27. Heavy jar with a flattened rim and a neck turning gradually outward. Large rim diameter. Coarse ware.

28. Heavy jar form with a round rim, vertical neck, straight-sloping shoulder; impressed strip sometimes attached below rim.

30–59: Jars (*jarres*)

30. Jar with a triangular lip, inward-curving vertical neck, slightly rounded shoulder. Rim sometimes slightly grooved. Creamware.

31. Jar with a band rim, vertical neck, sharply out-turned shoulder. Band rim high or low (note height). Usually creamware.

32. Jar with a beveled lip, beveled toward the interior; inward-sloping neck. Filter sometimes at bottom of neck. Shoulder usually rounded. Creamware.

33. Jar with a beveled lip, beveled toward interior; vertical neck; very thin walls. Overall small dimensions. Usually creamware.

34. Jar with a triangular lip and high, narrow, nearly vertical neck; very thin walls. Overall small dimensions. Usually creamware.

35. Jar with a triangular lip and high, narrow neck. Possibly high-necked liquid storage jar. Usually creamware.

36. Jar with a double-grooved rim. Lip rounded; two deep grooves below lip made by pressing a finger into the clay. Relatively narrow neck, sometimes vertical or turned outward into shoulder and body. Possibly high-necked liquid storage jar. Usually creamware.

37. Jar with a round rim and straight, vertical neck. Rim often with incised line below lip. Neck of varying height—short or tall. Shoulder extending outward from neck. Base unknown. Creamware. Strap handle sometimes connecting neck and shoulder.

38. Jar with a round rim and a neck ribbed below the lip. Neck generally vertical. Shoulder extending outward from neck. Usually creamware.

39. Jar with a round or slightly beveled rim. Creamware. Indeterminate form (form 32, 33, 37, or 38).

40. Jar with a round, out-flared rim, short vertical or slightly curved neck, shoulder extending outward from the neck. Body unknown. Creamware. Sometimes glazed.

41. Jar with a round lip and a relatively vertical neck. Rounded shoulder turning outward. Coarse ware. Previous types 40 and 41, formerly distinguished by wall thickness and neck height, now here; all three similar in rim and neck form.

42. Jar with a thin round lip; neck vertical but rounded; shoulder and body unknown. Usually coarse ware.

43. Jar with a round rim and a slightly incurved neck; rounded body sloping gently outward. Usually coarse ware. Possibly a cooking vessel.

44. Jar with a round rim and an outward-sloping neck. Creamware or coarse ware.

45. Jar with a flat rim and a high, relatively narrow, vertical neck, sometimes ridged; large strap handle sometimes attached to ridge below rim. Coarse ware.

46. Jar with a beveled lip, beveled outward, and a high, narrow, vertical neck, often ridged; large strap handle sometimes attached to the ridge below the rim. Coarse ware.

47. Jar with a round lip and a relatively narrow vertical neck. Coarse ware.

48. Jar with a round rim and thickening below the rim. Vertical neck. Shoulder and body unknown. Possibly similar to 41.

49. Jar with a round rim. Coarse ware. Indeterminate form.

50. Jar with a rounded, outward-flaring rim. Neck curving inward and then outward toward the body. Creamware to coarse ware. Highly variable.

51. Jar with a flat rim and a nearly vertical neck. Possibly an open form. Coarse ware.

52. Jar with a beveled lip, beveled toward the interior. No neck. Shoulder usually ribbed and nearly vertical or turning slightly outward. Body unknown.

53. Jar with a triangular lip and an incurved neck. Shoulder sloping outward. Possibly a cooking vessel.

54. Small jar with a round lip, very short neck, and sharply carinated shoulder. Creamware. Sometimes glazed.

55. Small jar with a beveled lip, beveled toward the interior; nearly vertical neck, rounded shoulder, inverted pear-shaped body. Sometimes with a small strap handle from neck to shoulder. Small ring base. Creamware. Overall small dimensions: rim = 6–7 cm; vase = 3–4 cm.

56. Tall, cylindrical jar with a flat base (form 82), carinated above the base to form an indentation; walls relatively thick and nearly vertical. Rim unknown.

57. Jar with a tall narrow neck and a round lip. Flask-like form.

58. Jar with a high, very narrow neck and a rounded, triangular lip. Possibly a flask or spout.

59. Jar with a flask-like neck (very narrow). Indeterminate form.

60–79: Plates and Bowls (*plats et bols*)

60. Bowl with a triangular lip. Short, nearly vertical neck, sharply carinated shoulder, straight inward-sloping body. Large rim diameter. Usually creamware, often glazed. Possibly a plate form.

61. Bowl with a triangular lip. Short curved neck, round shoulder, straight inward-sloping body. Large rim diameter (greater than 20 cm). Usually creamware, often glazed. Possibly a plate form.

62. Bowl with a rounded lip and a flange below the rim. Flange extends outward c. 1 cm. Inward-sloping body below flange. Usually creamware. Sometimes glazed. Possibly a plate form.

63. Bowl with a flattened lip, sometimes slightly beveled toward exterior; curved inward-sloping body. Walls relatively thick. Usually coarse ware. Often sooted. Probably a cooking vessel.

64. Bowl with a flattened lip; interior surface below lip sometimes grooved slightly; straight inward-sloping body. Usually coarse ware.

65. Small bowl with a beveled or round lip; curved inward-sloping body. Sometimes with combing or incising on handle below the rim. Usually creamware. Possibly a cup form.

66. Bowl with a round lip thickening below the rim on the exterior of the vessel. Straight inward-sloping sides. Cuplike form.

67. Bowl with a round, out-flaring rim. Body shape unknown.

68. Bowl with a simple round lip and a curved, inward-sloping body. Sometimes glazed or with an incised line below the rim. Creamware.

69. Bowl with a beveled lip, beveled toward the interior. Inward-sloping body. Similar to Form 33, but open rather than closed. Creamware.

70–79: Lamps (*lampes*)

70. Lamp? Creamware.

71. Lamp on a high ring base with a square foot. Narrow neck with a hole in the center. Small circular handle attached to the neck and base platform. Sometimes green glazed. Bhayr style.

72. Nosed lamp. Small round cuplike form with a long nose extending from cup.

73. . . .

74. . . .

75. Bowl with a triangular rim and a straight inward-sloping body.

76. . . .

77. . . .

78. Possible cup or lid. Flat lip bulging inward, sometimes with an incised line in a flat rim. Vessel curving inward from the rim.

79. Small cup with a round or beveled lip, a short vertical neck, an inward-sloping body.

80–99: Bases (*fonds*)

80. Flat base, wheel-made. Usually creamware.

81. Flat base, handmade. Usually coarse ware.

82. Flat base for tall cylindrical jar (form 56); carinated, relatively thick walls above base. Ribbed interior. Wheel-made. Creamware.

83. Ring base; ring well defined or poorly defined (smoothed). Usually creamware. Sometimes glazed on the interior.

84. Square ring base. Ring flattened on sides and bottom. Height of base interior less than 2 cm; exterior height shorter. Usually coarse ware.

85. High square ring base. Ring flattened on sides and bottom. Height of base interior greater than 3 cm; exterior height generally shorter. Usually coarse ware.

86. Ring base with walls above base extending sharply outward—nearly horizontally. Body sometimes carinated above base. Possibly belongs to a restricted form.

87. . . . .

88. . . . .

89. . . . .

90. Flanged inset base.

91. Flanged flat base.

92. Inset base. Inset carved into a flat base.

93. Flat base with beveled side, bevel restricted to the area just above the base. Vessel sides constricting slightly above beveled base and then opening up.

94. . . . .

95. Small convex base. Possibly for a noria pot. Relatively thick walls and a steeply sloped body.

96. Coarse low ring base, less than 2 cm high.

97. Coarse high ring base, greater than 2 cm high.

98. Base-like form resembling a pizza pan. Probably lid. Lip round; rim low; floor or base of form thin and flat. Coarse ware.

99. Base. Indeterminate form.

100–109: Handles (*anses*)

100. Small strap handle. Less than 1 cm wide at midsection. Creamware.

101. Medium strap handle. More than 1 cm wide at midsection. Creamware or coarse ware.

102. Grooved strap handles, 2 or 3 grooves along the upper surface of handle. Usually creamware.

103. Twisted strap handle. Clay coil twisted before being attached to the vessel. Creamware.

104. Strap handle with protuberance on the upper surface.

105. Round handle, elongated or circular.

106. Large strap handle, 2–4 cm wide. Usually coarse or very coarse ware.

107. Small horizontal or vertical handle, usually attached below the rim of handmade cooking vessels. Possibly decorative rather than functional because of handle's size.

108. Double-coiled handle. Two coils joined together. Strap handle with elbow. Handle with a sharp right angle. Usually coarse ware.

109. Small strap handle with snail's head appliqué; usually green glazed.

110–119: Lids, Spouts, Strainers (*becs, couvercles, filtres*)

110. Flat base lid with a round rim flaring horizontally outward; small conical handle on top. Lid is c. 10 cm in diameter. Usually creamware.

111. Flat base lid with round rim not flaring outward.

112. Flat rim lid.

113. Lid (?) with round knob on top.

114. Lid with round lip. Shoulder turning downward at 90-degree angle.

115. Lid. Indeterminate form.

116. Spout. Note size of the hole.

117. Strainer. Note the size of the neck, especially the diameter at the strainer.

118. *Meshmar* (brazier used mostly for cooking).

119. *Couscousier* (vessel used for cooking couscous). Piece with holes.

120–149: Glazed Decoration

120. Blue-green glaze, interior.

121. Blue-green glaze, exterior.

122. Blue-green glaze, interior and exterior.

123. Blue-green glaze, interior and exterior, incised below glaze.

124. Blue-green glaze exterior, green glaze interior.

125. Honey-brown glaze, interior.

126. Honey-brown glaze, exterior.

127. Honey-brown glaze, interior and exterior.

128. Blue-green glaze, exterior; honey-brown glaze, interior.

129. Honey-brown glaze, exterior; blue-green glaze, interior.

130. Green glaze, interior.

131. Green glaze, exterior.

132. Green glaze, interior and exterior.

133. Green glaze, exterior; blue-green glaze interior.

134. Green glaze, exterior; honey-brown glaze interior.

135. Black motif under or in tin white glaze, interior.

136. Black motif under or in tin white glaze, exterior.

137. Black motif under or in tin white glaze, interior and exterior.

138. Black motif under blue-green glaze, interior or exterior.

139. . . . .

140. Black glaze and dark paint.

141. Manganese under honey-brown glaze.

142. Incised decoration below glaze (note form number of color).

143. Manganese or green motif under honey-brown glaze, exterior; interior sometimes honey-brown glazed.

144. . . . .

145. Orange glaze.

146. Green motif in or under clear tin white glaze.

147. Yellowish-green glaze.

148. Manganese glaze under yellowish-green glaze.

149. Glazed; colors indeterminate.

150–154: Painted Decoration

150. Black or brown paint.

151. . . . .

152. Red Paint.

153. Black and white paint.

154. Black or white paint on buff (either paint or slip).

155–159: Slipped Decoration

155. Red slip.

156. White or buff slip.

157. . . . .

158. . . . .

159. . . . .

160–164: Incised Decoration

160. Incised.

161. Incised and punctuated.

162. Incised and impressed or carved motif.

163. Glazed above impressed or carved motif.

164. . . .

165–169: Combed Decoration

165. Horizontal bands.

166. Wavy line bands.

167. Horizontal and wavy line bands.

168. . . .

169. Ribbing.

170–174: Impressed Decoration

170. Twine impression.

171. Impression.

172. Rocker stamping (shell edge rocked back and forth on the surface).

173. . . .

174. . . .

175–178: Appliqué Decoration (application of clay to surface)

175. Finger-impressed strip.

176. Tool-impressed strip.

177. Appliqué strip—not impressed.

178. Punctuation (hole punched into the wall with a sharp, pointed tool).

179: Burnishing or Polishing

179. Burnishing.

180–200: Miscellaneous

180. Pottery waster (*rate*).

181. Trivet (*pernette*).

182. Architectural fragment.

183. Unidentifiable piece.

184. Noria vessel fragment—not base, but still diagnostic.

185. Thick clay nail-like object (probably associated with pottery production; possibly a trivet).

186. Disk—small round ceramic piece made from a pottery fragment. Possibly a gaming piece.

Paste Composition

There are several types of basic paste composition at Sijilmasa: creamware, coarse ware, and very coarse ware. The major distinctions between the types are based on paste texture and color as well as the type, size, and quantity of inclusions. There are also several variants within each group.

White creamware

Brown creamware

White coarse ware

Brown coarse ware

Coarse ware

High-calcite coarse ware

Very coarse ware

Creamware

There are four types of creamware: white cream, brown cream, white coarse, and brown coarse. These types are characterized by paste color (in the core of a sherd rather than on its surface), texture, and the presence of relatively small inclusions. White and brown creamwares have a very fine texture. In addition, the paste has a soft, soapy feel to it. It is easily scratched with a fingernail. Inclusions consist primarily of quartz and iron oxide particles; others may be present but are too small to identify with a hand lens (10X magnification). The inclusions are very small (c. 1–2 mm). Because of their small size, it is likely that the inclusions occurred naturally in the clay, and were not added as a tempering material by the potters. White and brown coarse wares are a variation of white and brown creamwares. They have a relatively fine texture, but they contain some larger inclusions (1–4 mm). These inclusions, which consist mostly of quartz, iron oxides, and vegetal material, are scattered throughout the paste. The paste colors are similar to those of the white and brown creamwares.

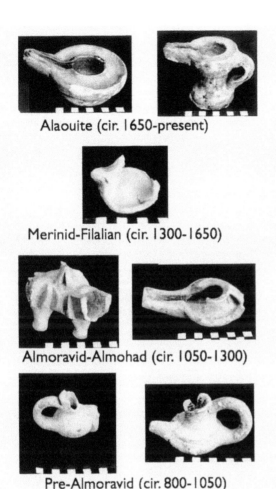

Alaouite (cir. 1650-present)

Merinid-Filalian (cir. 1300-1650)

Almoravid-Almohad (cir. 1050-1300)

Pre-Almoravid (cir. 800-1050)

Figure A2.1.
Time-sensitive
lamp typology.

Coarse Wares

Coarse wares are relatively coarse in texture and have thicker walls than creamwares. They contain two main types of inclusions: calcite and iron oxides, including possibly hematite, limonite, ironstone, and magnetite. The inclusions average about 2–3 mm in size. Their size and angular shape suggest that they were added as a tempering material by the potter. The inclusions constitute an estimated 10–15 percent of the paste. Coarse wares tend to be uniform in color: generally, reddish yellow.

Very Coarse Wares

Very coarse wares have a very coarse texture and very thick walls. Like coarse wares, they contain two main types of inclusions: calcite and iron oxides. The inclusions average about 4 mm in size, but range from 2 to 6 mm. They constitute an estimated 20–30 percent of the paste. This proportion appears to be the main distinction between coarse wares and very coarse wares, since inclusion type and size appear to be similar between these two paste groups. Very coarse wares tend to vary in color: white, pale yellow, reddish, and pink.

Vegetal Inclusions and Calcareous Depositions

Both cream and coarse pastes tend to contain vegetal matter, mostly chaff or straw-like materials that leave elongated voids on surfaces and interiors. There does not seem to be much organic material naturally present in the clay; few low-fired sherds have the gray core characteristic of heavily vegetal paste. In addition, both cream and coarse pastes tend to exhibit some calcareous deposition, which occurs when the pottery is buried for long periods of time in an area with calcareous groundwater. This practice typically occurs in arid or semiarid climates like that in southern Morocco.

Time-Sensitive Typology

Abdallah Fili, using the broad chronological categories of Taouchikht and the form and decoration types introduced to the project by Benco, developed a time-sensitive typology that reflects the four periods providing the chronological framework for the Sijilmasa story:[4]

Pre-Almoravid pottery

Almoravid-Almohad-Merinid pottery

Filalian pottery

Bhayr pottery

Notes

Prologue

1. Ibn Battuta has become perhaps more famous than ever. Enthusiastic and growing interest in this fourteenth-century world traveler has led to the production of a number of works on him over the last twenty-five years, beginning with Ross E. Dunn's *The Adventures of Ibn Battuta: A Muslim Traveler of the Fourteenth Century* and continuing with the works of the English writer Tim Mackintosh-Smith, who has brought Ibn Battuta to life in three books: *Travels with a Tangerine: From Morocco to Turkey in the Footsteps of Islam's Greatest Traveler*, *The Travels of Ibn Battutah*, and *Landfalls: On the Edge of Islam with Ibn Battutah*. Ibn Battuta's life and times have reached younger readers with the publication of James Rumsford's *Traveling Man: The Journey of Ibn Battuta, 1325–1354*. Ibn Battuta's increasing modern fame has continued with the contributions of L. P. Harvey's *Ibn Battuta* and David Waines's *The Odyssey of Ibn Battuta: Uncommon Tales of a Medieval Adventurer*. Ibn Battuta's modern literary recrudescence is reflected in the publication of Boussif Ouasti's *La Rihla d'Ibn Battuta, Voyageur Ecrivain*. More than that of any other medieval Arabic chronicler, Ibn Battuta's star continues to rise.

2. Ibn Battuta, *Tuhfat al-Nuzzar fi Ghari'ib al-Amsar wa-Aja'ib al-Asfar*. Said Hamdun and Noel King's *Ibn Battuta in Black Africa*, which selects only Ibn Battuta's journeys to East and West Africa, has generally been followed here, with a careful comparison with the Arabic text in *Muhadhabb Rihlat Ibn Battutah* and the translation of relevant portions of Ibn Battuta's African journey in J. F. P. Hopkins and N. Levtzion, *Corpus of Early Arabic Sources for West African History*, 279–304.

3. The descriptions of Sijilmasa by the Syrian al-Umari, who wrote his "Pathways of Vision in the Realms of the Metropolises" in 1337–1338, or at least the relevant sections of this combination of "universal history and world geography," are equally interesting to us here (Hopkins and Levtzion, *Early Arabic Sources*, 253). While al-'Umari did not visit Sijilmasa or travel to Mali, which he nonetheless describes in detail, in writing so close to the time of Ibn Battuta, he is an essential reference for the North African Islamic world of the mid-1300s.

4. The plague began to circulate throughout the Mediterranean basin, and out-

ward, from Sicily and Alexandria in October 1347. Ibn Battuta was in Aleppo, Syria, in June 1348 when reports of the wave of disease reached him from travelers arriving from the south.

5. From 1348, when Ibn Battuta learned of the spread of the Black Death while in Aleppo, to the fall of 1351, when he returned to the sultan's court in Fez, his travels took the following circuitous route. He journeyed to Damascus, Jerusalem, Cairo, Upper Egypt, and Jidda, reaching Mecca by mid-November 1348. He performed his last hajj, remaining in Mecca for more than four months, then returned to Egypt, from which he sailed westward to Gabès, in southern Tunisia, arriving in Tunis in June 1349. He took a Catalan merchant vessel, via Christian Sardinia, to Ténès, on the Algerian coast, and reached Fez by early November 1349. After several months at home in Morocco, Ibn Battuta crossed the Strait of Gibraltar in March or April 1350 and met his future scribe, Ibn Juzayy, in Granada. He returned to Sabta (Ceuta) on the Strait of Gibraltar toward the end of 1350, traveled around Morocco, and returned to Fez at the court of Sultan Abu Inan about a year later, toward late summer in 1351. Ibn Battuta then undertook the journey to Mali described in this chapter; see Dunn, *Adventures of Ibn Battuta*.

6. Most often spelled "Kairouan" in French transliteration.

7. See Abdelmalek Benabid, "Forest Degradation in Morocco," for a review of present forest conditions.

8. As quoted in Hamdun and King, *Ibn Battuta in Black Africa*, 74–75.

9. Ibn Battuta, *Muhadhabb Rihlat Ibn Battutah*, pt. 2, 280; Ibn Battuta, *Travels of Ibn Battuta*, 5:306, 309, 310.

10. Quoted in Hamdun and King, *Ibn Battuta in Black Africa*, 30.

11. D. Jacques-Meunié, "Sur l'Architecture du Tafilalt et de Sijilmasa," describes this gate as "vestiges d'une porte; des arcatures anciennes surmontent un portail restauré à une époque récente" (vestiges of a gate, ancient arcades over a portal restored in a more recent era). MAPS has not done any archaeological research on this gate to provide more specific dating.

12. Hopkins and Levtzion, *Early Arabic Sources*, 64. Al-Bakri (Abu 'Ubayd 'Abd Allah ben 'Abd al-'Aziz al-Bakri) (d. Almeria? 487/1094) is largely unpublished, but key selections on North Africa and West Africa were translated by William Mac-Guckin de Slane and published under the French title *Description de l'Afrique Septentrionale*. More recently, parts of al-Bakri have been translated into English and annotated by Hopkins and Levtzion, whose *Early Arabic Sources* brings together relevant portions of sixty-five medieval Arabic manuscripts, many of which link North African and West African history. Twelve of these are especially significant for the study of Sijilmasa; al-Bakri's is undoubtedly the most significant.

13. Boris de Rachewiltz reported that the second season of work at Sijilmasa in the early 1970s uncovered the remains of walls, a fountain, plant fossils, and human bones ("Missione Etno-Archeologica nel Sahara Maghrebino," 567). The excavations also produced fragments of fine glass, jewelry, and small tiles in faience.

14. *Wali*, often used in Arabic to mean "governor." The *wali* in 1351 would have been the direct representative of the sultan of Fez, Abu Inan.

15. Ibn Abi Zar, *Kitab al-Anis al-Mutrib bi-Rawd al-Qirtas fi Akhbar Muluk al-Maghrib wa-Tarikh Madinat Fas*, 81. Archaeological evidence for this is presented in chapter 4.

16. Ibn Battuta, *Travels of Ibn Battuta*, 5:288.

17. Quoted in Hamdun and King, *Ibn Battuta in Black Africa*, 30.

18. Al-Bakri, *Kitab al-Mughrib fi Dhikr Bilad Ifriqiya wa-'l-Maghrib*, 148; *Description de l'Afrique septentrionale*, 283.

19. International football (soccer) pitches vary in size but oft-used dimensions are 105 meters long and 68 meters wide (7,140 square meters, or 1.76 acres). Such is the commonly copied Old Trafford (Manchester).

20. For a discussion of camels and caravans, see Raymond Mauny, *Tableau Géographique de l'Ouest Afrique au Moyen Age d'après les Sources Écrites, la Tradition et l'Archéologie*, 287–291, 394–395.

21. Our research at Suq Ben Akla is described in chapter 10. A detailed ground survey conducted in the 1998 season was followed by periodic visits to the site over the next fourteen years; see also the conclusion.

22. Ibn Battuta, in his *Rihla*, provides the first mention of Timbuktu known in history; see Hopkins and Levtzion, *Early Arabic Sources*, 299.

23. A description of the silent trade, or silent barter, as it is also known, during the Middle Ages is provided by al-Mas'udi (writing in 947). The first reference to the silent trade is by the classical Greek historian Herodotus. There is also a reference as late as the fifteenth century in the writing of Ca' da Mosto (Cadamosto), the Venetian explorer who sailed with Prince Henry the Navigator and provides incisive detail on West African societies from 1455 to 1456, indicating a long continuity to the practice in the supply of gold from the Guinea Highlands and elsewhere along the West African coast.

24. Hopkins and Levtzion, *Early Arabic Sources*, 282. Teghaza is the salt-mining settlement mentioned earlier.

25. The literature on Ibn Battuta's visit to Mali has broadened as interest and knowledge of African history has deepened. Among the most useful, summarizing and discussing the situation of knowledge about Mali, is J. O. Hunwick, "The Mid-Fourteenth Century Capital of Mali."

26. Oualata is a UNESCO World Heritage Site in southeastern Mauritania. Iwalatan and Walata are variant spellings.

27. See David Conrad, "A Town Called Dakajalan: The Sunjata Tradition and the Question of Ancient Mali's Capital," which discusses the question of Mali's capital.

28. The miserable time that Ibn Battuta had in Takadda is well described in Dunn, *Adventures of Ibn Battuta*, 305–306.

29. Quoted in Hamdun and King, *Ibn Battuta in Black Africa*, 73.

30. This is conjecture. We argue simply, how could it not have happened in the Fez of the 1350s?

31. Hopkins and Levtzion, *Early Arabic Sources*, 282. The location of Qanjanfu has puzzled many scholars.

32. Ibid., 304.

33. André Miguel, in his *Encyclopedia of Islam* article on Ibn Battuta (3:758–759), provides both dates for his death, but most modern writers employ only the 770/1368-1369 date. Hopkins and Levtzion note: "Ibn Battuta died in Marrakech in 770/1368" (*Early Arabic Sources*, 279). A picturesque account of Ibn Battuta's tomb is in Mackintosh-Smith, *Travels with a Tangerine*, ch. 1, "Morocco: One End of the World."

Chapter 1

1. Hopkins and Levtzion, *Early Arabic Sources*, 22.
2. Ibid., 36.
3. Ibid., 41.
4. On the nature of the Arabic cosmographies, see Klaus Vogel, "Cosmography."
5. See Ronald A. Messier, *The Almoravids and the Meanings of Jihad*.
6. See James A. Miller, "Trading through Islam: The Interconnections of Sijilmasa, Ghana, and the Almoravid Movement." *Journal of North African Studies* 6 (2001): 29–58.
7. Ibid.
8. Timothy F. Garrard, "Myth and Metrology: the Early Trans-Saharan Gold Trade."
9. Harry Hazard, *The Numismatic History of Late Medieval North Africa*, contains an extensive bibliography on North African coins and mints.
10. Ronald A. Messier, "Quantitative Analysis of Almoravid Dinars."
11. Janet L. Abu-Lughod, "Islamic City: Historic Myth, Islamic Essence, and Contemporary Relevance."
12. William Marçais, "L'Islamisme et la Vie Urbaine"; George Marçais, "L'Urbanisme musulman"; G. Marçais, "La Conception des Villes dans l'Islam"; Robert Brunschvig, "Urbanisme Médiéval et Droit Musulman"; Gustave von Grunebaum, "The Structure of the Muslim Town"; Roger Le Tourneau, *Fès avant le Protectorat: Étude Économique et Sociale d'une Ville de l'Occident Musulman*; Le Tourneau, *Les Villes Musulmanes de l'Afrique du Nord*; Carlton Coon, *Caravan: The Story of the Middle East*, chapter titled "Town and City"; Jacques Berque, "Medinas, Villeneuves et Bidonvilles."
13. Jean Sauvaget, "Esquisse d'une Histoire de la Ville de Damas"; Ira Lapidus, *Muslim Cities in the Later Middle Ages*.
14. Frej Stambouli and Abdelkader Zghal, "Urban Life in Precolonial North Africa."
15. Nezar al-Sayyad, *Cities and Caliphs*.
16. Ibid., 7. Al-Sayyad claims that one can describe a city as Muslim only if one adds the qualifiers "Arab" and "early" (153).
17. Amira K. Bennison and Alison L. Gascoigne, *Cities in the Pre-Modern Islamic World*, 7.
18. Salma K. Jayussi, *The City in the Islamic World*, x, xiv.
19. The first mission was conducted May 29–July 3, 1971, and the second March 28–May 7, 1972, both under the direction of Boris de Rachewiltz.
20. Rachewiltz, "Missione Etno-Archeologica," 567.
21. Abdulaziz Touri, speech delivered at the Jour d'Hommage Ronald Messier, BNRM, May 23, 2011.
22. Al-Bakri, *Kitab al-Mughrib fi Dhikr Bilad Ifriqiya wa-'l-Maghrib*, 148; see also the French translation, *Description de l'Afrique septrionale*, 283–284.

Chapter 2

1. Al-Muqaddasi, a native of Jerusalem, devoted his life to geography, traveling far and wide following his hajj at the early age of twenty. His work *Ahsan al-Taqasim fi Ma'rifat al-Aqalim* (The best classification for the knowledge of the climes) appeared sometime in 985–990; see Hopkins and Levtzion, *Early Arabic Sources*, 53.

2. For the Arabs, the lands between the Sahara and the Mediterranean Sea and Atlantic Ocean, described by the arc of the Atlas Mountains and cupped in the north-western outline of Africa, form the "island of the west," *al-jazirat al-maghrib*. It is a metaphorical "island" (*jazirat*) of beneficent environments, or at least environments in which rain and snow fall, trees grow, and humanity can create landscapes of farms and towns, as opposed to the Sahara. So it is that the Maghrib, in lands dominated by the numerous folds of the Atlas, is like an island set between the desert and the sea. The term, which is widely used in Arabic, tends today to mean the entirety of Moroccan, Algerian, and Tunisian national space—in effect, the same space as Ifriqiya ash-shamalia, "North Africa," in its most common modern denotation in Arabic.

3. Al-Bakri's work *Kitab al-Masalik wa'l-Mamalik* (The book of routes and realms), dating from 1068, offers a glimpse of Sijilmasa in the third century of its existence and provides distinctive and elusive hints about the city and the nature of its people. It is the single most important early source of information on Sijilmasa's history; see Hopkins and Levtzion, *Early Arabic Sources*, 65.

4. The Maghrib consists of the northern sections of modern Tunisia, Algeria, and Morocco. The modern country names Algeria and Morocco emerge from the Maghrib as a distinctive region in the Arab World. Morocco's Arabic name, *al-maghrib*, is simply the term itself, which is understood to be in full *al-maghrib al-aqsa*, the "the most Maghrib," or the "farthest West."

5. French geographers developed the concept of the *pré-Sahara* to identify a desert threshold, a transition zone in which many of the characteristics of a Mediterranean-type environment still hold sway, but are highly attenuated by Saharan qualities, most notably very high average temperatures and very low precipitation totals. In this sense, the Tafilalt, Sijilmasa, and the entire southern-facing side of the Atlas Mountains are pre-Saharan. On the nature of the pre-Sahara, see Jean Despois and René Raynal, *Géographie de l'Afrique du Nord-Ouest*, 462–463.

6. Al-Mas'udi, born in Baghdad at the height of the Abbasid caliphate, wrote the *Muruj al-Dhahab wa-Ma'adin al-Jawhar* (The meadow of gold and the mines of jewels) as early as 947 and continued to add to it until his death in 956 in Fustat (Cairo). It is al-Mas'udi to whom we are indebted for among the first descriptions of the silent trade in gold between Africans "in the land of gold," "which is opposite Sijilmasa of the land of the Maghrib" (i.e., on the other side of the Sahara); see Hopkins and Levtzion, *Early Arabic Sources*, 32.

7. The Draa has been known to reach the Atlantic coast just south of Cap Draa very occasionally in human history.

8. Erfoud was created by the Army of France in the first push to capture the Tafilalt in the period just before World War I. It serves as the major administrative center of the Tafilalt, some fifteen kilometers (nine miles) south.

9. The Daoura has been known to flow deep into the Sahara in exceptional years. Jean Dubief, in "Les Pluies, les Crues et Leurs Effets au Sahara," describes the nature

of the Oued Saoura, which is analogous to the Daoura in that it is the combined flow of the Oueds Zousfana and Guir, the next Saharan rivers east of the Tafilalt. The Saoura flowed uninterruptedly at Beni Abbès, Algeria, 450 miles removed from any source of resupply, from October 1905 until the end of May 1906, and at times continued to flow more than twice that distance (130). See also Jean-Paul Ruhard, "Le Bassin Quaternaire du Tafilalt."

10. The Pleistocene is now recognized with fair exactness as extending from 2,588,000 to 11,700 years ago.

11. Peter U. Clark et al., "The Last Glacial Maximum."

12. Ibid.

13. James A. T. Young and Stefan Hasternrath, "Glaciers of Africa." The High Atlas Mountains are identified (p. G49) as having been glaciated during the last glacial maximum, but this is incorrect. Clear evidence of peri-glaciation exists on the lower northern slopes of Mount Toubkal, the chain's highest peak (4,165 meters; 13,644 feet), in the form of a rock glacier at the level of the village of Arremdt, but not full mountain glaciation; see James Miller, *Imlil*, 44–45, 60n8.

14. David Lubell, "Paleoenvironments and Epi-Paleolithic Economies in the Maghrib."

15. F. Gasse, "Hydrological Changes in the African Tropics since the Last Glacial Maximum," provides an excellent overview of climate and environmental change in both African hemispheres, focusing on hydrological changes during the Holocene. Steven Mithen, in *After the Ice*, attempts to put the Maghrib's post-Pleistocene environmental and human history into a worldwide focus; see especially ch. 51, "Sheep and Cattle in the Sahara: The Development of Pastoralism in the Sahara, 9500 to 5000 BC."

16. The dryas is an alpine flower whose pollen is present in large amounts in core samples from the period.

17. Gasse, "Hydrological Changes in the African Tropics," 200.

18. Within this span of 6,000 years, Gasse identifies a desiccation phase lasting 500 years between 8,500 and 8,000 YA ("Hydrological Changes in the African Tropics," 204). It must be stressed that there are large geographic and methodological gaps in our knowledge of Saharan paleoclimates. While there remains much debate about the periodization of the Neolithic Pluvial in the Sahara, and about its length, continuity, and genesis, it is now beyond doubt that a "Green Sahara" was a reality for several millennia in the period between 10,000 and 3000 YA. See I. S. Castaneda et al., "Wet Phases in the Sahara/Sahel Region and Human Migration Patterns in North Africa," and Christian-Albrechts-Universitaet zu Kiel, "The Green Sahara: A Desert in Bloom."

19. Gasse, "Hydrological Changes in the African Tropics," 200.

20. The significant gaps in our knowledge of the prehistoric climate of the Sahara after the last glacial maximum have attracted increasing numbers of researchers convinced that Holocene Saharan climate change is as significant in human prehistory as the retreat of the glacial ice in more northern latitudes.

21. The Continental Intercalaire aquifer extends from the Great Western Erg in Algeria east through Tunisia and into Libya, covering some 600,000 square kilometers (231,660 square miles, an area slightly smaller than Texas); see Abdelhamid Guendouz

and Jean-Luc Michelot, "Chlorine-36 Dating of Deep Groundwater from Northern Sahara."

22. Gabriel Camps, *Les Berbères*; see especially 27–41.

23. Carleton Coon's ideas on the origins of the Berbers are found in his controversial *The Origin of Races* and in *Caravan*.

24. Gabriel Camps, *Les Civilisation Préhistoriques de l'Afrique du Nord et du Sahara*.

25. Nick Brooks, "Cultural Responses to Aridity in the Middle Holocene and Increased Social Complexity."

26. See Gasse, "Hydrological Changes in the African Tropics," 199–200.

27. The southern margins of the Green Sahara in north-central Niger have been explored recently by a scientific team led by the University of Chicago paleontologist Paul Sereno. They found two distinctive cultures, the Kiffian and Tenerean, separated by a thousand years, 8000–7000 YA, when heat and aridity returned to the area. http://paulsereno.uchicago.edu/discoveries/people_of_the_green_sahara.

28. Michael Brett and Elizabeth Fentress, *The Berbers*; see especially ch. 1, "Berbers." This work can be considered the most definitive in English on Berber history and culture. A summary of explorations conducted by the Fazzan Project to reveal the nature of ancient Garamantes settlement and society is found in Kevin White and David Mattingly, "Ancient Lakes of the Sahara." (Fazzan is Libya's large southwestern desert region, approximately the size of France.)

29. Tifinagh, a traditional script of the Touareg people, was widely used throughout the Sahara and the Maghrib in the pre-Islamic period. A recent contribution to the study of Saharan rock art is David Coulson and Alec Campbell, *African Rock Art*.

30. Al-Umari, cited in Hopkins and Levtzion, *Early Arabic Sources*, 275. Al-ʿUmari spent much of his life in Mamluk Cairo, where, in 1337–1338, he wrote *Masalik al-Absar fi Mamalik al-Amsar* (Pathways of vision in the realms of the metropolises), an encyclopedic survey of the world. *Masalik al-Amsar* is particularly useful for its survey of Mali, since it records accounts of the visit of Mansa Musa to Cairo in 1324.

31. Quoted in Hopkins and Levtzion, *Early Arabic Sources*, 209. Al-Dimashqi (1256–1327) wrote *Nukhbat al-Dahr fi ʿajab al-Barr waʾl-Bahr* (The choice of the age; of the marvels of land and sea) by using earlier sources stretching back to al-Bakri and al-Idrisi, as did his fellow cosmographers over the centuries.

32. Figures from Guy Evans, "The Changing Dynamics of the Moroccan Oasis."

33. See Stephen O. Hughes, "Morocco: Nation Pays a High Price for Water," *New York Times*, Jan. 31, 1966. The role that the 1965 Ziz flood in the Tafilalt played in launching Morocco's *politique des grands barrages* is developed in Will D. Swearingen, *Moroccan Mirages*, especially ch. 6, "Fulfilling the Colonial Vision."

34. A parallel dam, Mansour ad-Dahbi, was built at Ouarzazate in the same time period, early 1970s, by the Soviet Union at the head of the Oued Draa. The situation is a mirror image of that of Errachidia and the Ziz, but perhaps more dramatic, given the growth of Ouarzazate as an international destination, a desert playground, and a center for the film industry. Mansour ad-Dahbi is a far more imposing structure, a large concrete arch-gravity dam (like Hoover Dam), whereas Hassan ad-Dakhil is a long, low, earth-fill dam.

35. Interviews at Qsar Rhazzi and Qsar Ouled Abdel Halim, May 23, 2010. The dam is operated by a committee composed of representatives from the Regional Agri-

cultural Investment Office–Tafilalt; the Regional Hydrologic Management Agency for the Guir-Gheris, Maider, and Ziz; and the Ministry of the Interior. James Miller was a member of a team of experts who inspected Hassan ad-Dakhil in May 2007 at the request of the Moroccan authorities and in the context of due diligence for the signing of the Millennium Challenge Corporation's Compact with Morocco in August 2007. Long-standing fears of a fissure in the base of the dam were allayed by the team's findings that the escape of water posed no threat to the integrity of the dam.

36. Basic information on *bayyoud* can be found in S. Freeman and M. Maymon, "Reliable Detection of the Fungal Pathogen Fusarium oxysporum f.sp. Albedinis, Causal Agent of Bayoud Disease of Date Palm, using Molecular Techniques."

37. Al-Idrisi, *Nuzhat al-Mushtaq fi Ikhtiraq al-Afaq*, published with French translation as *Description de l'Afrique et de l'Espagne par Edrisi*, by Reinhart Dozy and Michael Jan de Goeje, 70.

38. Hopkins and Levtzion, *Early Arabic Sources*, 65.

39. Survey conducted by Tony Wilkinson, then at the University of Chicago, now professor of archaeology at Durham University, UK.

40. Al-Mas'udi, from *Akhbar al-Zaman* (lost, but parts of which are found in his other works), cited in Joseph M. Cuoq, *Recueil des Sources Arabes Concernant l'Afrique Occidentale du VIIIè au XVIè Siècle*, 60–61.

41. Jean Margat, *Mémoire Explicatif de la Carte Hydrogéologique au 1/50,000 de la Plaine du Tafilalt*, 25.

42. Legends of the Sultan al-Khal abound in the Tafilalt and are often tied to his attempts to impede the flow of the Ziz to the oasis.

43. Dale R. Lightfoot and James A. Miller, "Sijilmasa: The Rise and Fall of a Walled Oasis in Medieval Morocco."

44. Hopkins and Levtzion, *Early Arabic Sources*, 64.

45. Ibid., 209; Leo Africanus, *The History and Description of Africa and of the Notable Things Therein*, 3:780–785.

46. This is the Alnif road, Route 3454.

47. Al-Bakri, *Kitab al-Mughrib fi Dhikr Bilad Ifriqiya wa-'l-Maghrib*, 148.

48. Mahmud Abderrazak Isma'il, *Al-Hawarig fi Bilad al-Maghrib min al-'Usul Hata Muntqasaf al-Qaren ar-Rabi al-Higeri* (1985), quoted in Lahcen Taouchikht, "Étude Ethno-Archéologique de la Céramique du Tafilalet (Sijilmassa)," 20.

49. Lightfoot and Miller, "Sijilmasa: Rise and Fall," 90. The Sultan al-Khal is famous in legend for trying to plug the Timedrine spring or springs.

50. Margat, *Mémoire Explicatif de la Carte Hydrogéologue*, 191.

51. Ibid.

52. Lightfoot and Miller, "Sijilmasa: Rise and Fall," 92.

53. Tony Wilkinson, field notes.

54. Miller, field notes, July 3, 1992.

55. In Hopkins and Levtzion, *Early Arabic Sources*, 65–66.

56. Unpublished report by the MAPS team member Nancy Mahoney, then a graduate student at Arizona State University.

57. Today, wheat has replaced barley as the preferred cereal grain in Morocco, and it is hard wheat, with its high gluten content, that is normally the basis of couscous.

58. Mahoney report.

59. Ronald A. Messier, "Sijilmâsa: L'Intermédiaire entre la Méditerranée et l'Ouest de l'Afrique."

60. *Filali* refers to people and things from the Tafilalt.

61. Mahmoud Abd ar-Raziq, *Al-Khawarij fi Bilad al-Maghrib Hatta Muntasif al-Qarn ar-Rabiʿ al-Hijri.*

62. Sijilmasa first appears in world literature as a standard point of reference among world locations in the *Surat al-Ard* (Picture of Earth) of al-Khuwarizmi (d. Mesopotamia, 846/847). The *Surat al-Ard* is largely an Arabic reformulation of Ptolemy's *Geographia*, the world's first (c. 150) gazetteer. Sijilmasa is identified as one of eight places (including also one of the earliest mentions of Ghana) in the "First Clime," often later known as the torrid zone. Sijilmasa's Midrar period is documented in detail by al-Bakri and is partially repeated by Ibn Idhari, a native of Marrakech, in his *Al Bayan al-Mughrib* (The amazing exposition), written in the early 1300s (Hopkins and Levtzion, *Early Arabic Sources*, 216–232). Ibn Khaldun, the most famous Arab historian of the medieval age, continued the thread of placing Sijilmasa among the great urban places in the world in his universal history, the *Kitab al-Ibar* (The book of examples) in 1374–1378, to which he continued to add until he died in Cairo in 1406. It is Ibn Khaldun's *Muqaddima*, the "introduction" to the full work, that is the best known of his endeavors (Hopkins and Levtzion, *Early Arabic Sources*, 317–342).

63. Paul Love, "The Sufris of Sijilmasa."

64. Known to us as the Almoravids through the Spanish *almoravides*, the movement started in a religious redoubt, a *ribat*, located along the western edge of the territory of the Juddala Sanhaja peoples in the southwestern Sahara in modern Mauritania. They are thus the people of the *ribat*, the *al-murabittun*, discussed in detail below in chapter 4.

65. Taouchikht, "Étude Ethno-Archéologique," 27.

66. Lightfoot and Miller, "Sijilmasa: Rise and Fall"; D. Jacques-Meunié, *Le Maroc Saharien des Origines à 1670*, 1:296–298.

Chapter 3

1. Leo Africanus, who has become ever more famous because of several popular modern accounts of his life, was born in Granada in 1494, two years after the conquest of the Nasrid kingdom, which marked the end of Muslim rule in Iberia. His families moved to Fez, where he was educated and grew up. As a youth, he traveled to Timbuktu, passing through Sijilmasa at some point. His peregrinations on the return voyage led him perhaps to Djerba, perhaps to Crete, where he was captured by Christian pirates and brought to the court of Naples. Word of his knowledge of Arabic, Islam, and the Mediterranean world spread, and he flourished under the patronage of Pope Leo X (d. 1521). Educated in the Christian tradition of the day, Hassan Wazzan became Johannes Leo de Medici, best known as Leo Africanus. He wrote a memoir of Africa, completed in 1526 and first published in Venice in 1550 as *Della Descrittione dell'Africa* and then in French (1556) and English (1600). The diverse themes of Leo's life and legacy were explored in a conference in 2003, published as *Léon l'Africain*, edited by François Pouillon. For us, Leo's significance is twofold: as a visitor to Sijil-

masa, he recorded the language of discovery in the regional context of North and West Africa; and at the same time, he offered both the last medieval description of the city and the first modern picture of it, largely in ruins and placed within a contemporary-seeming landscape of Tafilalt *qsur* (villages). Both traditions are reported in Daniel F. McCall, "The Traditions of the Founding of Sijilmassa and Ghana."

2. Dhu'l-Qarnain, who is identified in the Quran (in the Sura al-Kahf) seventeen times, was taken to be Alexander the Great by Muslim scholars until modern times; today there is much controversy on the matter.

3. Quoted in McCall, "Founding of Sijilmassa and Ghana," 15. Massa, a town known by that name both in antiquity and today, is located on the Atlantic Ocean south of Agadir. Jacques-Meunié considered the origins of Sijilmasa and concluded that the name "Sijilmasa" is neither Arabic nor Berber (see "Sur l'Architecture du Tafilalt et de Sijilmassa"). The Moroccan historian Larbi Mezzine considered the possibility of a Roman origin of "Sijilmassa," but discounted it in favor of a Berber origin and etymology. He suggests that it has the meaning of a place where there is water (see "Sur l'Étymologie du Toponyme 'Sijilmasa'").

4. *Mauri*, the origin of the English word "Moors," was the Latin designation for those ancient Berber peoples inhabiting modern Algeria and Morocco.

5. Thapsus is on the Tunisian coast just south of modern Monastir. Juba and Petreius died together at Zama, inland from Thapsus, in a suicide pact following their defeat at Thapsus. It is estimated that at Thapsus 10,000 Roman troops who sought to surrender to Caesar were in fact slaughtered by him.

6. A recent work on Juba II is D. W. Roller, *The World of Juba II and Kleopatra Selene*.

7. Daniel McCall suggests that Juba II called on the help of the Roman governor of Africa, Proconsularis, to help suppress this revolt; see McCall, "Founding of Sijilmassa and Ghana," 15–16.

8. On the puzzling death of Cleopatra Selene, see the account of her on the Egyptian Royal Genealogy website: http://www.tyndalehouse.com/Egypt/ptolemies/selene_ii_fr.htm.

9. *Garum* was a fermented fish sauce flavored with herbs; it became an essential condiment in Rome during the period under consideration here. *Garum* produced from small fishes along the Atlantic coast and the westernmost Mediterranean was especially favored. *Garum* might be likened to the fish sauces of Southeast Asia or even Worcestershire sauce, which is produced, in part, from anchovies.

10. Frédéric de La Chapelle, "L'Expédition de Suetonius Paulinus dans le Sud-Est du Maroc."

11. Abdallah Laroui describes the history of the Maghrib for the first two centuries after Roman annexation as "indistinguishable from the history—marked by continual revolts—of the Roman army in Africa" (*The History of the Maghrib*, 30–31). That is because textual sources at our disposal view this encounter from the perspective of the Roman army. From a Filalian perspective, though, it is the story of Berber resistance to Roman occupation, resistance that succeeded.

12. Garrard, "Myth and Metrology."

13. Jean Devisse challenges the validity of Garrard's argument by pointing to the existence of glass weights found at Tegdaoust and at Kumbi Saleh that date to the early

Fatimid period; see Devisse, "Routes de Commerce et Échanges en Afrique Occidentale en Relation avec la Méditerranée," 241.

14. Garrard, "Myth and Metrology," 447–448.

15. Richard W. Bulliet, *The Camel and the Wheel*, 113–114.

16. McCall, "Founding of Sijilmassa and Ghana," 16 and n. 42; Ziegler, Hallemans, and Mauny, "Mauritanie: Trouvaille de Deux Monnaies Romaines," 486–488.

17. Mohammed el-Mellouki, "Contribution à l'Étude de l'Histoire des Villes Médiévales du Maroc," 41.

18. Jacques-Meunié, "Sur l'Architecture du Tafilalt et de Sijilmassa," 142.

19. The sample can be dated to the period 220–450 with 95 percent probability.

20. Al-Bakri, *Description de l'Afrique Septentrionale*.

21. Ibid., 284–285.

22. With a 95 percent probability, these fragments are dated 575–670 and 590–800.

23. Al-Bakri, cited in Hopkins and Levtzion, *Early Arabic Sources*, 65.

24. Ibid., 64. Hopkins and Levtzion speculate on the names and locations of "Targha" and "Ziz," noting that both could have been in the Sus (southwest Morocco—Agadir), which seems unlikely for "Targha" in that "two days" journey. Perhaps, as they suggest, "Targha" may have been along the Oued Todghra, a tributary of the Oued Gheris. Of Ziz, it seems to have been located along the Oued Ziz in or near the Tafilalt. Al-Masʿudi identifies "Targha" as being in the land of the "Khawarij of the Sufriya" and notes that "Targha" has "an important silver mine," pointing to its location at the foot of the Atlas Mountains in the Todghra of today. Al-Bakri, like all the medieval cosmographers, drew on all available previous writers, passing on information from one generation to the next. That said, the question remains why these towns, especially a silver-mining town in the Todghra, which is indeed two days from Sijilmasa, would be depopulated with the founding of Sijilmasa.

25. J. Schacht, "Ikrima," *Encyclopedia of Islam*, 2nd ed., 3:1081–1082.

26. Ibn Kaldun, *Muqaddimah*, 1:333 and n. 54.

27. Ibid., 397.

28. Al-Bakri, *Description de l'Afrique Septentrionale*, 284.

29. This discussion of the Kharijite origins of Sijilmasa comes from Messier, *Almoravids and Jihad*, 29–30; see also Love, "Sufris of Sijilmasa."

30. Al-Bakri, *Description de l'Afrique Septentrionale*, 284. The only Islamic city older than Sijilmasa is Nakur, which was founded c. 740 on the Moroccan Mediterranean coast.

31. Al-Bakri, *Description de l'Afrique Septentrionale*, 282–283.

32. Al-Masʿudi, from *Akhbar al-Zaman*, in Cuoq, *Recueil des Sources Arabes*, 60–61; see also the discussion of the city wall in chapter 2.

33. Michael E. Bonine, "Islamic Cities in Morocco."

34. Mellouki, "L'Histoire des Villes Médiévales du Maroc," 96.

35. Oleg Grabar, "The Architecture of the Middle Eastern City from Past to Present," 35.

36. *The Holy Qurʾan*, trans. Abdullah Yusuf Ali, 116.

37. The error range is 680–980.

38. For a more detailed description of pre-Almoravid ceramics, see Ronald A.

Messier and Abdallah Fili, "The Earliest Ceramics of Sijilmasa." A detailed study of Almoravid and post-Almoravid ceramics is in progress.

39. Al-Bakri, *Description de l'Afrique Septentrionale*, 283.

40. Neil D. MacKenzie, *Ayyubid Cairo*, 78.

41. Choukri Heddouchi, "The Medieval Coins of Sijilmasa, Morocco," 27.

42. Al-Bakri, *Description de l'Afrique Septentrionale*, 288.

43. Heddouchi, "Medieval Coins of Sijilmasa," 71–72.

44. Al-Bakri, *Description de l'Afrique Septentrionale*, 289.

45. Chloé Capel is a PhD Student at Paris I–Sorbonne, working on a dissertation topic related to Sijilmasa.

46. Hopkins and Levtzion, *Early Arabic Sources*, 43.

47. M. Canard, "L'Impérialisme des Fatimides et leur Propagande."

48. Hopkins and Levtzion, *Early Arabic Sources*, 49.

49. Heddouchi, "Medieval Coins of Sijilmasa," 24; see also Sherif Anwar and Jere L. Bacharach, "Shi'ism and the Early Dinars of the Fatimid Imam-caliph al-Mu'izz li-din Allah (341–365/952–975)."

50. Ronald A. Messier, "Muslim Exploitation of West African Gold during the Period of the Fatimid Caliphate," 61–67.

51. Messier and Fili, "Earliest Ceramics of Sijilmasa."

52. Hanna Kassis, "Coinage of an Enigmatic Caliph." Edward von Zambaur claims that the first Fatimid coins were struck even earlier, in 297 (see Heddouchi, "Medieval Coins of Sijilmasa," 27), immediately following the first Fatimid invasion of Sijilmasa to rescue Ubayd Allah.

53. Khaled Ben Romdhane, "Le Métier de Monétaire d'après les Sources Arabes," 25–43.

54. The one Almoravid coin die extant today, located in the Musée Stéphane Gsell in Algiers, is from the Nul (Lamta) mint; see Georges Marçais, "Un Coin Monétaire Almoravide du Musée Stéphane Gsell."

55. Heddouchi, "Medieval Coins of Sijilmasa," 149–156.

56. *Princeton Encyclopedia of Classical Sites*, s.v. "Laurion," 489.

57. Al-Bakri, *Description de l'Afrique Septentrionale*, 301. There is much more about this in the next chapter.

58. From the chronicle of Abu Zakariya, cited in Mellouki, "L'Histoire des Villes Médiévales du Maroc," 444.

59. Ibid., 443.

60. Al-Bakri, *Description de l'Afrique Septentrionale*, 287.

61. Cited in Mellouki, "L'Histoire des Villes Médiévales du Maroc," 345.

62. Hopkins and Levtzion, *Early Arabic Sources*, 47.

63. Cited in Mellouki, "L'Histoire des Villes Médiévales du Maroc," 446.

64. Ibn Abi Zar, quoted in Hopkins and Levtzion, *Early Arabic Sources*, 242.

Chapter 4

1. For a comprehensive, scholarly, yet popular narrative of Almoravid history, see Messier, *Almoravids and Jihad*.

2. Ibn Abi Zar, cited in Hopkins and Levtzion, *Early Arabic Sources*, 242. That is

also the figure given in the Tornberg edition (81), considered to be the most authoritative edition of the *Rawd al-Qirtas*. The Beaumier translation (176), on the other hand, gives a figure of 1,500 camels, which seems much more reasonable.

3. Ibn Abi Zar, in Hopkins and Levtzion, *Early Arabic Sources*, 242.

4. The study of macrobotanical material was resumed in 1998 by the biologist Samantha Messier.

5. Documents in the Cairo Geniza show ample evidence of this among the Muslim population in Egypt; see S. D. Goitein, *A Mediterranean Society*, 1:122–123.

6. Ibn Abi Zar, quoted in Hopkins and Levtzion, *Early Arabic Sources*, 242.

7. Larbi Mezzine, *Le Tafilalt*, 271; Messier, *Almoravids and Jihad*, 27.

8. Ibn Abi Zar, quoted in Hopkins and Levtzion, *Early Arabic Sources*, 243.

9. On the Almoravids' conversion to Malikite Islam, see Messier, *Almoravids and Jihad*, 3–5, 191–192.

10. Ibn Idhari al-Marrakushi, *Kitab al-Bayan al-Mughrib fi Akhbar Muluk al-Andalus wa'l-Maghrib*, 14–15.

11. This is the pattern in precolonial North African cities described by Stambouli and Zghal in "Urban Life in Precolonial North Africa."

12. Ibn al-Athir, *Al-Kamil fi'l-Tarikh*, 621. Ibn Idhari also mentions this appointment, although he does not mention Yusuf specifically (*Kitab al-Bayan al-Mughrib fi Akhbar Muluk al-Andalus wa'l-Maghrib*, 15). He says that when Abu Bakr left Sijilmasa to march on Aghmat, he appointed over Sijilmasa one of his brothers with a numerous band of Lamtuna.

13. The encounter of Abu Bakr and Yusuf Ibn Tashfin is described by Ibn Idhari (*Kitab al-Bayan al-Mughrib fi Akhbar Muluk al-Andalus wa'l-Maghrib*, 58–59) and in *Al-Hulal al-Mawshiyya*, 16–17.

14. Jacques-Meunié, *Le Maroc Saharien*, 2:242.

15. There is an excellent discussion of this episode in Hanna Kassis, "Observations on the First Three Decades of Almoravid History (AH 450–480 = AD 1058–1088)."

16. Ibn al-Athir, *Al-Kamil fi'l-Tarikh*, 427; Messier, *Almoravids and Jihad*, 205.

17. Ibn Idhari, *Kitab al-Bayan al-Mughrib fi Akhbar Muluk al-Andalus wa'l-Maghrib*, 15.

18. For a more complete description of Almoravid administration, see Messier, *Almoravids and Jihad*, 85–92.

19. For this conflict between the Almoravid ulama and al-Ghazzali, see É. Lévi-Provençal, "Réflexions sur l'Empire Almoravide au Début du XIIe siècle," 319.

20. Abu Ya'qub Yusuf Ibn Yahya al-Tadili, *Kitab al-Tashawwuf ila Rijal al-Tassawuf*, 98. In the edition of the *Tashawwuf* edited by A. Faure, the name of the mosque is given as Ibn Abd al-Malik.

21. Ahmed Ibn al-Qadi al-Miknassi, *Jadouat al-Iqtibas fi Dhikri man Halla min al-A'lam Madinat Fas* (Rabat, 1973), 167, cited in Mellouki, "L'Histoire des Villes Médiévales du Maroc," 456.

22. Ibid.

23. Ibid.

24. Al-Tadili, *Kitab al-Tashawwuf ila Rijal al-Tassawuf*, 154.

25. Ibid., 95–101.

26. Ibid., 155.

27. J. F. P. Hopkins warns us against assuming that the Almoravids employed in

the Maghribi cities of the empire the regulations in the *hisba* (marketplace regulation) manual of Ibn Abdun that were applied in Seville (*Medieval Muslim Government in Barbary*, 136). On the other hand, he tells us that Almoravid *katibun* (secretaries) were Andalusian to a man (12). We later show that the Almoravids standardized monetary policy and that they enforced the same rule of censorship throughout the empire. So having considered Hopkins's word of caution, we are still inclined to believe that the Almoravids enforced uniform marketplace regulations throughout the empire.

28. Ibn Abdun, *Séville Musulmane au Début du XIIe Siècle*, 95, 106, 111.

29. Abdulaziz Touri and Mohammed Hammam, "Tradition Écrite et Architecture," 215–216. The text specifies that the individual will be responsible for the wall passing in front of his house. He will be assisted by the tribe in the reconstruction of the first four courses of the wall, but that the individual must complete the upper five courses on his own.

30. Julie Coco, "Caravans, Commerce, and Cities."

31. This is part of the geomorphological study done by Tony Wilkinson.

32. Larbi Mezzine, *Le Tafilalt*, 271–272.

33. This information on slavery also appears in Messier, *Almoravids and Jihad*, 199. Determining the volume of the trans-Saharan slave trade is nearly impossible. Raymond Mauny cites Ibn Battuta (wrote 1355) describing a single caravan going from Takadda to Touat as having 600 slaves (*Tableau Géographique*, 377–379). Al-Umari (cited in Mauny) says that Mansa Musa took some 12,000 slaves with him on his pilgrimage. *Tarikh es-Soudan*'s figure of 500 (also in Mauny) is likely to be much closer to reality. At the figure of 500–600 slaves per caravan, if 35–40 caravans crossed the desert yearly, Mauny estimates that some 20,000 slaves were transported across the Sahara annually. More recently, Ralph Austen places the number of slaves taken across the Sahara during the medieval period at 6,000 a year or more ("The Trans-Saharan Slave Trade," 66).

34. Al-Bakri, *Description de l'Afrique Septentrionale*, 301, cited in Hopkins and Levtzion, *Early Arabic Sources*, 69, and in Messier, *Almoravids and Jihad*, 62.

35. *Kitab al-Istibsar*, ed. Zaghlul, 216.

36. Cited in Hopkins and Levtzion, *Early Arabic Sources*, 229.

37. These products from the Sudan, the Sahara, and the Atlantic coast are listed in the works of Ibadi writers cited in ibid., 66–67.

38. Documents in the Cairo Geniza attest to the high value of books; see Goitein, *Mediterranean Society*, 1:196, 259, 266, 382n60. See also Messier, *Almoravids and Jihad*, 28, 199.

39. A significant number of these manuscripts have been collected, preserved or restored, and catalogued at the Centre de Documentation et de Recherches Historiques Ahmed Baba in Timbuktu. To date, the collection has over 16,000 holdings. See the West African Arabic Manuscript Database, "The 'Timbuctu' Records," http://westafricanmanuscripts.org/timbuktu.htm and the Tombouctou Manuscripts Project, http://www.tombouctoumanuscripts.org/.

40. The plate was identified as "probably Egyptian" by Joseph A. Greene at the Harvard Semitic Museum on the basis of photographs that we sent to him.

41. Al-Bakri, *Description de l'Afrique Septentrionale*, 281.

42. For a general description of the ceramics for this and the other two periods,

see the doctoral thesis of Lahcen Taouchikht, a native of the Tafilalt: "Étude Ethno-Archéologique de la Céramique du Tafilalet (Sijilmasa): État de Question." Taouchikht has done an extensive surface survey of the area, examining approximately 140,000 sherds. He generously shared his expertise and data with us.

43. Denise Robert-Chaleix, "Lampes à l'Huile Importeés Découvertes à Tegdaoust: Premier Essai de Classification," *Journal des Africanistes* 53 (1983): 62, cited in Taouchikht, "Étude Ethno-Archéologique," 191.

44. Taouchikht, "Étude Ethno-Archéologique," 192.

45. Pottery with distinctive Andalusian decoration (*verde y morado* and *cuerda seca complète*) was found in the excavation within the mosque, within the area of the public latrine, and most abundantly in the surface collection at Suq Ben Akla. Yet another provenience for imported ceramics was West Africa. Susan McIntosh examined samples of pottery excavated in Sijilmasa in 1988 and recognized three types as "strongly reminiscent of Middle Niger pottery," namely, geometric black on buff painted, a great deal of red slipped pottery, and much twine-impressed polychrome paint (personal communication).

46. Mauny, *Tableau Géographique*, 328–332.

47. Ibn Battuta, cited in Hopkins and Levtzion, *Early Arabic Sources*, 282.

48. Horace Miner, *The Primitive City of Timbuctoo*, 72.

49. Al-Bakri, *Description de l'Afrique Septentrionale*, 301, 339. Recent archaeological work at Tadmekka, Mali, by Sam Nixon, Thilo Rehren, and Maria Filomena Guerra discovered molds that produced blank coins as described by al-Bakri. Traces of gold associated with these molds are 97–98 percent pure gold, justifying al-Bakri's statement that the gold coins of Tadmekka were of "pure gold"; see Nixon et al., "New Light on the Early Islamic West African Gold Trade."

50. J. Devisse, "Or d'Afrique," 236. This statement is corroborated by the research of one of Devisse's graduate students, Rajae Benhsain, whose doctoral dissertation studied year by year, coin die by coin die, the monetary output of the Almohads; see her "Biens Sultaniens, Fiscalité et Monnaie à l'Époque Almohade."

51. Messier, "Muslim Exploitation of West African Gold," and "Quantitative Analysis of Almoravid Dinars." To the extent possible, we employed the die-count method, trying to establish whether coins of the same issue were struck from the same or different dies. The advantage of this is that two different dies then represent several thousand coins rather than just two. Our analysis showed that roughly two-thirds of the published dinars represent coin dies rather than individual coins. Our tabulation is intended to provide not a figure for the number of coins in circulation, but rather a basis for comparing the level of production from one period to another or from one mint to another.

52. Ronald A. Messier, "The Almoravids, West African Gold, and the Gold Currency of the Mediterranean Basin," 39.

53. Messier, "Quantitative Analysis of Almoravid Dinars."

54. Ibn Idhari, *Kitab al-Bayan al-Mughrib fi Akhbar Muluk al-Andalus wa'l-Maghrib*, 25.

55. Heddouchi, "Medieval Coins of Sijilmasa," 154–155.

56. Messier, "Quantitative Analysis of Almoravid Dinars."

57. Messier, "Almoravids, West African Gold, and Gold Currency."

58. The information on Almoravid coins circulating in Europe comes from J. Duplessy, "La Circulation des Monnaies Arabes en Europe Occidentale du VIIIe au XIIIe Siècle."

59. Henri L. Misbach, "Genoese Commerce and the Alleged Flow of Gold to the East, 1154–1253," 80.

60. Goitein, *Mediterranean Society*, 1:235.

61. Ibid., 1:236.

62. Ibid., 1:235–236.

63. Al-Bakri, *Description de l'Afrique Septentrionale*, 301. Recent analyses suggest that the purity of West African gold deposits, which are typically accessible through panning or surface mining, can reach 98 percent or higher; see Nixon et al., "Early Islamic West African Gold Trade."

64. Al-Umari, *Masalik al-Absar fi Mamalik al-Amsar*, 67, 81.

65. Eliyahu Ashtor, *Histoire des Prix et des Salaires dans l'Orient Médiéval*, 92.

66. Ibid., 91–94.

67. Eliyahu Ashtor, "Le Coût de Vie dans l'Egypte Médiévale."

68. Hady Roger Idris, *La Berberie Orientale sous les Zirides X–XIIIè Siècles*, 657n365.

69. The poet is Ibn Arfa' Ra'sufa, cited in Richard Fletcher, *The Quest for El Cid*, 34.

70. Ibid., 71–72.

71. Joan Evans, *Monastic Life at Cluny*, 32–34.

72. Giles Constable, *Crusaders and Crusading in the Twelfth Century*, 274.

73. Ibid., 274n235.

74. For a recent work on the Almohads, see Allen Fromherz, *The Almohads*.

75. For a more detailed account of the development of the Almohad challenge to the Almoravids, see Messier, *Almoravids and Jihad*, 140–144.

76. Haim Zeev Hirschberg, *The History of the Jews in North Africa*, 1:127–128.

77. Goitein, *Mediterranean Society*, 2:300.

78. Ibid.

79. Al-Bakri, *Description de l'Afrique Septentrionale*, 284.

80. *Kitab al-Istibsar*, ed. Fagnan, 165–166.

81. Hirschberg cites this information from Abraham Ibn Ezra's famous lament *Aha yarad* (*Jews in North Africa*, 1:123, 352). Hirschberg concludes: "The sources mentioned indicate that in the 12th century, both before and after the first Almohad persecution, Sijilmasa was a center of rabbinical learning, with scholars important enough for Maimonides to call them his opponents in debate after a lapse of fifty years."

82. "Les Mémoires d'al-Baidak," in *Documents Inédits d'Histoire Amohade*, ed. Évariste Lévi-Provençale, 173–174.

83. J. Schacht, "An Unknown Type of Minbar and Its Historical Significance," 156.

84. At the very end of the 2011 excavating season at Aghmat, Morocco, the Moroccan-American team under the direction of Ronald Messier and Abdallah Fili uncovered another set of rails for a movable *minbar*.

85. Ibn Abi Zar, *Kitab al-Anis al-Mutrib bi-Rawd al-Qirtas fi Akhbar Muluk al-Maghrib wa-Tarikh Madinat Fas*, 35.

86. Henri Terrasse, *La Mosquée al-Qaraouiyin à Fès*, 25–26.

87. Bonine, "Islamic Cities in Morocco."

88. David A. King has done a considerable amount of work on this question. We found the following articles most useful: "Science in the Service of Religion"; "Astronomical Alignments in Medieval Islamic Religious Architecture"; "Al-Bazdawi on the Qibla in Early Islamic Transoxania"; "Architecture and Astronomy"; "The Sacred Direction in Islam"; "Kibla," in the *Encyclopedia of Islam*, 2nd ed., 4:82–88; and with Gerald S. Hawkins, "On the Orientation of the Ka'aba."

89. We analyzed three carbon-14 samples from this unit. One was from the Almoravid-Almohad period, one was from before the Almoravid period, and one was from after the Almohad period.

90. Ahmed Ibn al-Qadi al-Miknassi, *Jadouat al-Iqtibas fi Dhikri man Halla min al-A'lam Madinat Fas*, 167, cited in Mellouki, "L'Histoire des Villes Médiévales du Maroc," 462.

91. Al-Tadili, *Kitab al-Tashawwuf ila Rijal al-Tassawuf*, 332, 378, 417.

92. Laroui, *History of the Maghrib*, 245.

93. Ibn Khaldun, *Kitab al-'Ibar wa Diwan al-Mubtada' wa'l-Khabar fi Ayyam al-'arab wa'l-'ajam Wa'l-Barbar*; edited and translated into French by William Mac-Guckin de Slane as *Histoire des Berbères et des Dynasties Musulmanes de l'Afrique Septentrionale*, 2:410.

94. Jacques-Meunié, *Le Maroc Saharien*, 1:287, which cites Charles de La Roncière, *La Découverte de l'Afrique au Moyen Age: Cartographes et Explorateurs*, 1:113.

95. Ibn Khaldun, *Histoire des Berbères*, 3:356; 4:70.

96. Heddouchi, "Medieval Coins of Sijilmasa," 36.

97. Laroui, *History of the Maghrib*, 245.

98. Jamil M. Abun-Nasr, *A History of the Maghrib in the Islamic Period*, 116–117.

99. Laroui, *History of the Maghrib*, 215.

100. Henri Dastugue, "Quelques Mots au Sujet de Tafilet et de Sidjilmassa," 371.

101. These dates were established by carbon-14 dating by MAPS.

102. Leo Africanus [Leon Africain], *Description de l'Afrique*, 2:430.

103. Ibn Khaldun, *Histoire des Berbères*, 4:191–193.

104. Charles André Julien, *History of North Africa from the Arab Conquest to 1830*, 133.

105. Jacques-Meunié, *Le Maroc Saharien*, 1:289–290.

106. Ibn Khaldun, *Histoire des Berbères*, 4:215.

107. Quoted in Jacques-Meunié, *Le Maroc Saharien*, 1:290, and translated by Ronald Messier.

108. Amin Maalouf, *Leo the African*, 157.

Chapter 5

1. Jacques-Meunié, *Le Maroc Saharien*, 1:297.

2. Donald Moore and Richard Roberts suggest that "listening for silences is equally important in changing and challenging the paradigms of the production of knowledge in our fields [African studies]" ("Listening for Silences," 322–323). In "Lis-

tening for Silences in Almoravid History," Sheryl L. Burkalter applies the theory to the Almoravids. We apply it here more narrowly to Sijilmasa; see Messier, "Listening for Silences in Sijilmasa's History."

3. Jacques-Meunié cites as the source of these contacts "Sources Inédites: Portuguese III," 59 (*Le Maroc Saharien*, 1: 455n46), that is, the third volume of *Les Sources Inédites de l'Histoire du Maroc*, 1st ser., *Archives et Bibliothèques de Portugal*, 5 vols., edited by Pierre de Cenival, David Lopes, Robert Ricard, and Chantal de La Véronne (Paris: Geunther, 1935-1935).

4. Leo Africanus [Leon Africain], *Description de l'Afrique*, 2:428-431.

5. Jacques-Meunié, *Le Maroc Saharien*, 1:297.

6. Jacques-Meunié states that this *qsar* was destroyed in 1830 (*Le Maroc Saharien*, 1:336n24). It was located on the east bank of the Ziz about one kilometer southeast of Tabouassamt.

7. Heddouchi, "Medieval Coins of Sijilmasa," 37.

8. Jacques Meunié, *Le Maroc Saharien*, 1:444-446.

9. The name "Almoravid" is derived from this word. The *murabitin* in this chapter should not be confused with the dynasty in the previous chapter.

10. Quoted in Jamil Abun Nasr, *The Tijaniyya*, 5-6.

11. Heddouchi, "Medieval Coins of Sijilmasa," 38-41.

12. Mohammed Esseghir Ben Elhadj Ben Abdallah al-Oufrani, *Nozhet-Elhadi (Histoire de la Dynastie Saadienne au Maroc, 1511-1670)*, cited in *La Grande Encyclopedie du Maroc*, 4:91.

13. Wilfrid J. W. Blunt, *Black Sunrise*, 40.

14. Jacques-Meunié, *Le Maroc Saharien*, 1:398-399.

15. Leo Africanus [Leon Africain], *Description de l'Afrique*, 96, cited in Jacques-Meunié, *Le Maroc Saharien*, 1:399.

16. Jacques-Meunié provides a detailed account of Abu Mahalli's story (*Le Maroc Saharien*, 2:598-616).

17. Ibid., 2:600.

18. Ibid., 2:601.

19. Ibid., 2:638.

20. Leo Africanus [Leon Africain], *Description de l'Afrique*, 2:428, 430.

21. Taouchikht, "Étude Ethno-Archéologique," 122-123.

22. Leo Africanus, *Description de l'Afrique*, 2:228.

23. Al-Bakri says that the baths built by al-Yas'a were not well constructed (*Description de l'Afrique Septentrionale*, 283).

Chapter 6

1. Oufrani, *Nozhet-Elhadi*, cited in Jacques-Meunié, *Le Maroc Saharien*, 2:645-646.

2. Ibid., 2:647-648.

3. Ibid., 2:649.

4. Dastugue, "Quelques Mots au Sujet de Tafilet et de Sidjilmassa," 363.

5. Ibid., 369-370. The interview was published in 1867.

6. Larbi Mezzine, "Relation d'un Voyage de Tagaza à Sigilmasa en 1096 H./1685 J.C.," 222n31.

7. Dastugue, "Quelques Mots au Sujet de Tafilet et de Sidjilmassa."

8. Mezzine, "Relation d'un Voyage," 212–233.

9. Ibid., 213n212.

10. Ross Dunn, *Resistance in the Desert*, 50–83.

11. Mezzine, "Relation d'un Voyage," 231.

12. Ibid., 224n37.

13. Ibid., 225n40.

14. T. S. Willan, *Studies in Elizabethan Foreign Trade*, 99, 102, 108, 111, 113–114, 135, 266.

15. Dastugue, "Quelques Mots au Sujet de Tafilet et de Sidjilmassa," 370.

16. Al-Naciri, *Kitab al-Istiqsa*, quoted in *La Grande Encyclopedie du Maroc*, 4:109.

17. Ibid., 4:110.

18. Dastugue, "Quelques Mots au Sujet de Tafilet et de Sidjilmassa," 371.

19. Dunn, *Resistance in the Desert*, 89.

20. Ibid., 89–90.

21. Ross Dunn, "The Trade of Tafilalt," 271.

22. Dunn, *Resistance in the Desert*, 292.

23. Mark Ellingham, Shaun McVeigh, and Don Grisbrook, *Morocco, the Rough Guide*, 20.

24. Dunn, *Resistance in the Desert*, 111–112. Dunn reports that a former Native Affairs officer who served in Erfoud in 1925 stated that the slave market at Abu Am was still in operation at the time (*Resistance in the Desert*, 132n20).

25. Dunn, *Resistance in the Desert*, 111.

26. Ibid., 115.

27. Ibid., 116. In 1907, Sultan Moulay Abd al-Aziz paid his *khalifa* Moulay Rashid his monthly salary of 1500 *duros* through the intermediary of Ibn Idris.

28. Ibid., 114.

29. Walter B. Harris, *Tafilet*, 283.

30. Harris estimates the total cost of the expedition at "nearly a million dollars" (ibid., 284).

31. Ibid., 287.

32. Dunn, *Resistance in the Desert*, 213.

33. Ibid., 221.

Chapter 7

1. Dale Eickelman, *The Middle East*, 104–106. Eickelman bases this analysis largely on Stambouli and Zghal, "Urban Life in Pre-colonial North Africa," which, as the title suggests, focuses on North Africa.

2. Bennison and Gascoigne, *Cities in the Pre-Modern Islamic World*, 7–11.

3. This is the pattern in precolonial North African cities described by Stambouli and Zghal ("Urban Life in Pre-colonial North Africa," 4–5).

4. Ibid.

5. Al-Bakri, cited in Hopkins and Levtzion, *Early Arabic Sources*, 65.

6. Paul Wheatley, *The Places Where Men Pray Together*, 335.

7. Bonine, "Islamic Cities in Morocco."

8. Gustave von Grunebaum, *Islam*, 146.

9. Abu-Lughod, "The Islamic City"; Dale Eickelman, "Is There an Islamic City?"; al-Sayyad, *Cities and Caliphs*.

10. Ibn Abdun, *Seville Musulmane au Début du XIIe Siècle*, 95.

11. Taouchikht, "Étude Ethno-Archéologique," 122–123; see also Taouchikht "La Céramique Médiévale de Sijilmassa," 233.

12. Abdallah Fili and Ronald Messier, "La Céramique Médiévale de Sijilmasa," 689–690.

13. Messier, "Sijilmasa: L'Intermédiaire," 184–185.

14. Heddouchi, "Medieval Coins of Sijilmasa," 149–156.

15. Ibn Hawqal, *Kitab Surat al-Ard*, ed. Zaghlul, 97.

16. Ibn Abi Zar, cited in Hopkins and Levtzion, *Early Arabic Sources*, 243.

17. Al-Sayyad, *Cities and Caliphs*, 6, 162n16.

18. Dale Eickelman, *The Middle East and Central Asia*, 95–96.

19. Ibid.

20. Stambouli and Zghal, "Urban Life in Pre-colonial North Africa," 5.

21. Sahih al-Bukhari, Hadith 9.107.

22. MacKenzie, *Ayyubid Cairo*, 78.

23. Abu-Lughod, "The Islamic City," 164–167.

24. Goitein, *A Mediterranean Society*, 2:289–293.

25. Abu-Lughod, "The Islamic City," 167–169.

26. Ibid., 169–171.

27. Touri and Hammam, "Tradition Écrite et Architecture." The text specifies that the individual will be assisted by the tribe in the reconstruction of the first four courses of the wall, but the individual must complete the upper five courses on his own. Each course was 80–85 centimeters (2.6–2.8 feet) high.

28. Ibid., 220n36; translated by Ronald Messier.

29. Bennison and Gascoigne, *Cities in the Pre-Modern Islamic World*, 172, citing David C. Powers, *Law, Society, and Culture in the Maghrib, 1300–1500*, 105.

30. Al-Bakri, *Description de l'Afrique Septentrionale*, 148; Mahmud Abderrazak Isma'il, *Al-Hawarig fi Bilad al-Maghrib min al-Usul Hata muntqasaf al-Qaren ar-Rabi al-Higeri* (1985), quoted in Taouchikht, "Étude Ethno-Archéologique," 120.

Appendix I

1. Love, "Sufris of Sijilmasa."

Appendix 2

1. Taouchikht, "Étude Ethno-Archéologique."

2. Nancy L. Benco, *The Early Medieval Pottery Industry at al-Basra, Morocco.*

3. Numbers followed by ellipsis points are left open for anticipated variations that did not materialize.

4. Abdallah Fili, "La Céramique Médiévale du Maroc"; Messier and Fili, "Earliest Ceramics of Sijilmasa."

Glossary

Foreign words are italicized unless they are commonly used in English or are proper nouns.

abid al-Bukhari   Slaves who swore an oath of loyalty to the sultan upon the book of hadith compiled by al-Bukhari.

Aid al-kabir   Also known as Aid al-adha. A major feast day in the Islamic calendar on which Muslims sacrifice a sheep to honor the prophet Abraham's willingness to sacrifice his young son Ismail.

Aid al-saghir   Also known as Aid al-fitr or the feast of the breaking of the fast. It celebrates the end of Ramadan.

Ait Atta   A tribal confederation in the southeastern corner of Morocco.

Ait Khabbash   A tribe of the Ait Atta. It dominated the region from the Tafilalt to Touat, controlling the trade routes going south from the Tafilalt across the Sahara to Timbuktu, as well as the route going north to Fez.

al-Mahdiya   The capital city of the Fatimids in Ifriqiya (modern Tunisia) from 921 until they moved their capital to al-Mansuriya in 946.

al-Mansuriya   The capital of the Fatimids until they moved their capital to Cairo in 969.

Alaouites   The ruling dynasty in Morocco from c. 1631 to the present.

Almohads   The ruling dynasty in Morocco from c. 1130 to 1147.

Almoravids   The ruling dynasty in Morocco from 1055/6 to 1146/7.

Amazigh   Many Berbers call themselves some variant of the word *imazighen* (singular: Amazigh), possibly meaning "free people" or "free and noble men."

Amerbouh   A stream (oued) that is part of the Oued Ziz basin. It runs from the vicinity of Erfoud, at the northern end of the Tafilalt, and rings the eastern edge of the Tafilalt plain before rejoining the Oued Ziz at the southern end of the Tafilalt. It is suspected that the mouth of the Amerbouh was blocked in Almoravid times in order to increase the flow of the Ziz through the Tafilalt in a hydroengineering project connected to the straightening of the Ziz and the heightening of agricultural productivity in and around Sijilmasa.

amin   An official appointed by the *muhtasid*, the marketplace supervisor, to ensure the accuracy of merchants' weights and measures. The *amin*'s job was to calibrate scales, check weights and counterweights, and mark with his seal those within the margin of tolerance.

amir A commander. Military commanders usually had administrative responsibilities, and political rulers had military responsibilities. The term "amir" refers to a ruler at some level—the title of princes of a ruling family, a tribal chief, etc.

Andalusia Anglicized term for the Arabic "al-Andalus," the southern parts of the Iberian Peninsula, which were under Islamic rule between 711 and 1492. Today it refers to the southern province of Spain.

Aterian A type (and period) of toolmaking by both early (archaic) and modern *Homo sapiens* in northern Africa, distinguished by bifacial and nosed flint points and scrapers in addition to snail shell beads; named after finds at Bir al Ater, an archaeological site (and city) in eastern Algeria south of Tebessa. Aterian toolmaking, which dates to no earlier than 85,000 BP (before the present), and in Europe is identified as Cro Magnon culture, is subsumed within the general period of Mousterian culture of the later half of the Paleolithic, datable in northern Africa (Morocco to Egypt) from about 200,000 to 35,000 BP. Aterian culture vanished from the Maghrib as the climate became increasingly colder and drier toward the end of the last glacial maximum, around 30,000 BP. Some hold that the bow and arrow was an invention of Aterian culture; small barbed flints mounted in rows on bone and wooden sickles indicate that Aterian peoples harvested wild grain.

Artemisia A genus of plants including the sagebrush and wormwood.

Awdaghust An important oasis town at the southern end of a trans-Saharan caravan route; it is mentioned in a number of early Arabic manuscripts. The archaeological ruins at Tegdaoust in southern Mauritania are thought to be the remains of the medieval Awdaghust.

Awlad Hussein One of the tribes of the Maʿqil Arabs.

Awlil One of the salt deposits on the coast of southern Mauritania north of the Senegal River.

bab The Arabic word for gate or door. It is often used as part of the name of city gates.

Bani Abd al-Wad Otherwise known as the Bani Zayyan or the Zayyanids. They constituted one of the Zanata tribes of the central Maghrib. Through military prowess and diplomacy, they managed to rule almost continuously from their capital at Tlemcen for over three centuries, from the second quarter of the thirteenth century through the mid-sixteenth century.

Bani Ahlaf One of the tribes of the Maʿqil Arabs.

Bani Gudala One of the tribes of the Sanhaja confederation of tribes in the western Sahara.

Bani Iznassin A tribe in the lower Moulouya valley.

Bani Khazrun A tribe of the Bani Maghrawa confederation that ruled in Sijilmasa before the Almoravid conquest.

Bani Marghrawa The tribal rulers of Sijilmasa and its environs from 976 to 1055/6.

Bani Midrar The tribal rulers of Sijilmasa and its environs from 758 to 963.

baraka A special blessing, gift, or power given by God. *Baraka* is sometimes believed to be bestowed upon a special person, through whom it may be extended to those associated with that person.

baya'a   From the verb "to sell." The *baya'a* is the expression of allegiance to a leader in Islam. In Morocco, the Alaouite dynasty continues the practice of having notables swear allegiance in an annual ceremony of *baya'a* at the time of the Fête du Trône (*Aid al-arsh*) to the king, where it is seen, despite current controversy surrounding the practice, as a foundational element of monarchical rule.

bayyoud   Date palm wilt. *Fusarium oxysporum f.sp. albedinis*, a filamentous fungi distributed in the soil, enters the root system of the date palm (*Phoenix dactylifera*) and travels up the xylem of the tree, eventually killing it. *Bayyoud* tends to whiten the date palm fronds with powdery mildew, thus the Arabic meaning of the word, "whitening." Detected in the date palms of Moroccan oases in the early twentieth century, *bayyoud* presents a persistent and unsolved scourge on the production of dates in Morocco, since areas infected by *bayyoud* are generally abandoned and no remedy to *bayyoud* has proved effective.

Berber   The indigenous ethnic group of North Africa west of the Nile Valley. They are continuously distributed from the Atlantic Ocean to the Siwa oasis in Egypt, and from the Mediterranean to the Niger River. Historically, they spoke the Berber language and local varieties of it, which together form the Berber branch of the Afro-Asiatic language family.

Bhayr pottery   Pottery that was produced in the Qsar Bhayr al-Ansar, to the immediate southwest of Sijilmasa. Produced in the eighteenth and nineteenth centuries, this pottery is a distinctive time marker for eighteenth- and nineteenth-century levels of occupation in Sijilmasa.

caliph   Literally, "one who comes after" or "successor." It refers to the successors of the Prophet Mohammed.

Capsian   A type (and period) of culture in North Africa, placed within the context of the broader Mesolithic culture, spanning the extent of the post-Pleistocene pluvial period in regional earth history, from perhaps as early as 15,000 and as late as 5,000 BC. Capsian culture prevailed across the northern Sahara in savanna environments where hunting and gathering populations practiced distinctive burial practices during more pluvial conditions as depicted in petroglyphs and parietal rock art. Named for cultural elements first identified at Gafsa (Roman "Capsa"), in south-central Tunisia.

dar al-imara   Literally, "house of the *amir*"; the site of government.

dar al-Islam   Literally, "house of peace." Those areas under an Islamic government, as opposed to the *dar al-harb* (literally, the "house of war"), referring to those areas where Islam does not have jurisdiction.

dar al-sikka or *dar al-saff*   Literally, "the house of striking"; a mint.

Dawi Mani   Bani Hilal tribe of the Moroccan-Algerian border area between Taghit and the Tafilalt region. It controlled most of the area east of the Oued Ziz.

Dila   A *zawiya*, or Sufi brotherhood, in the western Middle Atlas Mountains that strove first to overthrow the last of the Saadians and then to control the rest of Morocco.

dinar   An early Islamic gold coin weighing 1 *mithqal* (about 4.25 grams).

dirham   An early Islamic silver coin. The official exchange rate of gold to silver coins in the eleventh century was around 1:18, whereas the actual rate of exchange could reach 1:35 or 1:40, depending on a number of factors such as deterioration of the silver content, hoarding in time of panic, ore calamity, and so on.

faqih (pl., *fuqaha*)   A scholar of Muslim law, a theologian, an expert in *fiqh*, a legist, one whose legal opinions are accepted as a basis of law.

Fasi   An adjective meaning "of Fez."

Fatimids   An Isma'ili Shi'ite caliphate originally based in Tunisia. It extended its rule across the Mediterranean coast of Africa and ultimately made Egypt the center of its caliphate.

fiqh   Understanding; Islamic jurisprudence.

Filalian   Referring to people and things from the Tafilalt. In the context of this book, it refers more specifically to local rulers of the Tafilalt following the civil war that brought the control of Sijilmasa by the Merinid rulers of Fez to an end. The current ruling dynasty of Morocco, the Alaouites, are Filalians who rose to power in the Tafilalt in the mid-seventeenth century and then extend their rule to the rest of Morocco.

funduk   A caravansary, an inn, an enclosure to shelter travelers and their beasts of burden.

gamaman (sing., *gamoun*)   Agricultural zone; a series of enclosed fields within a larger enclosure.

Gao   A city in Mali on the Niger River, 320 km (200 mi) east-southeast of Timbuktu.

Gheris   One of the two main streams (oueds) of the Tafilalt, the other being the Ziz. The Oued Gheris rises in the Eastern High Atlas, is joined by the Oued Todghra at the foot of the mountains, and flows south and east to nearly meet the Oued Ziz at Erfoud. The Gheris forms the western margin of the Tafilalt oasis and runs roughly parallel to the Ziz throughout the oasis's extent. The Gheris was repeatedly dammed throughout the much of Sijilmasa's history. Some twenty-two dams are identifiable—all in ruins—along its course. Contemporary embankment dams in its northern sections add to the irrigation projects associated with Hassan ad-Dakhil to provide water for the Tafilalt.

GIS   A geographic information system designed to capture, store, manipulate, analyze, manage, and graphically present all types of geographic data.

hadith (sing. and pl.)   Sayings and traditions attributed to the Prophet Mohammed through an unbroken chain of reliable sources.

hajj   The Islamic pilgrimage to Mecca required of all believers.

hammada   A desert landform; a plateau that is normally swept bare of sand or gravel. Their scale ranges from small and isolated mountain-like rises to vast uplifts thousands of square kilometers in size. Similar to the mesas of the desert Southwest and Mexico, they are the most prominent landscape feature throughout the northwestern Sahara.

haraka   A movement; a military operation or uprising.

Hassan ad-Dakhil   A low earthen embankment dam on the Oued Ziz, constructed just upstream from the city of Errachidia. It was built by the U.S. Agency for International Development (USAID) assistance program for Morocco and was completed in March 1971. The dam has no hydroelectric-generation capacity and was built solely to regulate flooding and to improve irrigation for downstream users, including, most importantly, the date palm orchards of the Tafilalt. Instead, the dam has served mainly to provide an abundant source of water for the growth of Errachidia. Hassan ad-Dakhil, a descendant of the Prophet and a resident in Yanbu, Arabia, was the first Alaouite to come to Morocco, at the request of Berber-speaking pilgrims from Sijilmasa, where he arrived in 1266.

hijra Migration. The migration of the Prophet Mohammed and his Muslim followers from Mecca to Medina in 622. The Islamic calendar begins with this migration.

hisba Manual for marketplace supervision.

Holocene A geologic epoch that followed the long Pleistocene and its many substages and continues to today. The transition between the Pleistocene and the Holocene was marked by a sudden return to much colder temperatures, a change known as the Younger Dryas event. The Holocene witnessed the shift in human cultures from the Mesolithic, as demonstrated in the northern Sahara by the Capsian period throughout the first half of the Holocene, to the appearance of Neolithic cultures after 5,000 YA. In recent years, the Holocene has been described as another interglacial period, implying that earlier ideas about the Pleistocene being over may have to be recast.

Homo erectus "Upright man." *Homo erectus* appears in the fossil record from about 1.8 million BP and to about 300,000 BP. *Erectus* was present throughout the Maghrib. Important finds have been made in Morocco; most recently, a complete *erectus* mandible was found at the (endangered) Thomas Quarry in Casablanca in 2008. The prevalence of *erectus* in North Africa has given rise to the identification of a subspecies, *Homo mauritanicus.*

Homo sapiens The immediate evolutionary ancestor of anatomically modern humans, *Homo sapiens sapiens,* which cannot currently be dated earlier than 100,000 BP. *Homo sapiens,* which had slightly different anatomical characteristics, can be dated to at least 160,000 years ago in Africa and 200,000 years ago in China, despite origins commonly held to be in East Africa.

Homo sapiens sapiens A subspecies of *Homo sapiens* that includes all modern humans.

Ibadi A denomination in Islam. Historians as well as most Muslims believe that the denomination is a branch of the Khawarij or Kharijite sect. But Ibadis continue to deny any but a passing relation to the Kharijites and point out that they merely developed out of the same precursor group.

Iberomaurusian People (and their culture) appearing in the paleontological record of the Maghrib and Iberia around 16,000 YA, the beginning of the end of the Pleistocene. Iberomaurusians hunted Barbary sheep, wild cattle, gazelles, zebras, and deer; their diet included freshwater snails and wild plants. Iberomaurusian culture appears to have disappeared with the advent of the Younger Dryas event. The term was first used to identify finds in northwestern Algeria in 1909 by P. Pallary, and has been carried by some scientists of prehistoric North Africa, most notably Gabriel Camps.

irar A special type of date grown in the area around Sijilmasa. According to al-Bakri, the dates were of the best quality, "better than the dates of Basra."

Ibn Abd Allah, Mosque of The Friday mosque in Sijilmasa at the time of the Almoravids, identified in the *Kitab al-Tashawwuf ila Rijal al-Tassawuf,* although the text does not identify which person named Ibn Abd Allah is meant.

Ifriqiya In medieval history, the area comprising the coastal regions of modern western Libya, Tunisia, and eastern Algeria. This area included what had been the Roman province of Africa, whose name it inherited.

imam   A Muslim prayer leader; a leader of the religious community.

INSAP   Institut National des Sciences d'Archéologie et du Patrimoine; the National Institute for the Study of Archaeology and Patrimony in Morocco, established in 1987.

Jebel Mudawwar   "Round Mountain." An isolated mesa naturally fortified by virtue of its round crest enclosing an eroded interior, located 16 km (12 miles) west of Sijilmasa. Remains of stone fortifications and structures are apparent today.

jama'a   The supreme executive and judicial body of a village; it deliberated on all matters of concern to the inhabitants.

Kharijite, Kharijism   One of the three main sects of Islam, the other two being Sunni and Shi'ite. Kharijite Islam is the sect that was predominant in North Africa in the early centuries of Islam.

khettara   A gravity-fed, underground aqueduct, constructed by digging vertical shafts in a line and then connecting them by digging a horizontal tunnel through which water travels. This system is called *qanatir* in much of the Arab World.

kreb   A desert landform term used widely in the northwestern Sahara in association with *hamada*; the cliff of a *hamada*.

Kufic   A style of Arabic script that consists of square-shaped letters.

lacustrine   Of or related to a lake. The northern Sahara is dotted with lacustrine plains, former lakes filled by subsequent sedimentation. Lakes in the northern Sahara were part of the topography of the pluvial period in recent geologic history, the post-Pleistocene pluvial (12,000–5000 BP).

Lalla Maghnia, Treaty of   In 1845, it established the border between Algeria and Morocco, but only as far south as Taniat al-Sassi, some seventy miles inland from the Mediterranean coast.

Lamtuna   One of the main tribes of the Berber confederation of tribes known as Sanhaja. In another sense, it remains a caste name applied to nobles and a military aristocracy.

Ma'qil Arabs   A Yemeni nomadic tribe that migrated to the Maghrib in the thirteenth century.

madinat al-'amra   Literally, the "inhabited city." It refers to the northern part of Sijilmasa, which was enclosed within the restored citadel under Moulay Ismail.

madrasa   A theological university; in essence, the word for "school" in Arabic.

Maghrawa   A tribe from the Zanata Berber confederation. Its members controlled Sijilmasa first as clients of the Umayyads of Cordoba, then independently until they were defeated by the Almoravids in 1055.

Maghrib   In Arabic, the geographic West. "Maghrib" refers to the geographic region that today includes Morocco, Algeria, Tunisia, and western Libya. In medieval times, Arabs used the term to refer to northwestern Africa beyond the Atlas and toward the Atlantic and the Mediterranean.

Mahdi   The divinely guided one, the one who will conquer the world and restore it to true Islam. Ubayd Allah, the founder of the Fatimid dynasty in Tunisia in 909, was considered al-Mahdi by his followers, as was Ibn Tumart, the founder of the Almohad dynasty in Morocco.

makhzan or *bilad al-makhzan*   Literally, "storehouse" or "treasury"; as a political concept, it refers to the lands controlled by the central power in the premodern state, especially those where taxes were collected.

makus   Taxes on market purchases.

Maliki school, Malikite   One of the schools of *fiqh*, or religious law, within Sunni Islam. It derives from the work of Malik Ibn Anas. It has been the dominant school of law in North Africa since at least the tenth century.

MAPS   Acronym for the Moroccan-American Project at Sijilmasa.

marabout   A Muslim religious leader and teacher in the Maghrib, often a scholar of the Quran or a religious teacher. Marabouts may be wandering holy men who survive on alms, or leaders of religious communities. "Marabout" can also mean "saint" and refer to a Sufi teacher who leads a lodge or a school called a *zawiya*.

Mauretania   In antiquity, Mauretania was an independent kingdom in northwestern Africa named after the Mauri tribe, from which the term "Moors" is derived. After the defeat of Carthage by the Romans, Mauretania became a Roman province. Ancient Mauretania is not to be confused with the modern Mauritanian state.

Mauretania Caesariensis   A Roman province located in northwestern Africa. It was the easternmost of the North African Roman provinces, mainly in present-day Algeria and partly in Morocco, with its capital at Caesarea (hence the name Caesariensis).

Mauretania Tingitana   A Roman province coinciding roughly with the northern part of present-day Morocco and the Spanish cities of Ceuta and Melilla. The province extended from the northern peninsula, opposite Gibraltar, to Chella (or Sala) and Volubilis to the south, and as far east as the Oued Laou. Its capital was the city of Tingis, modern Tangier.

mechouar   The area surrounding the royal palace, which served as a place where allegiance, *bay'a*, was pledged to the sultan and where the sultan made public appearances.

mellah   From the word *malh*, Arabic for "salt," the *mellah* is the Jewish quarter in Moroccan cities.

Merinids   The ruling dynasty in Morocco from c. 1216 to 1471.

Merzouga   A small village in southeastern Morocco, about 35 km southeast of Rissani. The village is known for its proximity to Erg Chebbi, a Saharan erg, and it is for this reason a part of the itineraries of many tourists visiting Morocco. Merzouga has the largest natural underground body of water in Morocco.

Microlith   A small stone tool chipped by early humans, typically from flint or chert, and generally not more than a centimeter long. It was used for the sharp points—spears, arrows, blades—of hunting instruments. Microliths are often a key component of dating archaeological finds.

Midrariya   Adjective for the Bani Midrar.

mihrab   The niche in the *qibla* wall of a mosque indicating the direction toward Mecca and thus the direction of prayer.

mim **punch**   The punch that engravers used to form the Arabic letter *mim* on a coin die.

minbar   The chair from which the imam preaches the Friday noon sermon.

mithqal   unit of mass equal to 4.25 grams and used mostly for precious metals. The dinar was theoretically equal to 1 *mithqal*.

moto-pompe   French for "motor pump." A two-stroke diesel engine used to draw water from wells. In the Tafilalt, the use of the *moto-pompe* has proliferated since the impoundment of the Oued Ziz, the construction of the Hassan ad-Dakhil dam, and the subsequently insufficient flow of water in the modern irrigation infrastructure of the Tafilalt.

Moulouya   River in Morocco running 520 km (330 miles) from the Eastern High Atlas Mountains to the Mediterranean Sea in the northeastern part of the country. Its course facilitated traditional trade routes.

muhtasib   The supervisor of all marketplace activities.

muluk al-tawa'if   The "party kings" of Andalusia who formed independent city-states from the ultimate fall of the Umayyad dynasty of Cordoba in 1031 until the coming of the Almoravids in c. 1090.

murabit (pl., *murabitin*)   A person imbued with holiness, or *baraka*, to the point that he or she may be recognized as a holy person with a group of followers; the followers may become a recognized *tariqa*, or separate caste of holiness, organized into its own *zawiya*.

Numidia   An ancient Berber kingdom occupying the heartland of modern Algeria and western Tunisia. It began as a sovereign state under Masinissa (240/238 BC–c. 148) and was later absorbed into the Roman Empire.

noria   A waterwheel used to lift water from the lower level of an irrigation channel or oued to a higher level.

ORMVAT (Office Régional de Mise en Valeur Agricole du Tafilalet)   One of a group of similar offices established to develop irrigated agricultural regions (*"perimètres"*) in Morocco. It dates from 1966, at the time of the beginnings of the Hassan ad-Dakhil dam. Headquartered in Errachidia, it is responsible for agricultural development throughout the reach of the dam. The "Office," as it is known throughout the region, employs over 500 people and supervises over 60,000 hectares (148,260 acres) of private irrigated agricultural lands throughout Errachidia Province.

Oualata   A small oasis town in southeastern Mauritania that was important in the thirteenth and fourteenth centuries as the southern terminus of the trans-Saharan trade.

oued or **wadi**   A river or riverbed. In many cases, it refers to a dry riverbed that contains water only during times of heavy rain.

Paleolithic   A prehistoric period distinguished by the development of very primitive stone tools. It extends from around 2.6 million YA to the end of the Pleistocene, around 10,000 YA.

parietal art   Also called "cave art." The term refers to the drawings or incisions on rock walls or large rock surfaces by early humans. Parietal art is widespread throughout the Maghrib and is especially an indicator of changing human life and environmental resources in the northern Sahara over time.

petroglyph   A set of images or scenes depicted in parietal art. The term may refer to a work of art left on a single surface or a smaller section of a larger work. The difference between the terms "petroglyph" and "parietal art" is one of scale or focus. A petroglyph is art on a single rock face or on rock in a single place; parietal art refers to the field of study of art on rock surfaces.

Pleistocene   The geological epoch that lasted from about 2,588,000 to 11,700 YA, spanning the world's recent period of repeated glaciations.

qadi   A judge.

qa'id   A local governor or leader, especially in North Africa or Islamic Spain.

qa'id al-suq   Director of marketplace supervision, or what in medieval Sijilmasa was called the *muhtasib*.

Qadi Iyad ("Cadi Ayyad")   A Maliki scholar (1083-1149) who wrote during the Almoravid period.

qibla   The direction of Mecca, toward which Muslims pray.

qsar (pl., *qsur*)   A fortified village.

qubba   A dome.

Rashidun   Literally, "the rightly guided ones." When describing caliphs, it refers to the first four caliphs.

ratl (pl., *artal*)   A pound in weight.

Reconquista   Reconquest; refers here to the effort made by Spanish Christians to re-capture land that had been conquered by Muslims beginning in 711.

ribat   A fortified post, where horses were sometimes stabled. The garrison of a *ribat* combined military duties with agriculture and pious and ascetic practices. It was usually located on or near the frontier of *dar al-Islam*. Also, a fortified monastery or convent. At times, this word had a metaphorical meaning indicating a frame of mind, a spiritual resolve, that combined deep devotion to Islam, self-sacrifice, and the courage to face alone, or with a like group, those enemies that threatened the faith.

Rissani   A town in the center of the Tafilalt oasis to the immediate east of medieval Sijilmasa.

Rteb   A town on the west bank of the Oued Ziz, located approximately halfway between Erfoud and Errachidia.

Saadians   The ruling dynasty in Morocco from c. 1510 to 1659.

sahil   Literally, "coastal." The term takes on many meanings: near the coast, on the coast, a region along the coast (of a body of water). It also has the sense of near the desert, in that in Arabic, as in other languages, a desert can be likened to a large body of land, unpopulated, with edges toward a land with people. Thus, Sijilmasa has been referred to as *sahili*, coastal, "the edge of the desert," much as the word (spelled "Sahel") has come, in recent years, to mean the edge of the desert along the southern flank of the Sahara in lands stretching from Senegal to Ethiopia.

sawic   A nutritious staple made of wheat, ground dates, sugar, butter, and pepper. Portable and long-lasting, it was often a basic food of caravaners.

Sefrou   A small town in central Morocco, located 29 km (18 mi) southeast of Fez.

Sevener   A branch of Isma'ili Shi'ites. Seveners believed that Isma'il Ibn Ja'far was the seventh and last imam in the direct line of Ali.

sharif (pl., *shurfa*, *cherif*, or *chorfa* in common transliteration in Morocco)   One who claims descent from the Prophet.

shaykh   An elderly, venerable man; an elder; a chief of a tribe.

shaykh al-qabilah   Tribal leader elected by the tribe.

Shi'a, Shi'ite   The second-largest sect in Islam. "*Shi'a*" is the short form of the historic phrase "*Shi'atu Ali*," meaning followers, faction, or party of Mohammed's son-in-law and cousin Ali, whom the Shi'a believe to be Mohammed's successor.

sidi   Literally, "my master." A masculine title of respect, equivalent to the modern popular usage of the English "Mr."

sikka   The striking of official coinage; the official insignia or inscription that appears on the coinage.

solidus   Originally, a gold coin issued by the Romans and a weight for gold more generally, corresponding to 4.5 grams.

Suq Ben Akla   A market and staging area for large caravans, located west of Sijilmasa.

spatial analysis   Analysis of the provenience, placement, or distribution of archaeological features or artifacts.

stratigraphy   In archaeology, the layering of levels of occupation.

Sudan or *bilad al-sudan*   Literally, the "Land of the Blacks." In medieval Arabic literature, it referred to sub-Saharan Africa, not to be confused with the modern country Sudan.

Sufi   A Muslim mystic. The term comes from the Arabic *suf*, which means "wool" and probably refers to the wool clothes worn by communities of mystics.

Sufriya   By the mid-eighth century, a label being applied to Kharijites who had no Ibadi affiliation.

Sultan al-Khal (the "Black Sultan")   The Black Sultan has been identified as Sultan Abu Yusuf Ya'qub, who took Sijilmasa by storm in 1274 and allegedly destroyed the spring of Timedrine to punish the inhabitants. It can also refer to Sultan Abu'l-Hassan, who took the city by storm in 1333 after a long, painful, yearlong siege that left the city in despair. The Black Sultan can likewise refer to the last governor of Sijilmasa, whose name we do not know but who was killed by its inhabitants in 1393, as described by Leo Africanus.

Sunni   The largest branch of Islam. Its adherents are referred to in Arabic as *ahlu-s-sunnati wa-l-jama'a*, "people of the tradition of Mohammed." In English, they are known as Sunni Muslims, Sunnis, or Sunnites.

suq   A market.

Sus ("Souss")   A region in the southwestern part of the Maghrib.

Tabouassamt   One of the largest and most secure of the *qsur* in the Tafilalt, located about 5 km south of Rissani and the ruins of Sijilmasa, but on the opposite, that is, west, bank of the Ziz River.

Tafilalt   The large oasis in the southeast of Morocco, between the southern tip of the High Atlas Mountains and the Sahara, where Sijilmasa is located.

tafsir al-Quran   Exegesis of the Quran.

Tasagdalt   The stone fort identified by al-Bakri as the refuge of Ibn al-Fath when the Fatimid commander Jawhar took Sijilmasa in 958.

Tazaroualt   A *zawiya* in the Anti-Atlas Mountains that competed with the Dila *zawiya* for control of the Tafilalt.

tawhid   Oneness; the doctrine of monotheism in Islam.

Teghaza   An salt-mining center up to the end of the sixteenth century, now abandoned, located 857 km (533 mi) south of Sijilmasa.

Tegdaoust   The principal commercial entrepôt on the southern edge of the Sahara; it was in direct contact with Sijilmasa. The archaeological ruins at Tegdaoust in southern Mauritania are thought to be the remains of the medieval Awdaghust.

Tifinagh   Script traditionally used by the Touareg (Berber/Amazigh) people and widely used throughout the Sahara and the Maghrib in pre-Islamic times; adopted as the official Amazigh script in Morocco today.

Timbuktu (Timbuctu; Tombouctou)   A town in the modern West African nation of Mali situated 20 km (12 mi) north of the River Niger on the southern edge of the Sahara. It was established around the year 1100 and played a key role in the trans-Saharan gold trade. It came under the control of Morocco during the Saadian dynasty.

Timedrine   Spring located on the west bank of the Ziz, just north of Sijilmasa.

Tripolitania   A region that included Tripoli, the capital city of modern Libya, and a vast northwestern portion of the country. Founded by the Phoenicians in the seventh century BC, it was conquered by the Greek rulers of Cyrenaica, who were in turn displaced by the Carthaginians. The Romans captured Tripolitania in 146 BC. In the seventh century, Tripolitania was conquered by the Rashidun caliphate and was inherited by its descendants, the Umayyads and the Abbasids. It was taken by the Fatimids in the tenth century.

ulama (sing., *alim*)   Religious scholars in Islam.

Umayyads   The first dynasty formed in Islam (in 661) after the Rashidun caliphs. Their capital was Damascus. After the Abbasid Revolution in 750, the surviving Umayyads reestablished their regime in Andalusia, with their new capital in Cordoba.

usul al-fiqh   The sources of Islamic law.

vizier   Religious scholar in Islam.

wali   Someone who has *walaya* (authority or guardianship) over somebody else; an administrative title used to designate governors of administrative divisions. The division that a *wali* governs is called a *wilaya*.

wargiya   A type of kale commonly grown in the northern Sahara.

Wattasids   The ruling dynasty in Morocco from 1472 to 1549. Related to the Merinids, they settled in the Rif Mountains after the last days of the Almohad dynasty and held important posts under the Merinids intermittently during the fourteenth century.

Zanata   One of the three great confederations of Berber tribes. It was located mainly in the plains north of the Atlas Mountains.

zawiya   A school or a group of students following the teaching of a particular master; a Sufi brotherhood or the shrine of a saint.

Zirids   A Sanhaja Berber dynasty that governed Ifriqiya from 973 to 1148. Initially governing on behalf of the Fatimids, the Zirids became independent in 1048.

Ziz   The river that runs through the center of the Tafilalt oasis. Sijilmasa is located on the east bank of the Oued Ziz.

Bibliography

Medieval Arabic Sources

Baidak, al-. "Les Mémoires d'al-Baidak." In *Documents Inédits d'Histoire Almohade*, edited by Évariste Lévi-Provençal. Paris: Librairie Orientaliste Paul Geuthner, 1928.

Bakri, Ubayd Allah Ibn Abd al-Aziz al-. *Kitab al-Mughrib fi Dhikr Bilad Ifriqiya wa-'l-Maghrib*. In French: *Description de l'Afrique Septentrionale*. Edited and translated by William MacGuckin de Slane. Paris: Librairie d'Amérique et d'Orient Adrien Maisonneuve, 1965.

Al-Hulal al-Mawshiyya. Edited by I. S. Allouche. Rabat: Impr. Economique, 1936. In Spanish: *Coleccion de Cronicas Arabes de la Reconquista*. Translated by Ambrosio Huici-Miranda. Tetuan: Editora Marroqui, 1952. Edited by Suhail Zakar and Abd al-Qadir Zamamah. Casablanca: Dār al-Rashād al-Hadīdthah, 1979.

Ibn Abdun. *Séville Musulmane au Début du XIIe Siècle: Le Traité d'Ibn Abdun sur la Vie Urbaine et les Corps de Métiers*. Edited and translated by Évariste Lévi-Provençal. Paris: Maisonneuve et Larose, 1947.

Ibn Abi Zar. *Kitab al-Anis al-Mutrib bi-Rawd al-Qirtas fi Akhbar Muluk al-Maghrib wa-Tarikh Madinat Fas* [Book of the entertaining companion in the garden of paper on the history of kings in the Maghrib and of the city of Fez]. Edited and translated by C. J. Tornberg. Uppsala: Litteris Academicis, 1843.

———. *Kitab al-Anis al-Mutrib bi-Rawd al-Qirtas fi Akhbar Muluk al-Maghrib wa Tarikh Madinat Fas. Roudh el-Kartas: Histoire des Souverains du Maghreb et Annales de la Ville de Fes*. Translated into French by A. Beaumier. Paris: L'Imprimerie Impériale, 1860.

Ibn al-Athir. *Al-Kamil fi'l-Tarikh*. Edited by C. J. Tornberg. Leiden and Uppsala, 1851–1876. Reprint, Beirut, 1966.

Ibn Battuta. *Muhadhabb Rihlat Ibn Battutah*. Edited by Ahmad Alawamri and Mohammad Ahmad Jaad al-Moulay. Cairo: Dar al-Kutub, 1934.

———. *Tuhfat al-Nuzzar fi Ghari'ib al-Amsar wa-'aja'ib al-Asfar*. In English: *Travels of Ibn Battuta, AD 1325–1354*. 5 vols. Translated by H. A. R. Gibb and C. F.

Beckingham (vol. 5). Cambridge: Hakluyt Society, 1958–2000. Reprint, London: Routledge Curzon, 2005.

Ibn Hawqal, Abu'l-Qasim al-Nasibi. *Kitab Surat al-Ard* [Book of the picture of the Earth]. Edited by Sa'd Zaghlul. Beirut: Dar Maktabat al-Ayah, 1964. See also the Arabic text as edited by J. H. Kramers, Bibliotheca Geographorum Arabicorum 2, no. 1, 2nd ed. Leiden: Brill, 1938–1939.

Ibn Idhari al-Marrakushi. *Kitab al-Bayan al-Mughrib fi Akhbar Muluk al-Andalus wa'l-Maghrib* [Book of the amazing exposition of the history of al-Andalus and the Maghrib]. Edited by Ahsan Abbas. Beirut and London: Dar al-Thaqafah, 1967.

Ibn Khaldun. *Kitab al-'ibar wa Diwan al-Mubtada' wa'l-Khabar fi Ayyam al-'arab wa'l-'ajam wa'l-Barbar*. In French: *Histoire des Berbères et des Dynasties Musulmanes de l'Afrique Septentrionale*. 2 vols. Edited and translated by William MacGuckin de Slane. Algiers: 1847, 1851. Reprint, 4 vols., Paris: Librairie Orientale Paul Geuthner, 1925–1956.

Ibn Kaldun. *The Muqaddimah: An Introduction to History*. 3 vols. Translated by Franz Rosenthal. New York: Pantheon, 1958.

Ibn Tumart, Muhammad Ibn 'Abd Allah. *A'azzu ma yutlab*. Published with French translation as *Le Livre de Mohammed Ibn Toumert*. Edited and translated by Ignác Goldziher. Algiers: Fontana, 1903.

Idrisi, Abu 'Abd Allah Muhammad Ibn Muhammad al-Sharif al-. *Nuzhat al-Mushtaq fi Ikhtiraq al-Afaq*. Published with French translation as *Description de l'Afrique et de l'Espagne par Edrisi*. Edited and translated by Reinhart Dozy and Michael Jan de Goeje. Leiden: Brill, 1866. Reprint, Amsterdam: Oriental Press, 1969.

Kitab al-Istibsar. Edited and translated by Edmond Fagnan as *Afrique Septentrionale au XIIe Siècle de Notre Ère*. Constantine, Algeria: Braham, 1900.

———. Edited by Sa'd Zaghlul. Alexandria: Matba'at Jami'at al-Iskandariyah, 1958.

Leo Africanus. *The History and Description of Africa and of the Notable Things Therein*. 3 vols. New York: Burt Franklin, 1896.

——— [as Leon Africain]. *Description de l'Afrique [par] Jean-Léon L'Africain*. Translated by Alexis Épaulard. Paris: Adrien-Maisonneuve, 1956.

Mafakhir al-Barbar: Fragments Historiques sur les Berbères au Moyen-Age; Extraits Inédits d'un Recueil Anonyme Compilé en 712/1312 et Intitulé: Kitab Mafakhir al-Barbar. Arabic text edited by Évariste Lévi-Provençal. Rabat: Moncho, 1934.

Marrakushi, Abu Muhammad Abd al-Wahid al-. *Kitab al-Mu'jib fi Talkhis Akhbar al-Maghrib*. Cairo, 1963. Translated into French as *Histoire des Almohades* by Edmond Fagnan. Algiers: Adolphe Jourdan, 1893.

Qayrawani, Ibn Abi Zayd al-. *Ar-Risala*. Published with French translation as *La Risala, ou Épître sur les Éléments du Dogme et de la Foi de l'Islam selon le Rite Malikite*. Edited and translated by Leon Bercher. Algiers: Éditions populaire de l'Armée, 1968.

Tadili, Abu Yaqub Yusuf Ibn Yahya al-, known as Ibn Zayat. *Kitab al-Tashawwuf ila Rijal al-Tassawuf* [Book of longing for the life of saints]. Edited by Ahmed Toufiq. Rabat: Université Mohammed V, Publications de la Faculté des Lettres et des Sciences Humaines, 1984.

———. *Kitab al-Tashawwuf ila Rijal al-Tassawuf*. Arabic text edited by A. Faure as *Vies des Saints du Sud Marocain*. Rabat: Matbu'at Ifriqiyah al-Shamaliyah al-Fanniyah, 1958.

Umari, al-. *Masalik al-Absar fi Mamalik al-Amsar* [Pathways of visions in the realms of the metropolises]. Extracts. Edited and translated by Maurice Gaudefroy-Demombynes. Paris: Geuthner, 1927.

Ya'qubi, Ahmad Ibn Abi Ibn Ja'far Ibn Wahb Ibn Wadih al-. *Kitab al-Buldan* [Book of countries]. Edited by M. J. de Goeje. Leiden: Brill, 1892.

Yaqut, Ibn Abd Allah al-Hamawi. *Mu'jam al-Buldan* [Dictionary of countries]. Edited by F. Wustenfeld. Leipzig: In Commission bei F. A. Brockhaus, 1866–1873.

Zuhri, Abu Abd Allah Muhammad Ibn Abi Bakr al-. *Kitab al-Jughrafiya* [Book of geography]. Edited by Mahammad Hadj-Sadok. *Bulletin d'Études Orientales* 21 (1968): 1–194.

Modern Sources

Abd ar-Raziq, Mahmoud. *Al-Khawarij fi Bilad al-Maghrib hatta Muntasif al-Qarn ar-Rabi' al-Hijri* [Kharijites in the Maghrib to the mid-fourth century of the Hijra]. Casablanca: Dar al-Thaqafa, 1985.

Abu-Lughod, Janet L. "The Islamic City: Historic Myth, Islamic Essence, and Contemporary Relevance." *International Journal of Middle East Studies* 19, no. 2 (1987): 155–177.

Abun-Nasr, Jamil M. *A History of the Maghrib in the Islamic Period*. Cambridge: Cambridge Univ. Press, 1987.

———. *The Tijaniyya: A Sufi Order in the Modern World*. Oxford: Oxford Univ. Press, 1965.

Amilhat, P. "Les Almoravides au Sahara." *Revue Militaire de l'Afrique Occidentale Française* 15 (1937): 1–3.

Anwar, Sherif, and Jere L. Bacharach. "Shi'ism and the Early Dinars of the Fatimid Imam Caliph al-Mu'izz li-Din Allah (341–365/952–975): An Analytic Overview." *Al-Masaq: Islam and the Medieval Mediterranean* 22, no. 3 (2010): 259–278.

Arbitol, Michel. "Juifs Maghrébins et Commerce Trans-Saharien du VIII au XV Siècles." *Le Sol, la Parole et l'Écrit* 2 (1981): 561–577.

Ashtor, Eliyahu. *Histoire des Prix et des Salaires dans l'Orient Médiéval*. Paris: SEVPEN, 1969.

———. "Le Coût de Vie dans l'Égypte Médiévale." *Journal of the Social and Economic History of the Orient* 3 (1960): 56–77.

Austen, Ralph. "The Trans-Saharan Slave Trade: A Tentative Census." In *The Uncommon Market: Essays in the Economic History of the Atlantic Slave Trade*, edited by Henry Gemery and Jan S. Hogendorn, 23–76. New York: Academic Press, 1979.

Bean, Richard. "A Note on the Relative Importance of Slaves and Gold in West African Exports." *Journal of African History* 15, no. 3 (1974): 351–356.

Bell, Christopher. *Portugal and the Quest for the Indies*. London: Constable, 1974.

Benabid, Abdelmalek. "Forest Degradation in Morocco." In *The North African Environment at Risk*, edited by W. D. Swearingen and Abdellatif Bencherifa, 175–189. Boulder, Colo.: Westview, 1996.

Bencherifa, Abdellatif, and Herbert Popp. "L'Économie Oasienne de Figuig entre la Tradition et le Changement." In A. Bencherifa and H. Popp, eds., *Le Maroc: Espace et Société*, special issue, *Passauer Mittelmeerstudien* 1 (1990): 37–48.

Benco, Nancy L. *The Early Medieval Pottery Industry at al-Basra, Morocco.* Oxford: British Archaeological Reports, 1987.

Benhsain, Rajae. "Les Almoravides et l'Afrique Occidentale, XIe-XIIe siècle." *Arabica* 47 (2000): 1–36.

———. "Biens Sultaniens, Fiscalité et Monnaie à l'Epoque Almohade." In *Los Almohades: Problemas y Perspectivas*, vol. 2, edited by Patrice Cressier, Maribel Fierro, and Luis Molina, 585–615. Madrid: Conseco Superior de Investigaciones Científicas, 2005.

Bennison, Amira K., and Alison L. Gascoigne. *Cities in the Pre-Modern Islamic World.* London: Routledge, 2007.

Berque, Jacques. "Medinas, Villeneuves et Bidonvilles." *Les Cahiers de Tunisie* 6 (1958): 5–42.

Berthier, Paul. "En Marge des Sucreries Marocaines: La Maison de la Plaine et la Maison des Oliviers à Chichaoua." *Hespéris-Tamuda*, 1962:75–77.

Blunt, Wilfrid Jasper Walter. *Black Sunrise: The Life and Times of Mulai Ismail, Emperor of Morocco.* London: Methuen, 1951.

Bonine, Michael E. "Islamic Cities in Morocco." *Muqarnas* 7 (1991): 50–72.

———. "The Sacred Direction and City Structure: A Preliminary Analysis of the Islamic Cities of Morocco." *Muqarnas* 7 (1990): 50–72.

Boone, James, Emlyn Myers, and Charles Redman. "Archaeological and Historical Approaches to Complex Societies: The Islamic States of Medieval Morocco." *American Anthropologist* 92 (1990): 630–646.

Bovill, Edward William. *The Golden Trade of the Moors: West African Kingdoms in the Fourteenth Century.* London: Oxford Univ. Press, 1970.

Boxer, Charles R. *The Portuguese Seaborne Empire, 1415–1825.* New York: Knopf, 1969.

Brett, Michael. "Islam and Trade in the Bilad al-Sudan, Tenth-Eleventh Century AD." *Journal of African History* 24 (1983): 431–440.

Brett, Michael, and Elizabeth Fentress. *The Berbers.* Malden, Mass.: Blackwell, 1997.

Brooks, Nick. "Cultural Responses to Aridity in the Middle Holocene and Increased Social Complexity." *Quaternary International* 151, no. 1 (2006): 29–49.

Brunschvig, Robert. "Urbanisme Médiéval et Droit Musulman." *Revue des Études Islamiques* 15 (1947): 127–155.

Bulliet, Richard W. *The Camel and the Wheel.* New York: Columbia Univ. Press, 1990.

Burkhalter, Sheryl. "Listening for Silences in Almoravid History: Another Reading of 'The Conquest That Never Was.'" *History in Africa* 19 (1992): 103–131.

Cahen, Claude. "L'Or du Soudan avant les Almoravides: Mythe ou Réalité." *Le Sol, la Parole et l'Écrit* 2 (1981): 539–545.

Camps, Gabriel. *Les Berbères: Mémoire et Identité.* 2nd ed. Paris: Editions Errance, 1987.

———. *Les Civilisation Préhistoriques de l'Afrique du Nord et du Sahara.* Paris: Doin, 1974.

Canard, Marius. "L'Impérialisme des Fatimides et Leur Propagande." *Annales de l'Institut des Études Orientales* 6 (1942–1947): 162–199.

Castaneda, I. S., S. Mulitza, E. Schefuss, R. A. Lopes dos Santos, J. S. Sinninghe Damste, and S. Schouten. "Wet Phases in the Sahara/Sahel Region and Human Migration Patterns in North Africa." *Proceedings of the National Academy of Science* 106, no. 48 (2009): 20,159–20,163.

Chouraqui. André. *Marche vers l'Occident: Les Juifs d'Afrique du Nord*. Paris: Presses Universitaires de France, 1952.

Christian-Albrechts-Universitaet zu Kiel. "The Green Sahara: A Desert in Bloom." *Science Daily*, Oct. 7, 2008. Available at http://www.sciencedaily.com/releases /2008/09/080930081357.htm.

Clark, Peter U., et al. "The Last Glacial Maximum." *Science* 325 (2009): 710–714.

Coco, Julie. "Caravans, Commerce, and Cities: A Preliminary Archaeological Study of Souk Ben Akla; A Medieval Moroccan Caravanserai and Marketplace." Master's thesis, Middle Tennessee State University, 2000.

Conrad, David. "A Town Called Dakajalan: The Sunjata Tradition and the Question of Ancient Mali's Capital." *Journal of African History* 35 (1994): 355–377.

Conrad, David, and Humphrey J. Fisher. "The Conquest That Never Was: Ghana and the Almoravids, 1076. I. The External Arabic Sources." *History in Africa* 9 (1982): 21–59.

———. "The Conquest That Never Was: Ghana and the Almoravids, 1076. II. The Local Oral Sources." *History in Africa* 10 (1983): 53–78.

Constable, Giles. *Crusaders and Crusading in the Twelfth Century*. Burlington, Vt.: Ashgate, 2008.

Coon, Carlton. *Caravan: The Story of the Middle East*. New York: Holt, 1958.

———. *The Origin of Races*. New York: Knopf, 1962.

Coulibaly, Mamadou. "L'Attaque de Ghana (XIè siècle)." *Afrika Zamani* 2 (1974): 55–77.

Coulson, David, and Alec Campbell. *African Rock Art: Paintings and Engravings on Stone*. New York: Abrams, 2001.

Cuoq, Joseph M. *Recueil des Sources Arabes Concernant l'Afrique Occidentale du VIIIe au XVIe Siècle*. Paris: Éditions du Centre National de la Recherche Scientifique, 1975.

Dastugue, Henri. "Quelques Mots au Sujet de Tafilet et de Sidjilmassa." *Bulletin de la Société de Géographie* 13 (1867): 337–380.

Defrémery, Charles, and Beniamino Raffaello Sanguinetti. *Voyages d'Ibn Batoutah*. Paris: Imprimerie Nationale, 1874.

Delafosse, Maurice. *Haut Sénégal-Niger*. Paris: Larose, 1912.

Despois, Jean, and René Raynal. *Géographie de l'Afrique du Nord-Ouest*. Paris: Payot, 1967.

Deverdun, Gaston. *Marrakech des Origines à 1912*. Rabat: Éditions Techniques Nord Africaines, 1959.

Devisse, Jean. "La Question d'Audagust." In *Tegdaoust*, edited by Denis Robert, Serge Robert, and Jean Devisse, 1:109–156. Paris: Arts and Metiers Graphiques, 1970.

———. "Or d'Afrique." *Arabica* 43 (1996): 234–243.

———. "Routes de Commerce et Échanges en Afrique Occidentale en Relation avec la Mediterranée: Un Essai sur le Commerce Africain Médiéval du XIè au XVIè Siècle." *Revue d'Histoire Économique et Sociale* 50 (1972): 42–73.

———. "Trade and Trade Routes in West Africa." In El Fasi, *General History of Africa*, 3:367–435.

Dubief, Jean. "Les Pluies, les Crues et Leurs Effets au Sahara." In *Maghreb et Sahara: Etudes Géographiques Offertes à Jean Despois*, edited by Xavier de Planhol, 125–135. Paris: Société de Géographie, 1973.

Dunn, Ross. *The Adventures of Ibn Battuta*. Berkeley and Los Angeles: Univ. of California Press, 1986.

———. *Resistance in the Desert*. London: Croom Helm, 1977.

———. "The Trade of Tafilalt: Commercial Change in Southeast Morocco on the Eve of the Protectorate." *African Historical Studies* 4, no. 2 (1971): 271-304.

Duplessy, J. "La Circulation des Monnaies Arabes en Europe Occidentale du VIIIe au XIIIe Siècle." *Revue Numismatique* 18 (1956): 101-163.

Eickelman, Dale F. "Is There an Islamic City?" *International Journal of Middle East Studies* 5 (1974): 274-294.

———. *The Middle East: An Anthropological Approach*. Englewood Cliffs, N.J.: Prentice-Hall, 1989.

———. *The Middle East and Central Asia: An Anthropological Approach*. Upper Saddle River, N.J.: Prentice-Hall, 2002.

El Fasi, M., ed. *General History of Africa*. Vol. 3, *Africa from the Seventh to the Eleventh Century*. Paris, London, and Berkeley: UNESCO, Heinemann, and Univ. of California Press, 1988.

Ellingham, Mark, Shaun McVeigh, and Don Grisbrook. *Morocco, the Rough Guide*. 4th ed. London: Rough Guides, 1993.

Encyclopedia of Islam. 1st ed. 4 vols. S.v., "Sidjilmasa," G. Colin, 4:404-405. Leiden: Brill, 1913-1938.

Encyclopedia of Islam. 2nd ed. 12 vols. Leiden: Brill, 1954-2005. See following articles:

———. "Alawis," H. Terrase, 1:355-358, 1960.

———. "Awdaghost," G. Yver, 1:762, 1960.

———. "Azalay," J. Despois, 1:808-809, 1960.

———. "Dienné," R. Mauny, 2:251-252, 1965.

———. "Djawhar al-Sikilli," H. Monès, 2:494-495, 1965.

———. "Ghana," R. Cornevin, 2:1001-1003, 1965.

———. "Gudala," G. S. Colin, 2:1121-1122, 1965.

———. "Ibn Battuta," André Miguel, 3:758-759, 1971.

———. "Ikrima," J. Schacht, 3:1081-1082, 1971.

———. "Kharidjites," G. Levi Della Vida, 4:1074-1077, 1978.

———. "Kibla," David A. King, 4:82-88, 1978.

———. "Kumbi Salih," R. Mauny, 5:386-387, 1986.

———. "Litham," W. Bjorkman, 5:769-770, 1986.

———. "Maghrawa," T. Lewicki, 5:1173-1183, 1986.

———. "Matghrara," G. S. Colin, 6:815, 1991.

———. "Midrar," Ch. Pellat, 6:1038-1042, 1991.

———. "Al-Murabitun," P. Chalmeta, 7:583-591, 1993.

———. "Muritaniya," H. T. Norris, 7:611-628, 1993.

———. "Mzab," M. Rouvillois-Brigol, 7:826-827, 1993.

———. "Sidjilmasa," M. Terrasse, 9:545-546, 1997.

———. "Sufriyya," W. Madelung and K. Lewinstein, 9:769, 1997.

Evans, Guy. "The Changing Dynamics of the Moroccan Oasis: Errachidia and the Tafilalt." Unpublished Fulbright (Morocco) Student Grant Final Report, Sept. 5, 2011.

Evans, Joan. *Monastic Life at Cluny*. 1931. Reprint, Hamden, Conn.: Archon, 1968.

Farias, Paolo Fernando de Moraes. "The Almoravids: Some Questions Concerning the

Character of the Movement during Its Periods of Closest Contact with the Western Sudan." *Bulletin de l'Institut Fondamental d'Afrique Noire* 29B (1968): 794–878.

———. "Great States Revisited." *Journal of African History* 15, no. 3 (1974): 479–488.

———. "Silent Trade: Myth and Historical Evidence." *History in Africa* 1 (1974): 9–24.

Fili, Abdallah. "La Céramique Médiévale du Maroc: État de la Question." *Caetaria: Revista del Museo Municipal de Algeciras* 4–5 (2004–2005): 231–246.

Fili, Abdallah, and Ronald Messier. "La Céramique Médiévale de Sijilmasa." In *VIIe Congrès International sur la Céramique Médiévale en Méditerranée*, 689–690. Athens: Ministry of Culture, 2003.

Fisher, Humphrey. "Early Arabic Sources and the Almoravid Conquest of Ghana." *Journal of African History* 23, no. 4 (1982): 549–560.

Fletcher, Richard. *The Quest for El Cid*. New York: Oxford Univ. Press, 1989.

Freeman, S., and M. Maymon. "Reliable Detection of the Fungal Pathogen Fusarium Oxysporum f.sp. Albedinis, Causal Agent of Bayoud Disease of Date Palm, Using Molecular Techniques." *Phytoparasitica* 28, no. 14 (2000): 1–8.

Fromherz, Allen. *The Almohads: The Rise of an Islamic Empire*. London: Taurus, 2012.

Garrard, Timothy F. "Myth and Metrology: The Early Trans-Saharan Gold Trade." *Journal of African History* 23 (1982): 443–461.

Gasse, F. "Hydrological Changes in the African Tropics since the Last Glacial Maximum." *Quaternary Science Reviews* 19 (2000): 189–211.

Gautier, Émile Félix. *Le Passé de l'Afrique du Nord: Les Siècles Obscurs*. Paris: Payot, 1952.

Goitein, S. D. *A Mediterranean Society: The Jewish Communities of the Arab World as Portrayed in the Documents of the Cairo Geniza*, vol. 1, *Economic Foundations*. Berkeley and Los Angeles: Univ. of California Press, 1967.

———. *A Mediterranean Society: The Jewish Communities of the Arab World as Portrayed in the Documents of the Cairo Geniza*, vol. 2, *The Community*. Berkeley and Los Angeles: Univ. of California Press, 1971.

Goulven, J. "Notes sur les Origines Anciennes des Israélites du Maroc." *Hespéris* 1 (1921): 317–336.

Grabar, Oleg. "The Architecture of the Middle Eastern City from Past to Present: The Case of the Mosque." In *Middle Eastern Cities*, edited by Ira Lapidus, 26–46. Berkeley and Los Angeles: Univ. of California Press, 1969.

La Grande Encyolpédie du Maroc. Edited by Mustapha El Kasri and Hassan Sqalli. Vol. 4. Cremona, Italy: GEP, 1987.

Guendouz, Abdelhamid, and Jean-Luc Michelot. "Chlorine-36 Dating of Deep Groundwater from Northern Sahara." *Journal of Hydrology* 328 (2006): 572–580.

Hamdun, Said, and Noel King. *Ibn Battuta in Black Africa*. Princeton, N.J.: Marcus Weiner, 1994.

Hammoudi, Abdellah. "Substance and Relation: Water Rights and Water Distribution in the Dra Valley." In *Property, Social Structure, and Law in the Modern Middle East*, edited by Ann Elizabeth Mayer, 27–57. Albany: SUNY Press, 1985.

Harris, Walter B. *Tafilet*. Edinburgh: Blackwood and Sons, 1895.

Harvey, L. P. *Ibn Battuta*. London: Tauris, 2008.

Hazard, Harry W. *The Numismatic History of Late Medieval North Africa*. Numismatic Studies 8. New York: American Numismatic Society, 1952.

Heddouchi, Choukri. "The Medieval Coins of Sijilmasa, Morocco: A History of the Mint and Its Minting Techniques." Master's thesis, Middle Tennessee State University, 1998.

Hirschberg, Haim Zeev. *The History of the Jews in North Africa*. Vol. 1. Leiden: Brill, 1974.

Hiskett, Mervyn. *The Development of Islam in West Africa*. London: Longmans, 1984.

The Holy Qur'an: Text, Translation and Commentary. Translated by Abdullah Yusuf Ali. Brentwood, Md.: Amana, 1983.

Hopkins, J. F. P. *Medieval Muslim Government in Barbary*. London: Luzac, 1958.

Hopkins, J. F. P., and Nehemia Levtzion, eds. and trans. *Corpus of Early Arabic Sources for West African History*. Cambridge: Cambridge Univ. Press, 1981. Reprint, Princeton, N.J.: Markus Wiener, 2000.

Hrbek, I. "The Emergence of the Fatimids." In El Fasi, *General History of Africa*, 3:314–335.

Hrbek, I., and J. Devisse. "The Almoravids." In El Fasi, *General History of Africa*, 3:336–66.

Hughes, Stephen O. "Morocco: Nation Pays a High Price for Water." *New York Times*, Jan. 31, 1966.

Huici-Miranda, A. "El-Rawd al-Qirtas y los Almoravides: Estudio Critico." *Hespéris-Tamuda* 1 (1960): 515–541.

———. "Un Nuevo Manuscrito de 'al-Bayan al-Mugrib.'" *Al-Andalus* 24 (1959): 63–84.

———. "La Salida de los Almoravides del Desierto y el Reinado de Yusuf B. Tashfin." *Hespéris* 47, nos. 3–4 (1959): 155–182.

Hunwick, John, "Gao and the Almoravids: A Hypothesis." In *West African Culture Dynamics*, edited by R. Dumett and B. Swartz, 413–430. The Hague: Mouton, 1980.

———. "The Mid-Fourteenth Century Capital of Mali." *Journal of African History* 14, no. 2 (1973): 195–206.

Ibn al-Qadi al-Miknassi, Ahmed. *Jadouat al-Iqtibas fi Dhikri man Halla min al-A'lam Madinat Fas*. Rabat, 1973.

Idris, Hady Roger. *La Berbérie Orientale sous les Zirides X–XIIIè Siècles*. Paris: Librairie d'Amérique et d'Orient Adrien-Maisonneuve, 1962.

Ilahiane, Hsain. "Small-Scale Irrigation and Social Stratification in the Ziz Valley, Southeast Morocco." Draft paper prepared for the Middle East Studies Association meeting, Portland, Oregon, Nov. 1992.

Insoll, Timothy. "Archaeological Research in Gao and Timbuktu, October and November 1996." *Saharan Studies Association Newsletter* 5, no. 1 (1997): 14–18.

———. "Archaeological Research in Gao, the Republic of Mali." *Saharan Studies Association Newsletter* 2 (1994): 8–11.

———. "Iron Age Gao: An Archaeological Contribution." *Saharan Studies Association Newsletter* 4, no. 2 (1996): 16–18.

———. "Islam, Archaeology, and History: Gao Region (Mali), ca. AD 900–1250." *Cambridge Monographs in African Archaeology* 39. BAR International Series 647. Oxford: Tempus Reparatum, 1997.

———. "Medieval Gao: An Archaeological Contribution." *Journal of African History* 3, no. 1 (1997): 1–30.

Jacques-Meunié, D. "Abbar, Cité Royale du Tafilalt." *Hespéris* 46 (1959): 68–72.

————. "Hiérarchie Sociale au Maroc Présaharien." *Hespéris* 45, nos. 3–4 (1958): 239–269.

————. *Le Maroc Saharien des Origines à 1670.* 2 vols. Paris: Librairie Klincksieck, 1982.

————. "Sur l'architecture du Tafilalt et de Sijilmassa." *Comptes Rendus de l'Académie des Inscriptions et Belles-Lettres* 106, no. 2 (1962): 132–148.

Jayussi, Salma K. *The City in the Islamic World.* Leiden: Brill, 2008.

Julien, Charles-André. *History of North Africa from the Arab Conquest to 1830.* Edited by Roger Le Tourneau. Translated by J. Petrie. English edition edited by C. C. Stewart. London: Routledge and Kegan Paul, 1970.

Kassis, Hanna. "Coinage of an Enigmatic Caliph: The Midrarid Muhammad Ibn al-Fath of Sijilmasah." *Al-Qantara* 9 (1988): 489–494.

————. "Observations on the First Three Decades of Almoravid History (AH 450–480 = AD 1058–1088): A Numismatic Study." *Der Islam* 62 (1985): 311–325.

King, David A. "Architecture and Astronomy: The Ventilators of Medieval Cairo and their Secrets." *Journal of the American Oriental Society* 104, no. 1 (1984): 97–133.

————. "Astronomical Alignments in Medieval Islamic Religious Architecture." In *Ethnoastronomy and Archaeoastronomy in the American Tropics,* edited by Anthony Aveni and Gary Urton, 303–312. *Annals of the New York Academy of Sciences* 385. New York: New York Academy of Sciences, 1982.

————. "Al-Bazdawi on the Qibla in Early Islamic Transoxania." *Journal for the History of Arabic Science* 7, nos. 1–2 (1983): 3–38.

————. "The Sacred Direction in Islam: A Study of the Interaction of Religion and Science in the Middle Ages." *Interdisciplinary Science Reviews* 10, no. 4 (1985): 315–327.

————. "Science in the Service of Religion: The Case of Islam." *Impact of Science on Society* 159 (1991): 245–262.

King, David A., and Gerald S. Hawkins. "On the Orientation of the Ka'aba." *Journal for the History of Astronomy* 13 (1982): 101–109.

Koribaa, Nabhani. *Les Kharidjites: Démocrates de l'Islam.* Paris: Publisud, 1991.

Kritzeck, James, and William H. Lewis, eds. *Islam in Africa.* New York: Van Nostrand-Reinhold, 1969.

La Chapelle, Frédéric de. "Esquisse d'une Histoire du Sahara Occidental." *Hespéris* 11 (1930): 35–95.

————. "L'Expédition de Suetonius Paulinus dans le Sud-Est du Maroc." *Hespéris* 19 (1934): 107–124.

Lange, Dierk. "The Almoravid Expansion and the Downfall of Ghana." *Der Islam* 73, no. 2 (1996): 313–351.

————. "The Almoravids and the Islamization of the Great States of West Africa." In "Itinéraires d'Orient: Hommages à Claude Cahen," edited by Raoul Curiel and Rika Gyselen. Special issue, *Res Orientales* 6 (1994): 65–76.

————. "Les Rois de Gao-Sané et les Almoravides." *Journal of African History* 32 (1991): 251–275.

Langewiesche, William. *Sahara Unveiled.* New York: Pantheon, 1995.

Lapidus, Ira M. *A History of Islamic Societies.* New York: Cambridge Univ. Press, 1988.

————. *Muslim Cities in the Later Middle Ages.* Cambridge, Mass.: Harvard Univ. Press, 1967.

La Roncière, Charles de. *La Découverte de l'Afrique au Moyen Age: Cartographes et Explorateurs*. 2 vols. Cairo: Imprimerie de l'Institut Français d'Archéologie Orient, 1924-1925.

Laroui, Abdallah. *The History of the Maghrib: An Interpretive Essay*. Princeton, N.J.: Princeton Univ. Press, 1977.

Le Chatelier, Alfred. *L'Islam dans L'Afrique Occidentale*. Paris, 1899.

Le Tourneau, Roger. *Fes avant le Protectorat: Étude Économique et Sociale d'une Ville de l'Occident Musulman*. Rabat: Éditions La Porte, 1987.

———. *Les Villes Musulmanes de l'Afrique du Nord*. Algiers: La Maison des Livres, 1957.

Lévi-Provençal, Évariste, ed. and trans. *Documents Inédits d'Histoire Almohade*. Paris: Librairie Orientaliste Paul Geuthner, 1928.

———. *Islam d'Occident: Études d'Histoire Médiévale*. Studies in African History 7. Paris: Maisonneuve, 1948.

———. "Réflexions sur l'Empire Almoravide au Début du XIIe Siècle." In *Cinquantenaire de la Faculté des Lettres d'Alger*, 307-320. Algiers: Société Historique Algérienne, 1932.

Levtzion, Nehemia. *Ancient Ghana and Mali*. London: Methuen, 1973.

———. "Ibn-Hawqal, the Cheque, and Awdaghost." *Journal of African History* 9, no. 2 (1968): 223-233.

———. "The Jews of Sijilmasa and the Saharan Trade." In *Communautés Juives des Marges Sahariennes du Maghreb*, edited by Michel Abitbol, 253-263. Jerusalem: Institut Ben-Zvi, 1982.

———. "Was Royal Succession in Ancient Ghana Matrilineal?" *International Journal of African Historical Studies* 1 (1972): 91-93.

Lewicki, Tadeuz. "L'État Nord-Africain de Tahert et ses Relations avec le Soudan Occidental à la Fin du VIII et au IX Siècle." *Cahiers d'Études Africaines* 2, no. 8 (1962): 513-535.

———. "Un État Soudanais Médiéval Inconnu: Le Royaume de Zafun." *Cahiers d'Études Africaines* 11, no. 44 (1971): 501-525.

———. "L'Exploitation et le Commerce de l'Or en Afrique de l'Est et du Sud-Est au Moyen Age d'après les Sources Arabes." *Folia Orientalia* 18 (1977): 167-186.

———. "The Role of the Sahara and Saharians in Relationships between North and South." In El Fasi, *General History of Africa*, 3:276-313.

———. *West African Food in the Middle Ages: According to Arabic Sources*. New York: Cambridge Univ. Press, 1974.

Lewis, Bernard. "The African Diaspora and the Civilization of Islam." In *The African Diaspora*, edited by Martin L. Kilson and Robert I. Rotberg, 37-56. Cambridge, Mass.: Harvard Univ. Press, 1976.

———. *Race and Slavery in the Middle East: An Historical Inquiry*. New York: Oxford Univ. Press, 1990.

Lightfoot, Dale R., and James A. Miller. "Sijilmassa: The Rise and Fall of a Walled Oasis in Medieval Morocco." *Annals of the Association of American Geographers* 86, no. 1 (1996): 78-101.

Love, Paul M. "The Sufris of Sijilmasa: Toward a History of the Midrarids." *Journal of North African Studies* 15, no. 2 (2010): 173-188.

Lubell, David. "Paleoenvironments and Epi-Paleolithic Economies in the Maghrib (ca. 20,000 to 5000 BP)." In *From Hunters to Farmers: The Causes and Consequences of Food Production in Africa*, edited by J. D. Clark and S. A. Brandts, 41–56. Berkeley and Los Angeles: Univ. of California Press, 1984.

Maalouf, Amin. *Leo the African*. Translated by Peter Sluglett. London: Quartet, 1986.

MacKenzie, Neil D. *Ayyubid Cairo: A Topographical Study*. Cairo: American University in Cairo Press, 1992.

Mackintosh-Smith, Tim. *Landfalls: On the Edge of Islam with Ibn Battutah*. London: John Murray, 2010.

———. *The Travels of Ibn Battutah*. London: Picador, 2002.

———. *Travels with a Tangerine: From Morocco to Turkey in the Footsteps of Islam's Greatest Traveler*. London: John Murray, 2001.

Marçais, George. "Un Coin Monétaire Almoravide du Musée Stéphane Gsell." *Annales de l'Institut d'Études Orientales* 2 (1936): 180–188.

———. "La Conception des Villes dans l'Islam." *Revue d'Alger* 2 (1945): 517–533.

———. "L'Urbanisme Musulman." In *5e Congrès de la Fédération des Sociétés Savantes de l'Afrique du Nord*. Algiers, 1940. Reprinted in G. Marçais, *Mélanges d'Histoire et d'Archéologie de l'Occident Musulman*. Vol. 1. Algiers: Imprimerie officielle, 1957.

Marçais, William. "L'Islamisme et la Vie Urbaine." *Comptes Rendus de l'Académie des Inscriptions et Belles-Lettres* 72, no. 1 (1928): 86–100.

Margat, J. S. *Mémoire Explicatif de la Carte Hydrogéologique au 1/50,000 de la plaine du Tafilalt*. Notes et Mémoires du Service Géologique 150. Rabat: Editions du Service Géologique du Maroc, 1962.

———. "Note sur la Morphologie du Site de Sigilmassa (Tafilalt)." *Hespéris* 45–46, nos. 3–4 (1959): 254–260.

Masonen, Pekka. "Conquest and Authority: Ancient Ghana and the Almoravids in West African Historiography." *Saharan Studies Newsletter* 3, no. 1 (May 1995): 4–9.

Massignon, Louis. *Le Maroc dans les Premières Années du XVIè Siècle: Tableau Géographique d'après Léon l'Africain*. Algiers: Adolphe Jourdan, 1906.

Mauny, Raymond. *Tableau Géographique de l'Ouest Africain au Moyen Age d'après les Sources Écrites, la Tradition et l'Archéologie*. Dakar: Institut Fondamental de l'Afrique Noire, 1960.

Mauny, Raymond, V. Monteil, A. Djenidi, S. Robert, and J. Devisse, eds. and trans. *Textes et Documents Relatifs à l'Histoire de l'Afrique: Extraits Tirés des Voyages d'Ibn Battuta*. Dakar: Faculté des Lettres et Science Humaines, University of Dakar, 1966.

McCall, Daniel F. "Islamization of the Western and Central Sudan in the Eleventh Century." *Boston University Papers on Africa* 5 (1971): 1–30.

———. "The Traditions of the Founding of Sijilmassa and Ghana." *Transactions of the Historical Society of Ghana* 1 (1961): 3–42.

McDougall, E. Ann. "The View from Awdaghust: War, Trade, and Social Change in the Southwestern Sahara, from the Eighth to the Fifteenth Century." *Journal of African History* 26 (1985): 1–31.

McIntosh, Susan Keech. "West African Savanna Kingdoms." In *The Oxford Companion to Archaeology*, edited by Brian Fagan, 748–750. New York: Oxford Univ. Press, 1996.

McIntosh, Susan Keech, and R. J. McIntosh. "Archaeological Reconnaissance in the Region of Timbuktu, Mali." *National Geographic Research* 2 (1986): 302–319.

Mellouki, Mohamed el-. "Contribution à l'Étude de l'Histoire des Villes Médiévales du Maroc: Sigilmassa des Origines à 668 (H)/1269 (J.C.)." PhD diss., Aix-en-Provence, 1985.

Mercier, Ernest. "Sidjilmassa selon les Auteurs Arabes." *Revue Africaine* 11 (1867): 233–242, 274–284.

Messier, Ronald A. *The Almoravids and the Meanings of Jihad.* Santa Barbara, Calif.: Praeger, 2010.

———. "The Almoravids, West African Gold, and the Gold Currency of the Mediterranean Basin." *Journal of the Economic and Social History of the Orient* 17 (1974): 31–47.

———. "The Grand Mosque of Sijilmasa: The Evolution of a Structure from the Mosque of Ibn Abd Allah to the Restoration by Sidi Mohammed ben Abdallah." In *L'Architecture de Terre en Méditerranée*, edited by Mohammed Hammam, 287–296. Colloques et Séminaires 80. Rabat: Université Mohammed V, Publications de la Faculté des Lettres et des Sciences Humaines, 1999.

———. "Listening for Silences in Sijilmasa's History." In *Moroccan History: Defining New Fields and Approaches; Proceedings of the 1st Moroccan History Days, School of Humanities and Social Sciences.* Ifrane, Morocco: Al-Akhawayn University, 2005.

———. "Muslim Exploitation of West African Gold during the Period of the Fatimid Caliphate." PhD diss., University of Michigan, 1972.

———. "Le Plan de Sijilmasa Révélé par GIS." In *Actes des Premières Journées d'Archéologie et du Patrimoine*, edited by Mohammad Hammam, 99–107. Rabat: Université Mohammed V, Publications de la Faculté des Lettres et des Sciences Humaines, 1997.

———. "Quantitative Analysis of Almoravid Dinars." *Journal of the Economic and Social History of the Orient* 23, nos. 1–2 (1980): 104–120.

———. "Sijilmasa: Five Seasons of Archaeological Inquiry by a Joint Moroccan-American Mission." *Archéologie Islamique* 7 (1997): 61–92.

———. "Sijilmasa: L'Intermédiaire entre la Méditerranée et l'Ouest de l'Afrique." In *L'Occident Musulman et l'Occident Chrétien au Moyen Age*, edited by Mohammed Hammam, 181–196. Rabat: Université Mohammed V, Publications de la Faculté des Lettres et des Sciences Humaines, 1995.

———. "The Transformation of Sijilmasa." *Studi Magrebini* 4 (2006): 247–257.

Messier, Ronald A., and Abdallah Fili. "The Earliest Ceramics of Sijilmasa." In *La Céramique Maghrébine du Haut Moyen Âge (VIIIe–Xe Siècle): État des Recherches, Problèmes, et Perspectives*, edited by Patrice Cressier and Elizabeth Fentress, 129–146. Rome: Collection de l'École Française de Rome, 2011.

Messier, Ronald A., and Neil MacKenzie. "Sijilmasa: An Archaeological Study, 1992." *Bulletin d'Archéologie Marocaine/al-Nashra al-Athariya al-Maghribiya* 19 (2002): 257–292.

Meyers, Allan R. "Class, Ethnicity, and Slavery: The Origins of the Moroccan Abid." *International Journal of African Historical Studies* 10 (1977): 427–442.

Mezzine, Larbi. "Relation d'un Voyage de Tagaza à Sigilmasa en 1096 H./1685 J.C." *Arabica* 43 (1996): 211–233.

———. "Sijilmassa." In *Le Mémorial du Maroc*, 2:25. Rabat: Nord Organisation, n.d.

———. "Sur l'Étymologie du Toponyme 'Sijilmasa.'" *Hespéris* 22 (1984): 19–25.

———. *Le Tafilalt: Contribution à l'Histoire du Maroc aux XVIIè et XVIIIè Siècles.* Rabat: Université Mohammed V, Publications de la Faculté des Lettres et des Sciences Humaines, 1987.

Miller, James A. *Imlil: A Moroccan Mountain Community in Change.* Boulder, Colo.: Westview, 1984.

———. "Revealing North-South Relations in the Eleventh Century." In *Hispaniens Norden Im 11 Jahrhundert; Christliche Kunst im Umbruch,* edited by Achim Arbeiter, Christiane Kothe, and Bettina Marten, 73–84. Petersberg, Germany: Michael Imhof, 2009.

———. "Trading through Islam: The Interconnections of Sijilmasa, Ghana, and the Almoravid Movement." *Journal of North African Studies* 6 (2001): 29–58.

———. "La Viabilité de l'Environnement dans les Oasis du Tafilalet: De l'Ancienne Sijilmassa au Tafilalet d'Aujourd'hui." In *L'Afrique du Nord Face aux Menaces Écologiques,* edited by Abdellatif Bencherifa and Will D. Swearingen, 3–19. Colloques et Séminaires 50. Rabat: Université Mohammed V, Publications de la Faculté des Lettres et des Sciences Humaines, 1995.

Miner, Horace. *The Primitive City of Timbuctoo.* Garden City, N.Y.: Anchor, 1965.

Misbach, Henri L. "Genoese Commerce and the Alleged Flow of Gold to the East, 1154–1253." *Revue Internationale d'Histoire de la Banque* 3 (1970): 67–87.

Mithen, Steven. *After the Ice: A Global Human History, 20,000–5,000 BC.* Cambridge, Mass.: Harvard Univ. Press, 2004.

Moore, Donald, and Richard Roberts. "Listening for Silences." *History in Africa* 17 (1990): 319–325.

Nixon, Sam, Thilo Rehren, and Maria Filomena Guerra. "New Light on the Early Islamic West African Gold Trade: Coin Moulds from Tadmekka, Mali." *Antiquity* 85, no. 330 (2011): 1353–1368.

Norris, H. T. "New Evidence on the Life of Abdullah B. Yasin and the Origins of the Almoravid Movement." *Journal of African History* 12, no. 2 (1971): 255–268.

———. *Saharan Myth and Saga.* Oxford: Oxford Univ. Press, 1972.

Ouasti, Boussif. *La Rihla d'Ibn Battuta, Voyageur Ecrivain.* Paris: L'Harmattan, 2006.

Oufrani, Mohammed Esseghir Ben Elhadj Ben Abdallah al-. *Nozhet-Elhadi.* Translated as *Histoire de la Dynastie Saadienne au Maroc, 1511–1670* by O. Houdas. Paris: Leroux, 1889.

Pejmi, Karel. "A Contribution to the Historical Climatology of Morocco and Mauritania." *Studia Geographica et Geodaetica* 6 (1962): 257–279.

Pouillon, François, ed. *Léon l'Africain.* Paris: Karthala, 2009.

Powers, David C. *Law, Society, and Culture in the Maghrib, 1300–1500.* Cambridge: Cambridge Univ. Press, 2002.

Princeton Encyclopedia of Classical Sites. S.v. "Laurion," C. W. J. Eliot, 489. Princeton, N.J.: Princeton Univ. Press, 1976.

Rachewiltz, Boris de. "Missione Etno-Archeologica nel Sahara Maghrebino." *Africa: Rivista trimestrale di studi e documentazione dell'Istituto italiano per l'Africa e Oriente* 27, no. 4 (1972): 519–568.

Robert, D., S. Robert, and B. Saison. "Recherches Archéologiques: Tegdaoust-Koumbi Saleh." *Annales de l'Institut Mauritanien de Recherch Scientifique* 2 (1976): 53–84.

Rogerson, Barnaby. *Morocco*. Chester, Conn.: Globe Pequot, 1989.

Roller, D. W. *The World of Juba II and Kleopatra Selene: Royal Scholarship on Rome's African Frontier*. New York: Routledge, 2003.

Romdhane, Khaled Ben. "Le Métier de Monétaire d'après les Sources Arabes." In *Mélanges Offerts à Mohamed Talbi à l'Occasion de son 70è Anniversaire*, 25–43. Tunis: Publications de la Faculté des Lettres de la Manouba, 1993.

Ruhard, Jean-Paul. "Le Bassin Quaternaire du Tafilalt." In *Ressources en Eau du Maroc*, 3:352–415. Rabat: Éditions du Service Géologique du Maroc, 1977.

Rumsford, James. *Traveling Man: The Journey of Ibn Battuta, 1325–1354*. Boston: Houghton Mifflin, 2004.

Sauvaget, Jean. "Les Épitaphes Royales de Gao." *Bulletin de l'Institut Fondamental de l'Afrique Noire* 12, no. 2 (1950): 418–440.

———. "Esquisse d'une Histoire de la Ville de Damas." *Revue des Études Islamiques* 8 (1934): 421–480.

Savage, Elizabeth. *The Human Commodity: Perspectives on the Trans-Saharan Slave Trade*. London: Cass, 1992.

Sayyad, Nezar al-. *Cities and Caliphs: On the Genesis of Arab Muslim Urbanism*. Westport, Conn.: Greenwood, 1991.

Schacht, J. "An Unknown Type of Minbar and Its Historical Significance." *Ars Orientalis* 2 (1957): 149–173.

Semonin, Paul. "The Almoravid Movement in the Western Sudan: A Review of the Evidence." *Transactions of the Historical Society of Ghana* 7 (1964): 42–59.

Shatzmiller, Maya. *L'Historiographie Mérinide*. Leiden: Brill, 1982.

Shellington, Kevin. *History of Africa*. Hong Kong: Macmillan, 1989.

Smith, William. *A New Classical Dictionary of Greek and Roman Biography, Mythology and Geography Partly Based upon the Dictionary of Greek and Roman Biography and Mythology*. New York: Harper and Brothers, 1895.

Stambouli, Frej, and Abdelkader Zghal. "Urban Life in Precolonial North Africa." *British Journal of Sociology* 27, no. 1 (1976): 1–20.

Sutton, J. E. G. "Archaeology in West Africa: A Review of Recent Work and a Further List of Radiocarbon Dates." *Journal of African History* 23, no. 3 (1982): 291–313.

Swearingen, Will D. *Moroccan Mirages: Agrarian Dreams and Deceptions, 1912–1986*. Princeton, N.J.: Princeton Univ. Press, 1987.

Talbi, M. "The Independence of the Maghrib." In El Fasi, *General History of Africa*, 3:246–275.

Taouchikht, Lahcen. "La Céramique Médiévale de Sijilmassa: Approche Générale." *Actes du 5ème Colloque sur la Céramique Médiévale en Méditerranée Occidentale*, 227–234. Rabat: Institut National des Sciences d'Archéologie et du Patrimoine, 1995.

———. "Étude Ethno-Archéologique de la Céramique du Tafilalet (Sijilmasa): État de Question." PhD diss., University of Provence, Aix Marseille I, 1989.

Terrasse, Henri. *La Mosquée al-Qaraouiyin à Fès*. Paris: Librairie Klincksieck, 1982.

Touri, Abdulaziz, and Mohamed Hammam. "Tradition Écrite et Architecture: Acte Coutumier d'un Village du Dades, 'Irigiwt.'" *Hespéris-Tamuda* 24 (1886): 212–229.

Trimingham, Spencer. "The Expansion of Islam." In *Islam in Africa*, edited by James Kritzeck and William H. Lewis, 13–34. New York: Van Nostrand-Reinhold, 1969.

———. *A History of Islam in West Africa*. New York: Oxford Univ. Press, 1970.

———. *The Influence of Islam upon Africa*. New York: Praeger, 1968.

Vila, Jacinto Bosch. *Los Almoravides*. Tetuan: Editora Marroqui, 1956.

Vogel, Klaus. "Cosmography." In *The Cambridge History of Science*, vol. 3, *Early Modern Science*, edited by Katharine Park and Lorraine Daston, 469–496. Translated by Alisha Rankin. Cambridge: Cambridge Univ. Press, 2006.

von Grunebaum, Gustave. *Islam*. Westport, Conn.: Greenwood, 1955.

———. "The Structure of the Muslim Town." In *Islam: Essays in the Nature and Growth of a Cultural Tradition*, 141–158. Memoir 81. Ann Arbor, Mich.: American Anthropological Association, 1955.

Waines, David. *The Odyssey of Ibn Battuta: Uncommon Tales of a Medieval Adventurer*. London: Tauris, 2012.

Wheatley, Paul. *The Places Where Men Pray Together: Cities in Islamic Lands*. Chicago: Univ. of Chicago Press, 2001.

White, Kevin, and David Mattingly. "Ancient Lakes of the Sahara." *American Scientist* 94, no. 1 (2006): 58–65.

Willan, Thomas S. *Studies in Elizabethan Foreign Trade*. Manchester, UK: Univ. of Manchester Press, 1959.

Willis, John Ralph, ed. *Slaves and Slavery in Muslim Africa*. Vol. 1, *Islam and the Ideology of Enslavement*. Vol. 2, *The Servile Estate*. London: Cass, 1985.

———, ed. *Studies in West African Islamic History*. Vol. 1, *The Cultivators of Islam*. New York: Cass, 1979.

Young, James A. T., and Stefan Hasternrath. "Glaciers of Africa." In *Satellite Image Atlas of Glaciers of the World*, edited by Richard S. Williams Jr. and Jane G. Ferrigno, chap. G-3. U.S. Geological Survey Professional Paper 1386. Denver: U.S. Geological Survey, 1991. Available at http://pubs.usgs.gov/pp/p1386g/africa.pdf.

Ziegler, Lt., J. Hallemans, and R. Mauny. "Mauritanie: Trouvaille de Deux Monnaies Romaines." *Libyca: Archéologie-Epigraphie* 2, no. 2 (1954): 486–488.

Index

www.ingramcontent.com/pod-product-compliance
Ingram Content Group UK Ltd.
Pitfield, Milton Keynes, MK11 3LW, UK
UKHW030713300425
458010UK00002B/205